With My Shoes Off

Katherine G. Howard

VANTAGE PRESS
New York   Washington   Atlanta   Hollywood

Dedicated to
My Grandchildren

DAMON HOWARD BALL
KATHERINE JOYCE HOWARD
ERIC SEVAN HOWARD
ALEXANDRA GRAHAM HOWARD

Contents

List of Illustrations

Acknowledgment

A special one to Mr. Edward Weeks, Atlantic Monthly Press, for his editorial assistance and his encouragement to "keep on."

With My Shoes Off

Mr. and Mrs. Charles P. Howard (Katherine and Charles).

I

A SOUTHERN HERITAGE

A steel engraving of Dante and Beatrice always hung in my Mother's room. There was a stain in the right-hand corner. When I remarked on it once my Mother said casually, "Oh, yes, I was looking at that picture all the time you were being born. It was raining hard and the roof of the summer cottage leaked, and the rain seeped down the wall and stained the picture." This was on September 30, 1898, in Guyton, Georgia.

My family lived in Savannah and I've always wished I had been born there, a recognizable city of good repute instead of an unheard of place with the unlikely name of Guyton. But my older brother Gregory had malaria fever, so Mother went to a summer resort on higher ground until cooler weather came in October. There I was born. The doctor's fee was twenty-five dollars, everything normal, no complications. I always felt they got a bargain.

My Father, Joseph Lewis Graham, had hoped I would be a boy, but he accepted what he got, and wired his mother in Augusta, Georgia, "Katherine Montague Graham born this morning." I have a copy of it on Central of Georgia stationery. My Father was then General Claim Agent for that railroad and President of the National Claim Agents Association of the United States and Canada. Mother put in "Montague" because it was a family name, and she said she thought it would look well on a wedding invitation.

During the first seven years of my life I spent a great deal

1

of time visiting Grandmother Graham in Augusta. One of my most vivid recollections is the daily afternoon drive. At four o'clock, Nelson drove the horse and carriage to the front door of Grandmother Graham's house. Soon Grandmother, Aunt Isabelle, and I would come down the front steps, past the roses blooming in the front yard, ascend the steps to the carriage, and go for the regular afternoon drive.

Nelson had been a slave to Grandmother before the Civil War, and had stayed on to work for her afterwards. There were thrilling stories about Nelson. When the river overflowed its banks and Augusta was flooded, he tried to drive the horse to safety, was swept off the horse's back, and clung to a telephone pole until the waters receded. Days later, someone returned the horse and Grandmother had to buy him back, which she cheerfully did. She told, too, of having to stay on the second floor, the first floor being inundated. She watched from the windows as fires raged, even in the flood.

Grandmother didn't talk much about the Civil War, but she did tell of the hardships: sugar was $100 a barrel, and so was flour, and $100 was an enormous sum then; coffee was made from ground acorns. We looked with interest at the sofa in the parlor, where a wounded Confederate soldier had lain. They tended him carefully and nursed him back to health.

Grandmother Graham's house was a fascinating place to me. She cheerfully broke the rules I had to adhere to at home in Savannah. There we were forbidden to eat bananas—they were not digestible for children. Grandmother let me have all I wanted. I could eat a whole one, ask for another, and be told "Yes." She often took me in her lap and gave me bread and jam in front of the fire in the dining room.

Then, too, she had a parrot, a parrot that could talk, and say, "Hello, Isabelle!" He could sit on Grandmother's shoulder, or on her wrist, and eat bread dunked in cocoa from her cup.

It was Grandmother Graham who taught me the Lord's Prayer, one summer evening on the small porch which opened off her bedroom.

I think of her always in her bedroom, seated in a rocking chair in the bay window, surrounded by newspapers, which she read voraciously. Over her mantelpiece was a picture of her brother, Major John Stephens, in his Confederate uniform. She said that she never smiled again after his death, which I could see was not so.

But I was a child divided, as we always spent our summers with my maternal Grandmother Nowell in Reading, Massachusetts. Through the years I remember the "Nora" in her kitchen, the homemade doughnuts in the crock in her pantry, the pear tree in the back yard, and how Grandmother would put the pears in a drawer to ripen. Over the back door there was a trumpet vine, and in the living room there was a carpet-covered box on rollers with toys inside, and a box of buttons to make necklaces with.

But what was my Yankee grandmother really like? Mother of one daughter, her oldest child, my Mother, and five handsome sons, she was a little jealous of my Mother's closeness to her father, both of them being possessed of great charm.

I can remember her sitting in her rocking chair on the porch, making a braided rug. A big basket of woolen stuff was beside her.

As I played with my blocks, I looked up at her and said, "Grandmother, how old are you?" "Fifty years," she said. "And do you have a hundred dollars in the bank?" "Yes," she said. Just that, "Yes." (How could anyone be so old and have so much money, I thought.)

"Grandmother," I asked, "what are we going to have for dessert?" I was hoping it would be blueberry pudding with hard sauce. She replied, "Anything we have, Katherine, is good enough for you."

In 1907 the great change in our lives came. My Father was offered two positions: one as President of the Atlanta and West Point Railroad, now part of the Southern Railroad System, which was the connecting link between Atlanta and Birmingham; the other, with the then small and relatively unknown R. J. Reynolds Tobacco Company in Winston-Salem, North Carolina. He chose the latter, and thus got in on the ground floor of what became one of the nation's most successful corporations. The slogans, "I'd walk a mile for a Camel" and "Winstons taste good like a cigarette should" are known the world over. It was a fortunate choice.

It was a great change for me as far as school was concerned. In Savannah I had gone to the Haskell-Pape, a private school where I was happy. The reading class was best of all.. I remember the small group of students sitting on a window seat as they read aloud. Red geraniums lined the window sill.

In Winston-Salem I was sent to the West End Public School, which was a big, ugly red brick building with double desks clamped to the floor. My deskmate smelled of snuff. The teacher was stern, and, it seemed to me, unjust. I was not good at arithmetic. I was struggling with percentages when my mother and several of my friends' mothers decided to take us out of the West End School and send us to Salem Academy, the Moravian school in the Salem part of Winston-Salem. The academy is the oldest girls' school in the United States, founded in 1772. Boarding pupils came from all over the South, but my friends and I were day pupils. I spent eight happy years at Salem Academy and Salem College.

At Salem a girl could be a "special" student and take what she wanted, so I gave up mathematics. But special students could still be a part of the class and could progress from class to class. I continued as a special student. Years later my mother was at the Meadowbrook Golf Club, explaining to friends about my education. Charlie Howard, in his tennis whites, was nearby and overheard the conversation. He exclaimed to himself, "What a hell of a way to raise a daughter." He had no idea he would marry that daughter not too many years after that.

Just before my senior year, when I wanted to graduate with my class, I was told that if I made up and passed algebra and geometry, I could do so. I was tutored in the summer, and given the necessary credits.

I had majored in art. My Mother was an accomplished artist, so it seemed natural for me to follow along those lines. Salem had excellent courses in design, drawing, painting, sculpture.

At Salem, chapel was held every morning with the President, faculty and student body present. The seniors, wearing caps and gowns, marched in singing the opening hymn, and then were seated on the platform. It was always a dash for me. Claude, our chauffeur, drove me to Salem. I would sleep until the last minute, rush through breakfast, grab my books; Claude would go as fast as possible, probably twenty-five miles an hour. As the procession was starting down the aisle, I would struggle into my gown, put on my cap somehow or other, and enter singing vigorously "Awake, my soul, stretch every nerve and press with vigor on."

It became a leitmotif of my life.

There was a rule at Salem College that only boarding pupils could hold the top class and college offices, but when I graduated as a day student, I was Vice-President of my class, and held the second highest academic rank, and I was Vice-President of the College Student Government Association.

So the years at Salem went happily by—basketball, Cotillion Club, dramatics, student government, a struggle with physics, success in English, Latin, and History, good work in drawing, painting, design, sculpture.

In 1917 soon after the United States entered the First World War, Katherine Montague Graham graduated from Salem College with a Fine Arts diploma. We "came out" at the Debutante Ball, given by the eligible men at the Twin City Club. One of the older men, in his late twenties, was in love with me and wanted to marry me. He promised me a car with my initials on it.

Then into my life came Lieutenant Frederick Atwood. War had been declared. We were having sugarless and meatless days. My Father didn't seem to think we were suffering too much when we had shad on meatless days.

Frederick was the son of one of mother's art school friends in Massachusetts. He was stationed in Charlotte, North Carolina, and came up to spend a weekend with us. He had dark hair and dark eyes. He was dynamic and vital. He was the first man I loved. When he came into a room, it was brighter and happier because he was there. His smile illuminated everything. He and I fell in love with each other, and it was agreed that when he came home from the war, we would be married. My father approved of him.

Frederick was majoring in government at Harvard when he volunteered and became a second lieutenant in the infantry. He came for weekends in Winston-Salem at our house from February, when the early forsythia was just coming out, until April, when we said good-bye and he went off to France.

It was then that I decided to go to a northern college until he came back.

Going to college was so simple then. I wrote off for

Katherine Graham coming home from school, age seven, Savannah, Georgia.

Katherine Graham—Captain, Basketball team—age sixteen.

Joseph Lewis Graham, Winston-Salem, North Carolina.

Mrs. Joseph L. Graham.

catalogues for Smith, Wellesley, and Vassar. Wellesley was "out" because I would have to take a course in mathematics, and I knew I couldn't do it. Smith was all right. They would accept a science in place of mathematics, and I could take zoology. I didn't seem to consider Vassar very seriously. Winston-Salem girls didn't go to northern colleges. As Will, who wanted to marry me, said, "Katherine, any girl who has been to Salem has got all the education she needs." I told Will that I couldn't marry him, that I was going off to college and that I was in love with Frederick Atwood. He said, "I wish you hadn't told me that."

In August came the telegram:

2nd Lieutenant Frederick M. Atwood, Co. F, 2nd battalion, 58th infantry, killed in action, August 5, 1918, while leading his platoon during attack by his battalion to cross the Vesle River.

I was prostrate with grief. I shut myself up in my room and sobbed and sobbed. My Mother said, "I didn't know you cared so much." Life had lost its meaning. There was nothing to live for. After some days, a friend of my Father, seeing my griefstricken face, said, "Katherine, the man you loved has been killed. To you, it seems the end of everything, but as an older man, let me tell you that love comes more than once. You will never forget Frederick, but you will find love again."

It was fortunate that I was going away to college—away to new surroundings, new challenges. In September I left for Northampton. My dresses were down to my ankles. We wore hats. Before college opened, I submitted my reports (straight A's in almost every subject), my science notebook, and my art portfolio. I intended to major in art.

The Latin professor gave me full credit for all my Latin courses. Professor Bassett knew Salem College and gave me full credit for all my history courses. The science professor thought my science notebook a little inadequate, but still accepted it and gave me credit. So did the French teacher, but this was a mistake. I wasn't prepared for the advanced class to which I was assigned. I had to ask to go back to a conversational French class. Before I knew it I had so many credits they suggested I go into graduate school. But I was eighteen going on nineteen; I had never had resident college life; I wanted that. So it was settled that I would be a full member of the Junior Class.

I knew that when I graudated, I wanted a job. I was still thinking of a career in art. I even knew that I wanted a salary of $5,000, a lot of money then. I asked the head of the art department what sort of work my art degree might lead to. "Why," he said brightly, "you might get a job in a museum." My face fell. I could feel myself shut up with those plaster casts and statues. Sunshine, light, and people would be left outside. I felt as if I would be enclosed in a sepulchre. I thanked him, picked up my portfolio, walked out and decided to major in Government and American History. Actually, the professor's casual remark changed the course of my life. I did major in Government and American History. I did marry a man who was dedicated to government, and I was to take a major part in local, state, and national politics myself.

As I sat in John M. Greene Hall the first morning of the college session, sitting alone at the rear of the hall, I watched the student body as they filed past me, and I didn't know anyone. I was on my own. This was what I wanted. I was tired of being known everywhere in Winston-Salem as Mr. and Mrs. Joseph L. Graham's daughter. I wanted to try my own wings. Winston-Salem was a conforming place. I had conformed. Now I was making a start, unknown and unplaced. At Smith I wasn't looking for social life or for men.

In time I became a member of the Smith College Debating Team, which defeated our male opponents in the intercollegiate debate. It was held in that same John M. Greene Hall, where I had sat alone and unknown not too long ago. The debate was sheer hard work in an unknown field. The subject of the debate was "Resolved that Trade Union Agreements Should Be Made Through Collective Bargaining." I didn't know what collective bargaining was, nor did I know anything about trade unions. Certainly Reynolds Tobacco Company and Hanes Knitting Mills in Winston-Salem were not unionized at that time.

I was still new and eager to meet a challenge, so when I was chosen to speak for Smith College, I accepted. This meant hours and hours of research in the stacks of the Library. It meant writing off for more material, correlating it, developing

11

my arguments in writing. Then it had to be, for me, committed to memory. Better, of course, to speak extemporaneously from notes, but I wasn't up to that then. Being the speaker for the negative I spoke after my opponent. An English teacher in the audience told me the next day that when I first began, she didn't recognize my voice, but as I got into my argument I warmed up and became natural. I remember looking out over that great audience in John M. Greene Hall, every seat taken, and feeling the strength and power begin to come. After the affirmative and negative presentations, we withdrew from the stage for a few minutes. When we came back for the rebuttal, I couldn't wait to say my piece. My opponent had led right into something I knew all about. He referred to the company union at the General Electric plants. The previous weekend my roommate's weekend guest had been the son of the President of General Electric. I talked to him about G.E.'s policies. He told me a bit and sent me full information which I read, learned, and inwardly digested. In the rebuttal, spoken without notes, the words poured out. I knew what I was talking about. I marshalled my facts; the words came freely and fluently; and I won the debate for Smith College.

When the debate was over, I threw myself into working for the senior play. I tried out for Portia and Bassanio in "The Merchant of Venice," which our class would present on two evenings in Commencement Week. Agnes Grant, the leading dramatic star in our class, got Portia, and I was chosen for Bassanio. Professor Eliot, son of Harvard's former President, was our coach. He had to show me how to seize and embrace Portia. She weighed about thirty pounds more than I did! The senior play was to me the best part of the senior year. Even today I look at the photographs and marvel at the beauty of the scenery and costumes, designed by members of the cast, and remember my pleasure in my part.

I was also Chairman of the Class Book Committee. Somehow or other I got that done, along with final examinations.

When I invited one of my housemates to a tea to meet my Mother, who had come for commencement, she said wearily, "I wish Kay wouldn't always be running a three-ring circus."

II

THE BEAU FROM MASSACHUSETTS

After I received my B.A. degree, Mother and I went to Boston for a short stay before returning to Winston-Salem.

I had had three jobs offered me: one, from Smith College, to stay on in the Department of Government and work for an M.A.; one came from my former art teacher at Salem, to teach art in a Pennsylvania school; a third was from the DuPont Corporation in Wilmington, Delaware. The first two I promptly declined. The DuPont one appealed to me. I wanted a job and an apartment of my own.

Mother and I were staying at the Women's City Club in Boston. We were invited to go out to the Meadowbrook Golf Club in Reading for the Saturday night Baked Bean Supper and dance. It was a family club with excellent tennis courts and a good nine-hole golf course. There would be homemade baked beans, both pea and kidney; as well as salad, blueberry and apple pie, and coffee. After supper the tables would be cleared away and a good three-piece orchestra would play for dancing.

Ordinarily I would have been pleased to go, but I was feeling let down from all the Commencement activities, and "Besides," I said to my mother, "I won't know anyone and no one will dance with me." But Mother wanted to go and so we did.

After supper, the Club President, Charlie Howard, was introduced to me, and we danced. I thought, as we danced, that he took himself rather seriously. He had graduated from Harvard and the Law School. He had been overseas in active duty in the Meuse-Argonne, had come out of the war as a Captain. Now he had his own law firm and was Selectman of the Town of Reading. He seemed impressively old—thirty-two years to my twenty-one.

I liked the way he danced the two-step, the fox trot, and, most of all, the waltz. He was strong and vital, with a fine sense of rhythm. All the time we danced we were talking, really talking—about President Wilson, whom we both admired; about the League of Nations—a tragedy that it was defeated. One of the things I instantly liked about Charlie was the fact that we could talk about all kinds of things. It was such a change! He expected a girl to have a brain. (His mother had taken a medical degree from the University of Michigan and had practiced medicine before she was married. His sister was a Phi Beta Kappa at Wellesley, and beautiful too.)

There was no insincere chitchat. I liked that. He bumped me into a post as we were dancing. I teased him about it. We had a good time. After a while, he said good-bye and went home. He had saved my evening.

The next day he telephoned to ask me to go with him to the Harvard Class Day Exercises and the Harvard-Yale baseball game. It didn't surprise me. In the South people always show courtesies like that to visiting girls. When he sent me a corsage of red roses to wear, I attributed it to the same reason.

Before the Wednesday arrived, he sent me a note saying that as we were sitting where the sun would be in my eyes, I had best wear a hat with a brim, or carry a parasol. But I only had one hat, a pretty and becoming one with accordion-pleated blue grosgrain ribbon, turned up in front.

So Charlie called for me. Wearing the heavenly blue hat and the crimson roses pinned at my waist, I tripped down the Women's City Club steps. A long, low-slung sports car was drawn up at the curb. I made for that, but no. Charlie steered me across Beacon Street and the Common and down into the subway. I couldn't have been more surprised. I had never been out with a man who didn't call for me in a car.

Charlie was fun and gay, with a marvelous sense of humor. We talked about Professors Taussig and Munro. He had studied under Professor Munro, and we had used his textbook at Smith.

Charlie didn't have any "line" at all. He never once said that I was "the most attractive girl he had ever met." Charlie's failure to pay me any compliments at all intrigued me. That afternoon, to me, he was a polite Yankee being courteous to a visiting Southerner.

Sure enough, the sun was in my eyes. I took off my hat and turned it around so that the brim shaded my eyes. Charlie looked startled. I don't think he was so shocked again until I took my shoes off at the Republican National Convention of 1952.

At the end of a week, Mother went back to Winston-Salem, but I was invited to visit friends near Boston and on Cape Cod.

Charlie and I found quite a lot to do. We went to tennis matches at the Longwood Cricket Club. We went to lunch at the Copley Plaza or Young's Hotel or at the Parker House, where all the colored waiters knew him. Being a law partner, Charlie could take time off when he pleased. One day, when my hostess, Mrs. Thomas, and I were bound for the seashore for the day, Charlie "just happened" to be at the corner where we would pass. When Mrs. Thomas saw him, she stopped and invited him to join us. He jumped in. Sitting in the front seat beside me, the closest physical proximity we had had up to this time, my white angora sweater shed on his blue coat, which seemed to embarrass him.

Charlie and I played tennis at the Meadowbrook Golf Club. He let me win. When we shook hands across the net, the look in his eyes told me he loved me.

Just before I was to leave, at the end of two weeks, he took me to see the exhibition golf matches at the Belmont Country Club. Francis Ouimet was playing. We followed the players. When the match was over, Charlie led me to a secluded pine grove. There he told me that he loved me and asked me to marry him.

I was unprepared for this. I was fresh from college. I felt that so much had been done for me that I had a debt to pay. I wanted to justify myself. In the fortnight I had found an extraordinary congeniality with this attractive and forthright older man. I might be ready for love, I thought, but not for marriage, and in those days you didn't take one without the other. I asked for time to think it over.

When I told Mrs. Thomas, she was aghast. She felt responsible for me. She had thought Charlie was interested in someone else. What would my family say? To cap it all, she said, "But, Katherine, how would you get along with the Howards? They are all so intellectual." This amused me, for in the South I had been considered a little too intellectual for my own good.

Back home in Winston-Salem, I still contemplated the DuPont job. The position offered me was to screen the applicants for their training course, and it appealed to me. But my feeling for Charlie deepened. When he wrote and said I had to choose the job or him, I was in a state for days. By October, when he came to see me in Winston-Salem, I took one look when he stepped off the train, and I knew the answer.

Now the question was not whether I loved him enough to marry him right away, but whether my family would permit my marrying him.

From the beginning my Mother had liked and admired Charlie and so had my New England grandfather, who was a friend of his parents. But my Father took a dislike to him. It began on this first visit to Winston-Salem. After meeting him at the station, we drove to the house, and soon sat down to lunch. Charlie set out to be amusing and entertaining. He told stories exceedingly well, but the choice of his subject that day was unfortunate. He recounted pranks at Harvard, dropping a bag of water from an upstairs window on a professor as he stepped out the door below; locking with bolt and chain the grilled gates at the head of the subway stairs which emerged at Harvard Square, etc. I could see my Father becoming more and more stiff. His code did not allow for practical jokes. He thought they were stupid, silly, and not in good taste. He was not amused.

It was warm. As Charlie talked gaily on, he picked up his iced tea glass. Down clattered the coaster which had adhered to the glass. Charlie paused, looked disconcerted, continued his stories, lifted his glass. Down clattered the coaster again. Oh dear! Things were not going well.

But that evening Daddy invited Charlie to have a drink with

him before dinner. This was a man-to-man ceremony, not a general cocktail hour as we have now.

"What would you like to drink?" asked my Father.

"Bourbon, if you please," Charlie replied.

"How will you take it?"

"Straight," said Charlie.

My Father paused, poured, and gave him a look of approval and respect.

But my Father's doubts remained. He told Charlie that I was just out of college, had not seen the world, was emotionally immature, that I should see more of the world and meet other people before I settled down. However, he did not object when we became engaged in September. He did insist that the engagement should not be announced, and we had to promise to wait a year to be married. My Father hoped that in that time I would change my mind.

I wore my engagement ring on a ribbon around my neck, inside my dress. Charlie had designed the ring himself, and had Bigelow-Kennard make it, a sapphire, because of my blue eyes, and because it was my birthstone, held by prongs on each side set with twenty-one small diamonds because I was twenty-one years old. The prongs were his arms embracing me.

Charlie came back to the South at Christmastime to visit and share in the festivities. He would escort me home from a dance, and then walk back downtown to the Hotel Zinzendorf where he stayed.

Two comments came to me from the kitchen:

"Mister Charlie looks like he's worn a tuxedo all his life."

The other one: "Miss Katherine, Mr. Charlie ought not to be walking back downtown late at night. He looks too rich." (In Winston-Salem no one ever walked.)

Charlie carried himself well. He was erect, and walked with a spring in his step. He had been on the cross-country team at Harvard, and had served in the infantry in the war, so recently over. He liked walking. He was tall, slender, athletic. His eyes were blue, and he had blond hair and strong features. In some ways he resembled my family. But in spite of physical resemblance, Charlie and my Father were fundamentally different. My father was reserved and an introvert—quite

17

serious. Charlie liked to tell jokes and stories. He belonged to many clubs and organizations and often became President, but fundamentally he was every bit as serious as my father.

At Eastertime Charlie returned. Then the long summer of waiting began. My engagement had been announced at a luncheon in the spring, and plans were now being made for the wedding in September. Mother went away for several weeks' vacation. Daddy and I were alone. One evening he had a long talk with me.

"Katherine," he said, "you are making a mistake to marry Charlie. I am a judge of men. He is a pleasant, intelligent person, but he will not go far in life.

"You are young. You are immature in matters of the heart. You may find as you grow older that other men are interested in you. Your marriage might be wrecked. I advise you not to go through with it. If you do, I shall change my will and leave you out of it."

This was a staggering announcement. To be cut off was a devastating thought both financially and emotionally. I was stunned.

We sat there in the library after dinner, talking in deadly seriousness. I didn't storm or shout or protest. There wouldn't have been any use. When my Father made up his mind, he did not yield to threats or cajolery.

I, too, had made up my mind. I was not going to be pressured by material considerations. Charlie and I loved each other. We would make our own way.

When I had recovered from the shock of his words, I said, "Daddy, Charlie and I love each other, and I am going to marry him."

No more was said, but he set matters in motion. Before we were married, I knew he had indeed written me out of any inheritance from him.

At the same time he wrote to Charlie telling him that he thought the marriage inadvisable and recounting to him all my faults. Charlie wrote my Father a dignified and well-phrased reply. He did not agree with my Father's characterization of me—in fact, he resented it. Charlie's reply made an impression on my Father but he did not change his mind.

My Father changed his tack. He asked me if I didn't want to study law—an unheard-of idea for most Southerners. I said that I'd rather get married. Then my husband must be good enough to be Secretary of State. Why must I marry Charlie Howard, he wanted to know?

My friends in Winston-Salem could not understand why Charlie didn't come to Winston-Salem to live, like the other men who married Winston-Salem girls. The Grahams were a prominent family. My father was a director of the R. J. Reynolds Tobacco Company. Mr. and Mrs. Graham were part and parcel of everything that went on in Winston-Salem. Why did he insist on taking me up North? They knew we had bought a white house with a garden and a stone wall and an apple tree. But it was considered not the thing at all that there was not going to be a cook in that kitchen. "Katherine isn't even going to have a servant!"

But none of these things troubled me. Charlie and I loved each other. The future was ours, and we would make it together.

III

SENATOR HOWARD

As I walked down the aisle of St. Paul's Episcopal Church on the arm of my Father, my eyes sought out Charlie Howard, waiting for me at the foot of the altar steps. At last we were getting married! I also noted that one of the candles on the altar was drooping in the heat.

There had been various contretemps, one of the last ones being a warning from Bishop Nash that all the decorations and the musical program might have to be changed. This was sent out to all brides being married that fall. He felt weddings were getting too ostentatious. My Mother met the Bishop at the train and took him straight to the church. "Now, Bishop Nash," she said, "I want the decorations to be just the way you want them to be. If they are too elaborate, we will change them." Whether he succumbed to Mother's charm, or just appreciated the opportunity to register his disapproval, he did say that the beautiful flowers and smilax were quite all right, but that the secular song, which was to have been sung in the middle of the service, must be changed to the singing of "The Lord's Prayer." That was easily arranged.

In the usual Southern custom, the wedding was an evening one—at eight o'clock, Saturday, September 15, 1921. Who could have imagined that the City Fathers would also decide to open "The Great White Way" of the new city lights on that same evening and that everyone from the surrounding countryside would swarm into the city. Or that the best man,

Professor Henry Thomas Moore, later President of Skidmore College, would be forced to abandon his car and walk from the Hotel Zinzendorf to St. Paul's Church because of the traffic jam? In full evening regalia, his six-foot, two-inch stature enhanced by a tall silk hat, he hurried along the crowded sidewalk, while farmers from the surrounding county said, "My ain't he the Big One!"

Meanwhile Charlie and the Bishop paced the floor in the vestry room, turning the corners in military fashion and glaring at each other. Where was the Best Man? Fortunately, fearing late arrivals, I had told the organist not to start the wedding march till quarter past eight. By that time Henry arrived at last with the ring. The service could proceed.

I was wearing a beautiful wedding dress in the style of 1921—dropped waistline, flat bust, skirt fourteen inches from the floor—adorned with silk velvet flowers appliqued by hand, pearl passementerie from my Mother's wedding dress, and a lace bertha from my Grandmother's. It also had a handsome court train.

Then to the Forsythe Country Club for the wedding reception. We had Meyer Davis's Orchestra down from New York to play at the reception, and the wedding cake was from Sherry's in Baltimore. There was a full moon shining in the warm September sky. Charlie and I danced the first dance together to the strains of "Poor Butterfly."

But why was Bob Hanes looking at me so strangely? He was head of the Trust Department of the Wachoria Bank and Trust Company. Was he trying to figure out why Mr. Joseph L. Graham had just changed his will and disinherited his daughter? Was he wondering how I was feeling, and what had brought this about?

It was no wonder that Hanes was puzzled. He had met Charlie in the First World War when Captain Howard and Captain Hanes were both traveling to Avignon. They had found mutual interests, and he knew Charlie to be an officer and a gentleman. What could Mr. Graham have against this New Englander?

Dr. and Mrs. Howard had come down for the wedding and received with us at the reception. It was easy to see that Dr. Howard was a man of distinction, and Hanes learned that he was the former director of the Massachusetts General Hospital, now retired. He couldn't understand it.

My Father and Dr. Howard had drinks together and liked each other. Daddy was impressed with Dr. Howard's forceful and genial personality and his standing as the leading authority on hospital administration in the country.

Looking back on it, I wonder that my Father's opposition didn't trouble me more at the time. What did trouble me was the thought of losing my identity as "Kay Graham." I wondered what lay ahead for Mrs. Charles P. Howard.

Pelted with rice, we drove away to spend the night in a suite in a hotel in Greensboro, which Charlie had decked with red roses. As I kissed my Father good-bye, he slipped $100 into my pocketbook, my dowry.

At the time of our marriage Charlie's law practice was going well so he planned a month's honeymoon: first, Washington and Mt. Vernon; then New York and the Biltmore Hotel, and tea dancing and evenings at the theater.

Finally on to Reading where we picked up country clothes for a visit to Goshen, New Hampshire. Some years before, Charlie's mother had bought the New England farmhouse, built in 1830, with 100 acres of land. Now it is one of the places I love best in the world. But at that time I was ignorant of the country and of country ways. I didn't know how to cook. I had never encountered a wood stove, or a house without running water or electricity. It was the end of September. The dark came early and the days were cold and crisp, or damp and cold.

Charlie made the fires and brought the water. To hurry the cooking, I took the lids off the stove so the aluminum pots would be over the flame. They got all sooty. I felt obliged to scrub the bottoms of Mother Howard's kettles, so I would leave them as shiny as I found them. Charlie accepted what he got without complaint.

After a week, my birthday arrived. It was cold and dark. It didn't seem very gay. I didn't know how to make a cake, and we had no ice cream. I was tired with the unaccustomed work. After our dinner of lamb chops, I sat on Charlie's lap and he said, "Darling, I didn't get you a present. Here is the camera we brought along. I am giving it to you." That did it! I dissolved into tears. Then out of his pocket came the present he had bought me, a sapphire and pearl bar pin which he had gotten for me in New York. Charlie taught me about fields and streams, and how cozy it is to light a fire in the stove in the bedroom in the morning and hear the crackle of the logs as they blaze while you lie in bed and the room warms up.

From Goshen we went to the Ravine House in Randolph, New Hampshire. We started off in the morning with our box lunches, across the meadow and up the trail. "Don't stop," said Charlie, "keep climbing." We did. I said to myself, "This will be like life; you climb up and up, and it is hard, but you keep going. Then finally you reach the top and you are rewarded for your efforts. Today when we finally get there, the view will be magnificent." It was early October and the foliage was brilliant. We sat and ate our lunch in the sunshine. Then onward and upward. But as we approached the summit of Mt. Adams, a blinding snowstorm swirled around us, and we crouched behind a rock to protect ourselves from the wind and the storm. No view. Was life going to be like this?

Before our week was up, a crisis developed at the law office, and we had to cut short our honeymoon and return to Reading, where the realities of life began to impinge upon us. Charlie had married me with a thriving law practice and a small income from his grandfather's trust. Now the depression of 1921 was making itself felt. His law practice was not so remunerative. His grandfather's holdings were largely in real estate and people could not pay their rents, so the income from that shrank. My hundred dollars had not lasted very long.

We were soon very hard up. Charlie's law practice shrank because of the depression. But more than that, Charlie began to suspect that he was putting a lot more money from his fees into the joint account of the firm than he was able to draw on. We went over bank statements and deposit slips and recorded fees. Charlie put a stop order on Fickett and Howard checks. One evening when we went to dinner in an out-of-the-way restaurant north of Reading, there was Charlie's partner, who lived on the South Shore, with an attractive woman, not his wife. Needless to say, the four of us were surprised and embarrassed.

Next day when Charlie went to his office, Fickett, who handled the funds, insisted that Charlie would find everything in order when he finished going over the accounts. Charlie wanted to believe him, for they had been friends in Harvard College and Harvard Law School.

But one morning Fickett did not appear at the office. Not all day—not the next day—no, his wife did not know where he was. He disappeared into thin air. Various members of the bar have told Charlie since that Fickett dropped in to see them just before he left, and borrowed from them $100 to $500 to "tide him over an emergency." It was the last they saw of him. This happened in the spring of 1922, and there has never been any trace of him since.

This was a knockdown for Charlie, emotionally and financially. His friend, his partner, had stolen his money and absconded. It was a blow to the prestige of the firm. Fickett's clients had to be dealt with. How much of their money had he gotten away with—how much money, if any, was left? The office payroll had to be met. It was a grim time. For the first time I saw Charlie under stress, and I was proud of the way he met it.

In the time of crisis I tried to economize on food. One day I walked downtown to the market and bought a beef heart. Following the cookbook, I boiled it. Then I made a stuffing. I stuffed the heart, got a needle and thread and sewed it up, put it in the oven and basted it as it baked for hours.

When Charlie came home to a table set with fine linen and sterling silver and candles, I put it on a silver platter and proudly bore it in.

"What is it?" said Charlie.

"Beef heart!" I replied happily.

"Oh, darling," my husband said. "I never could eat innards!"

This time I didn't dissolve into tears.

The house had an inadequate heating system. Of course it was a coal furnace. Charlie would feed it in the morning, let it blaze up, then before he went to Boston, he would bank it for the day.

One day it was terribly cold in the house. Even with a

wool dress and my heavy white athletic sweater on, with the "S" I had won for Varsity basketball at Salem College, I was cold.

I called Charlie at the State House. "Charlie," I said, "I'm freezing. What shall I do?"

"Well, darling," he replied, "just put the shades way up and let the sunshine in!"

Reading was a change from Winston-Salem. It was a fine New England town, with what seemed to me a classless society. When the expressman came to deliver a belated wedding present, he would say, "How's Charlie?" I was surprised by his use of the first name, but I liked the informality.

I loved my house, which Charlie had given me as a wedding present. In the living room there was a Franklin stove and a sunny bay window. With some of our wedding money we had bought an empire sofa, a Boston rocker, and a table.

Charlie's aunt gave us our mahogany dining room furniture, table, chairs, a Sheraton sideboard, even a rug! His mother and father had given us custom-made mahogany bedroom furniture. In my own house it was a pleasure to use and display our wedding presents.

I made a flower garden, and Charlie planted a vegetable garden to help with the budget. I was learning to cook. One day I exclaimed to a friend that I had just learned how to boil onions. She looked surprised and said, "What do you do?" "Why," I said, "you bring them to a boil, then pour off the water, put in fresh water and cook until done. In this way you avoid the strong taste." The story as to how I cooked onions was repeated and I realized that as the Southern bride of Charlie Howard, I was under scrutiny.

I went with Charlie to Town Meetings. He was Selectman and later Moderator, and how much I learned at these meetings in old Security Hall! Against a stage setting of castles and trees used for theatrical performances, Charlie and Mr. Charles, the Town Clerk, would be sitting at a plain, pine table on the platform. Charlie would rise, bang the gavel, and say, "The day and hour named in the warrant having arrived, the meeting will be in order! The clerk will read the warrant."

Ponderous Mr. Charles would unfold himself, rise, and begin the reading of the warrant, which was, in effect, advance notice of the projects for which money was to be appropriated. A selectman would then stand and say, "Mr. Moderator, I move that further reading of the warrant be dispensed with." When that motion was carried, he would say, "I move that we take up Article I." We were underway. A New England town meeting is the purest form of democracy. The citizens meet to appropriate funds for the School Committee, roads, welfare, zoning, and sewer projects. Prior to the meeting the different committees have made up their budgets for the year, and after they have been reviewed by the Finance Committee, they would be acted upon at town meeting. As with all such meetings, there were certain predictable characters—Louis Lyons, later curator of the Nieman Fellows at Harvard, and radio and TV commentator, was then a resident of Reading. Young and redheaded, he would sit in an aisle seat on the left-hand side. He asked searching questions and was apt to be critical. Mr. Berle sat in an aisle seat on the right-hand side of the center aisle, and could be counted on for a long discussion of almost any subject; and Mr. John Devaney was always against spending a lot of money on schools. He had made a success of life with very little education—why couldn't others do the same?

Charlie, as Moderator, ruled with light, but firm, touch. He knew parliamentary procedure backwards and forwards. When a vote was a foregone conclusion, he didn't wait for the nays, after the ayes were clearly unanimous. He knew the people by name—and by reputation too—and often he would make an amusing quip.

In Reading, all my New England ancestry came to the fore. In each of us there are many strains of inheritance, and my Southern upbringing still conditioned me. When I was young in Savannah my colored nurse would say to me, "Don't do that, honey. Little ladies don't act like that." We spoke gently and courteously. We didn't raise our voices or slam doors. We tried to be as pretty as we could and we aimed to please everyone, but the male sex in particular: fathers (not brothers) and all other men. Your success in life depended upon being pleasing to a man. But always there was in me a strong desire to do things myself, not just be dependent on a man's pleasure. This sent me off to Smith College, induced

me to defy my Father and marry Charlie. Later I was to find
that even in spite of our strong love I couldn't just live
through him. I had to do things myself.

Who were these New England ancestors? The three who
interested me most were Aquila Chase, whose name I have
seen on the little statue in Newbury, Massachusetts, with the
others who landed there in 1636, one of whose descendants,
John Kirby Chase, married my great grandmother Adelaide
Ann Titcomb, whom I knew and remember. When she was
four years old, she was chosen to present a welcoming
bouquet to General Lafayette, when he visited this country in
1824. In Kittery, Maine, she presented him with a bouquet of
flowers. He picked her up and kissed her. When I was seven,
she kissed me! Aquila Chase moved from Newbury to
Hampton, New Hampshire. He is called "an historic founder
of New Hampshire." Tristram Coffin appealed to me because
of his fascinating name, and the fact that he was the Chief
Magistrate of Nantucket with governing powers in the period
between 1671 and 1680.

Perhaps the most colorful was Samuel Nowell, from
whom my mother was descended on her father's side. Dis-
guised as an Indian, he met with other like-minded "liberty
boys" at the old South Meeting House in Boston, proceeded
from there to throw the English tea into Boston Harbor, this
act being one of the events leading up to the American Revolution. "No taxation without representation" was the cry.

The blood of these early leaders and protestors runs
strong in my veins.

Now, following the crisis in his law office, Charlie decided
to run for the State Senate. Ever since he had studied
Government under Graham Wallas at Harvard, Charlie had
felt that at some time in his career he wanted to devote himself to public service. This seemed to be the moment. It was
his way of saying that he had received a knockdown in Boston, but he meant to stand up and show the world that he
could be his own man. It was not something that we thrashed
out together. Jesse Morton, then Reading's Town Counsel,
and later Judge of the Woburn District Court said to me,
"Charlie ought not to run for the Senate. He should get
elected to the House of Representatives first. He'll never make

it now!" Charlie's Father did not approve either. He said that if Charlie wanted to go into politics, why didn't he run for District Attorney, which would be a help in his legal profession. But no, Charlie wanted to run for the Senate, and he announced his candidacy. Despite his disapproval, Dr. Howard lent Charlie $1,000. for campaign expenses, which were minimal then compared to present days. He approached good friends like Henry Shattuck, who was already in the Legislature, and he drew on his own savings. All in all, it was a small amount.

This was my introduction to politics. In the beginning, there was no organization except three good friends of Charlie's and me as the fourth member. Charlie said one morning, "We've got to get all these announcements of my candidacy mailed. Couldn't you call up some people to come over and help address them?" I called some neighbors and we sat around our dining room table for days addressing, stuffing, stamping, and sealing the letters.

The Howards had moved to Reading only a few years previously, when Dr. Howard retired. Charlie was, therefore, relatively a newcomer to the District. It was important that he call on the leaders and introduce himself to the Chairmen of the Republican Town Committees, and Republican State Committee members. Wives at that time did not usually campaign with their husbands. Women's suffrage had just been enacted. Politics was almost exclusively a man's world. But I went along with Charlie. Sometimes I would sit in the car when he went in to talk with a party leader and ask for his support. Sometimes, if it were a tough customer, he might take me in to help soften the opposition.

We worked day and night. The week before the Republican Primary election, Charlie asked me to help make arrangements for election day. We set up a Headquarters and made schedules for cars to meet the trains as they arrived from Boston, and to take people to the polls. We made it known that older people and invalids could call Howard Headquarters and be driven to the polls and home again.

On the Saturday before the election, a scurrilous handbill was circulated all over the district by Charlie's opponent, accusing Charlie of being "a State Street lawyer, robbing widows and orphans." I was sick at heart but it was too late to try to answer it. Charlie and I worked feverishly. Finally the day arrived.

The voting in Reading was in Security Hall. Charlie explained to me that there would be boards set up for him with duplicate voting lists. These would be covered by our friends. As a person gave his name to the teller, we would check it off on our list, and at the end of the day, we would telephone and send cars for those who had not yet voted. Charlie and I got volunteers to cover the boards for all the voting hours. I went down when the polls opened (I could not yet vote in Massachusetts, because I had not lived in the state for a year) to find that the volunteers were just standing around not doing anything. So, as the candidate's wife, I took charge and told them what to do. All day long I was there, directing as the shifts came and went. Charlie was off going to all the polls in the Seventh Middlesex District, which ran from Reading up to Ayer, including Carlisle, Bedford, Burlington, Chelmsford, North Reading, Saugus, part of Lowell, and part of Lynn. It was both rural and industrial.

When the polls closed in Reading, Charlie was there. There had been a tremendous turnout. Sometime during the evening one of the men counting votes came back to say, "It looks good, Charlie, running about 90 percent for you." Sure enough, he was triumphantly nominated in the primary and elected in November. By November I could vote. In the privacy of a voting booth, a wooden cubicle with a shelf and a pencil attached to a string, I studied the ballot and marked my choices. Having campaigned with Charlie all summer and fall, I knew all the candidates: Channing Cox for Governor, Alvan T. Fuller for Lieutenant Governor, Frederick Cook for Secretary of State, John Jacob Rogers for Congressman, Nathaniel Bowditch for County Commissioner and Charles P. Howard for Senator, Seventh Middlesex Senatorial District.

It was a proud moment when, after his election, he took his seat in the Senate. He became one of its most effective members. The Republicans controlled the Senate and House and the constitutional offices of Governor, Lieutenant-Governor, and Secretary of State. Frank Allen, later Governor, was President of the Senate. Charlie soon found out which was the power group in the Senate and became a part of it. He was Chairman of the Committee on Labor and

Industry, served on the Judiciary Committee, and on the Rules Committee, the most powerful one in the Senate. John E. Thayer, Gaspar Bacon, and Eben Draper were fellow senators. There was a good deal of rivalry between them, for privately each one hoped to succeed Frank Allen when he moved up the stepladder to become Lieutenant Governor.

Charlie would discuss the bills with me. The Democrats were attacking the Republicans about legislation affecting the cotton mills. At that time, Massachusetts had the most advanced labor legislation in the country. I said, "The worst labor legislation in the country is in the South, where the Democrats have complete control of the legislative processes." This found its way into the discussion on the floor of the Senate.

It surprised me that Charlie, an idealist, a Harvard graduate, could be so successful with many of the very realistic politicians with whom he served. His humor and camaraderie served him in good stead. He had no "side." The Democrats liked him, and he liked them. It seemed to me that the Senators must spend a lot of time in the Senate cloakroom, for he would come home at night with, to me, the most appallingly risqué stories.

He offered, and got enacted into law, a bill for the psychiatric examination of prisoners. Governor Cox gave him the quill pen with which he signed the bill. He served with his friend, Representative Henry Shattuck, on the Coal Commission appointed by the Governor to find the causes and the remedy for the anthracite coal shortage, affecting industry, utilities, and homes in New England.

Those winter days of 1923 were busy and active and interesting ones. In addition to serving in the Senate, Charlie was Moderator of the town meetings in Reading, and he had his law office at 53 State Street. He had replaced Fickett with Robert Bushnell, later Attorney General of Massachusetts, and a colorful political figure. Stanley Snow was legal assistant to both of them.

All through the Primary and election campaigns I was joyfully pregnant, just naturally and happily carrying a much-wanted baby. I was in excellent health and spirits. The bigger I got, the more pleased I was, but it would surprise me when I would be making the twin beds, and my stomach would not quite clear the space between.

Charlie's mother and father left to go South on a vacation. But on a morning in March Charlie telephoned me. His father had dropped dead while changing a tire on an isolated road in Virginia on the homeward trip. I was knocked in a heap. Dr. Howard and I had had real rapport; I loved him. Now he was gone.

I just sat in the living room grieving. Bibulous, the fiery Airedale Dr. Cecil Drinker had given Dr. Howard, sensed that something was wrong. He came and put his head in my lap and mourned too.

Dr. Howard's death raised practical problems. Would Mother Howard want to go to her own home, or would she, knowing that a baby was soon to arrive, want to come to us? We opened her house and made it ready for her, and we prepared our guest room too. She elected to come to us. She was prostrate with grief. Each morning in the last month before our baby was born, I took a breakfast tray upstairs to her.

A week or so before the expected date, Mother came to stay. One morning as we were washing the breakfast dishes, pains started and I timed them by the clock. This must be it. I telephoned Charlie, who had just reached Boston. He turned around and came right home to drive Mother and me to the New England Hospital.

Mother said to Dr. Nute, "You'd better give her some chloroform to slow things down; the baby is apt to come quickly." Probably I had a high tolerance of pain, for as Dr. Nute and I talked about the beauty of the flowers in Alaska, my firstborn came popping into the world. In the confusion there must have been a breach of asepsis, for within a few days, I was at death's door with septicemia. No antibiotics then! My temperature soared to 106°, day after day after day. And all the time I nursed my baby, Margaret Nowell Howard, born April 28, 1923.

Charlie would come each day. I was too sick to talk. I was just happy that he was there. As my condition worsened, they sent for my family, who stood round my bedside, my Father and Mother, my brother Gregory. The Howard plot in the cemetery was not big enough so they bought an addition to bury me in.

But I turned the corner; my fever dropped; my appetite returned. Now it was late May and I was moved to the outdoor porch of the New England Hospital for Women and Children. Margaret was in a bassinet beside me. If she didn't make little sounds, I would fear that she was dead.

Then Charlie came to tell me that now that I was out of danger, he had to go with the Coal Commission to Pennsylvania to inspect the anthracite mines. I hated to have him go. It was one of the first times when official duties took him away from me when I wanted him and needed him. As any woman whose husband is in politics knows, it happens all the time.

A month later, at the end of June, I was well enough to go home to our house on Summer Avenue with our baby. She was plump and healthy, with blond hair and blue eyes, a very pretty baby and I loved her dearly. As I was recuperating after my return from the hospital, Charlie said to his Mother, "Katherine isn't strong. She gets so tired."

Mother Howard replied, "She has to get tired to get strong."

It seemed to me that the Howards were stronger physically, and more dominant in personality, than I, but I was not going to be downed. My strength grew to meet their strength.

The following year, in 1924, Charlie was reelected to the Senate. Again, I had campaigned with him, just going along as his wife, meeting people. Perhaps standing at the back of the hall, handing out cards while he spoke from the platform, doing the same things I had done in the previous campaign, then home over the Middlesex County dirt roads, talking over the meeting.

One morning the telephone rang. It was Charlie, calling from the State House. "Katherine," he said, "the Governor has asked me to become Budget Commissioner of Massachusetts, and Chairman of the Commission of Administration and Finance. Shall I take it?"

I was overcome. My first reaction was to laughingly say, "Charlie, how can you be Budget Commissioner? You've never kept a budget, and you wouldn't even look at the one I kept!" But then I congratulated him on the tremendous honor, and I was happy that we would have a settled income. The salary at that time was $7,500, and the term of office was four years. It is the top administrative post in the State Government, and the Commissioner is the Governor's right-hand man. He is now usually referred to as the Deputy Governor.

IV

WINSTON-SALEM IN THE SPRING

Each year I visited my parents, taking little Margaret with me. After my Father retired, he and Mother would visit us in the late spring and fall, as they came and went to Europe. When March would come, and spring in New England was still a long way off, my Father would send me a check and say, "Come on down to Winston-Salem for two or three weeks and meet spring here."

Charlie would say, "Fine, and I'll send you a check to come home."

My Father would meet me at the railroad station. We would drive through the town, and finally up our driveway.

In my mind's eye, Mother is standing at the top of the front steps waiting to greet me. She is wearing a tailored white wool dress, with a tiny line of red at neck and sleeves. Her blue eyes are sparkling and there is a welcoming smile.

Behind her the front door is open.

Claude opens the car door, and I leap up the steps. My Father comes up more slowly. We go into the hall, then into the living room where a fire is burning in the grate. There are flowers on the tables. Anna comes in from the kitchen to say, "Welcome home, Miss Katherine." Claude takes my bag upstairs to my room. I step outside with Mother to see the gardens, bright with spring flowers.

In the living room there are family portraits and water colors on the walls, oriental rugs on the floor, a fine mahogany table my Father had before his marriage, and the Victorian sofa which had come from my great-grandfather Chase's house on Nesmith Street, in Lowell. There are various easy chairs too, and a walnut rocker where my Father would sit after dinner and smoke his cigar. I sat with him and talked after dinner for the duration of the cigar.

My Father was an intellectual, largely self-educated because his family in Augusta, Georgia, had no money to send him to college just after the Civil War. He still remains in my mind as one of the most knowledgeable men I have ever known. He read history and literature. He knew facts and dates. He was never muddled. He knew what he knew.

Shakespeare was his great love. He would often read aloud to us, and he would assign to me in the morning passages which I had to learn and repeat to him in the evening. It might be "the quality of mercy is not strained . . ." and the ensuing speech of Portia in *The Merchant of Venice*. Or perhaps it would be Polonius' advice to his son from *Hamlet*, or "Now is the winter of our discontent. . . ."

He made it a rule that I read the *New York Times*, which came daily to our house. When the President made an important speech, he insisted that I read, not just the newspaper account of what he said, but the message itself. He also received the *Congressional Record* and would read passages of it to me. I remember his coming out on the front porch, *Congressional Record* in hand, saying, "Katherine, listen to this!" It was something very amusing which a Congressman had inadvertently said in the midst of a speech.

Across the hall from the living room was the library with another fireplace and built-in bookshelves. There was a set of Dickens, and Prescott's *History of Mexico*, and the encyclopedia, and the best of the modern books as they came out. Here, too, was Mother's Governor Winthrop desk, and here too, I had my first kiss, quite unexpectedly, while listening to "Throw Me a Rose" on the phonograph!

Soon it would be dinner time. Anna would have cooked beefsteak and french fried potatoes, snap beans, cooked with a little salt pork, hot biscuits, salad, and for dessert, floating island and a Lady Baltimore cake. Claude would have finished cutting the grass and would have put on his white coat to serve dinner.

36

Our house was of the English style. It stood on a rise with a great oak tree in front, and it looked off to glorious sunsets in the west. To the right were locust trees with their fragrant white blossoms in the spring, and to the left, a black walnut tree. This was the view from my bedroom. At the rear was a grassy lawn with flower beds around the edges, enclosed with a hedge. Then the grounds went down in terraces to the roadway behind the house.

My Father was a Director of the Reynolds Tobacco Company. Mr. Reynolds had built it from a small operation manufacturing snuff, chewing and pipe tobacco, to one of the most successful coporations in the country. My father and his associates prospered with the firm.

He and Mother were close friends of the Reynolds. In the years before Mr. Reynolds's death, he and my Father would play golf together every afternoon at "Reynolda," the Reynolds' estate. At four o'clock "Mr. R.J." would stop for my Father, who would be on the front lawn of our house in plus fours and practicing an approach shot. On other occasions, my Father wore the conservative "city" clothes of his day, with the high, stiff, rounded collar attached to the white shirt, which was always worn; and, of course, the clean white linen handkerchief in his pocket, but not visible.

Early in life my Father had decided he wanted to make a certain very adequate sum of money. He set a goal and achieved it in his early fifties. He had always known that after that, he wanted to travel in comfort and ease. Late in the twenties, he resigned from the Reynolds Tobacco Company and got out of the stock market. He was in no trouble when the crash came in October 1929.

He and Mother were doing what he had always dreamed of, traveling abroad for months at a time. They would settle down at a comfortable hotel. He would read. Mother would paint. They visited museums, met interesting people. They would return to America, stay in Winston-Salem a few months, come to Boston, then off again.

In these years the rapport between my Father and Charlie was growing stronger. There had never been any angry break or recriminations on our part. We had been too busy and too happy to be bitter. We had never asked him for help. My father was pleased at Charlie's success in the Senate (Charlie was serving his second term when he was asked to become Budget Commissioner), and my father was pleased at his being Commissioner of Administration and Finance. He could see that we were happy and his first grandchild gladdened his heart. He now found Charlie's stories (no longer about Harvard pranks) amusing. He couldn't wait for Charlie to come home at the end of the day. Charlie would have anecdotes about the State House, jokes from the Senate cloakroom, stories of the dramatic events always taking place under the Golden Dome.

Gradually, I made some tentative references to the will. I had begun to give it more serious thought as the relationship between my Father and me became warmer, and more accepting. He no longer felt it necessary to "bring me up," though he still admonished me to dress well and take my place in the world.

While he was mulling things over, he gave me a generous monthly allowance to be used for clothes, hair, entertainment, theater—nothing to go into household bills. Each month I would write and thank him and tell him how I had spent the money.

Finally Father made up his mind, as we learned when he consulted Charlie about the provisions for a new will. A letter from Winston-Salem began: "March 3, 1930, Dear Charlie, I enclose a draft of my new will. I wish you would look it over with your lawyer's eye, and see if it needs changes. If so, please make notes and let me have them by March 10, if possible. . . ."

When the will was signed and sealed, my Father had left Charlie a nice sum of money in his own right and had made him an Executor. I was reinstated, sharing equally with my two brothers.

Both my older brother and I felt that we had taken the brunt of the family upbringing. By the time my younger brother John came along, our parents had relaxed. He also had a smooth, easy, noncontroversial personality which helped.

I was much more apt to argue with my Father, and I had a stubborn streak. He could hurt my feelings, and sometimes he did. But I respected him. I felt he was a difficult man to get along with, but I wanted to get along with him. In later life I felt that some of my ability to work with men and to have their respect for me and their friendship for me was because of my Father. I learned to consider his feelings, to respect his moods, and to match my wits with his.

He was a stern disciplinarian. I always felt that in my upbringing I had been repressed. My Father was so eager for perfection in his children that we had a great deal of advice, most of it very good, and criticism, which at the time I resented but which I now know helped me a lot.

Daddy never swore. He never told an off-color story. In the South of my growing-up days, ladies did not drink or smoke. Gentlemen did not tell risqué stories in their presence. Divorce did not exist. Families went to church together and had Sunday dinner together. It was a tight, homogeneous society.

But my Father did not go to church. He was frankly an agnostic. Mother went to the Episcopal church and we went with her. Today I can hear her voice singing familiar Episcopal hymns. It did not seem to bother my Mother that our Father did not go to church too; nor did it bother the children.

Joseph L. Graham's hands were beautiful. He had long tapering fingers and beautiful nails. They were not the hands to fix a lock, or drive a nail, or make any simple household repairs. Indeed, he did not intend to do any of these things and no one expected him to. If he wanted the thermostat put up or another lump of cannel coal put on the fire in the grate, he would ring for Claude.

As to my Mother, her blue eyes sparkled all through her life. She was a joyous and optimistic person. She believed and we believed that the world was getting better and better. God was in his heaven, and all was right with the world. What wasn't just right, was, in the progress of the world, improving.

Mother was a graduate of the Boston Museum's School of Fine Arts. She was always proud of the fact that she had studied under Benson, Tarbell, and DeCamp, the greats of that day. They could have been proud of her too. She painted all of her life, fresh, vivid watercolors. As a child in Savannah, I would sometimes go with her to the park and draw a crayon picture while she painted. When my Father retired and they traveled, her paints and watercolor pad went with her. After he died, and she spent her summers at Marblehead Neck, she would have breakfast in bed, read French for half an hour, and then she might say, "I just have to go and paint this morning!" This would be her way of saying that, much as she enjoyed bridge luncheons and the garden club, she needed to use her own talent.

She had one-man shows in Marblehead and in Winston-Salem, Charlotte, and Chapel Hill in North Carolina. She exhibited in Boston, Atlanta and in Washington. When one of her pictures on exhibit had a star in the corner denoting that it was sold, she was pleased. She liked to compete professionally.

Mother walked with a quick, light step. She had a fine carriage. Perhaps this was due to the fact that as a young girl she had walked on Singing Beach in Manchester with her father, a light board attached to her shoulders to keep them straight, and some heavy object on her head to hold it erect. Even today I can hear her step on the stairs.

My New England Mother and my Southern Father had met in Thomasville, Georgia. Mother had gone there with her grandmother, Adelaide Anne Titcomb Chase, of Lowell, Massachusetts, for a winter vacation. When my Father met her, she was sitting by a window, the sun lighting up her blond hair, and her eyes bluer than blue. He fell in love with her then and there. Describing her to his sister and sister-in-law, he said, "And she has naturally curly hair!" They snorted and replied, "She probably wears kid curlers at night, just the way we do!" But when she went to visit the Grahams, a rainy day came, and in the dampness, while their hair went limp, hers became curlier and curlier, with lovely tendrils around her face, and they were convinced.

A word about my two brothers . . . Gregory, my older brother, was unbelievably handsome—a striking figure, the sort of person you would turn around to stare at as he passed by. As my older brother, two years my senior, he was more of a teaser than a protector. We each had our own circle of friends, but naturally we attended the same dances. Once, when my escort was taken sick and my brother was going "stag," my mother pressed him into taking me.

"All right," he said, "but I'll never take a girl to a dance unless I can turn her loose on the ballroom floor, and know that she can take care of herself." How many times in the future did I remember his words. In the Texas Delegate fight, on the Campaign Train, in my job in Washington, at NATO deliberations, I was turned loose on the ballroom floor and had to take care of myself.

But in the matter of my disinheritance, Gregory said to me, "Never mind if you are left out. John and I will see that you get your third."

John was seven years younger than I. When I was fourteen and dating, he was just a child. When I was twenty-one and engaged, he was a young fourteen. But from the time that he came to Harvard Law School, we became close friends. Our lives have paralleled each other's in some ways. We both felt that the highest form of public service was in politics and in government. He is a Democrat. I chose the Republican Party. We soon found that during campaigns we could not talk politics, but when it was over, whichever side won, we would fall happily on each other's neck. He served under President Truman as Assistant Secretary of the Treasury and under President Eisenhower as a member of the Atomic Energy Commission.

When I married in 1921, perhaps one reason I did not worry about being disinherited was that my Father's inevitable death at some future time seemed so far off. Two years later, death stood by my own bedstead. Ten years later my Father died, and the year after, my older brother died.

In the case of both my Father and me, modern drugs would have made all the difference. My septicemia could have been quickly cured. My Father's death from erysipelas could have been prevented. He was only sixty-three. But he was one of the rare people who knew what he wanted in life and was able to achieve it. And I know that in the end he was happy about Charlie and me.

V

THE UNHAPPY YEARS

I loved our own snug, small home at 109 Summer Avenue. I loved the Franklin stove and the paper-white narcissus on a mahogany table in a sunny window, and the garden outside which I had made. It did have drawbacks: the heating was inadequate and there was only one bathroom, but it was mine. After Dr. Howard's death, Mother Howard said she could not live alone and asked us to move across the street to her house. This meant taking on a Victorian mansion with handsome, high-studded rooms on the first floor, a wide staircase leading to the second floor with five large bedrooms, and two additional ones of great size on the third floor. Then there was the vast kitchen with the big black iron stove, the soapstone sink and washtubs. Out beyond were the back entry, the storage rooms, the attic, the woodshed, the root cellar, and, of course, the regular cellar with the coal furnace. It was a big order for a housewife of twenty-five!

The house was situated on five acres of land with innumerable apple trees, cherry trees, grapes and grape arbors, and a handsome barn. We didn't discuss the move very much. Charlie decided that was what we should do, and we did it. He thought it would be a better place to raise children. I gave up my wedding-present home with rather a heavy heart. Mother Howard presented her house to Charlie and turned over the running of it to me. For help I had my sixteen-year-old maid, Ivy. Nowadays when my children taunt me by saying what an easy time I had because I always had maids, I just smile. It is impossible to explain.

So we moved, crowding our furniture and wedding possessions in together with the big mahogany pieces, or storing ours in the attic. At 122 Summer Avenue the wallpaper was dark. In the dining room the woodwork was golden oak and a Tiffany lamp hung over the dining table. It all depressed me.

Charlie was back in his old home. Mother Howard had her own room and her own chair and table and light where she had always sat to read, or knit, or crochet. She kept herself busy with clubs, and she was a wonderful grandmother.

She and I never quarrelled. She was careful not to interfere. I learned much from her. But, oh, how I longed for my own house, and my husband and child all to myself. Gnawing at my heart always was the desire for more children.

Margaret was a joy. She was an imaginative child. We went hunting fairies together and set a trap for a fox in Middlesex Fells. She loved Peter Pan and Wendy and all the other stories I read to her. Charlie took her on walks to find mayflowers and jacks-in-the-pulpit.

Charlie and I had planned for four children. My illness had gotten us off to a poor start, but two years later I was pregnant again. Then a miscarriage, then an operation, and, after that, another miscarriage, then a third, serious one when things went wrong and I lost an inordinate amount of blood. I was at home, and Dr. Dow, the family physician, came; he called in Dr. Richmond to help in the emergency. Margaret was terrified when the maid told her that her mother might not live.

But sometime in the next afternoon I regained consciousness. I was cold. Dr. Dow was sitting by my bedside, with his hand inside my thigh, probably on a pulse. "I'm cold," I said. "If Charlie were here, he would know how to warm me up." Charlie was just then in the next room. Dr. Dow smiled.

After that I was terribly thin and very weak. I had no appetite. My Father wrote to me, "If you gain to 130 pounds, I will give you $100." "And if you get over 130 pounds, I'll divorce you," Charlie said. I drank ginger ale with cream, and eggnogs. Charlie took me to Turk's Head Inn in Rockport and got the best room, overlooking the ocean. At dinner he would say lovingly, "Eat your bread and butter. Finish up your potato." Gradually I gained weight to 130 pounds, collected my $100 and Charlie didn't have to divorce me.

Charlie went off to Boston at 8:30 in the morning and often was not at home until 11 o'clock in the evening, or after. In his last term of office, Governor Fuller did not want to accept speaking engagements and sent Charlie in his stead. Night after night Charlie went to the Union Club, put on his tuxedo, and sat in the Governor's place at the head table at some banquet. Charlie could write a compelling statement in half an hour, and on his feet he was quick and resourceful. He became known as a forceful and dynamic speaker and was in demand. All this didn't leave enough time for me. Even on Saturday mornings he would go to Boston to catch up on his own affairs at his law office.

We had too little social life together. It was the prohibition era, and as a public official, Charlie would not patronize a bootlegger, nor make bathtub gin. And Mother Howard, living with us, would not fit in to most parties, she was too stern and aloof. And I wasn't mature enough to say, "Mother Howard, we are going to have a party which you probably wouldn't enjoy. Wouldn't you rather have a tray?"

I realized that I had to begin to make my own life. I became Vice-Chairman of the Republican Town Committee, which met in the evening, and President of the League of Women Voters in Reading. One of the League's most interesting activities was the mock Town Meeting, which we held each year. We enacted the procedures of the upcoming regular one and debated the articles in the warrant. Thus we were thoroughly familiar with the issues to come before the Town Meeting.

I had begun to make friends in Boston. Once a week I worked at the Pennywise Thrift Shop on Huntington Avenue, as a volunteer, along with Mrs. Paul Hubbard and Polly De Camp Moffatt. Mrs. Hubbard also asked me to become a Director of the House of Mercy, of which Mrs. Ernest Codman was President and Mrs. Brandegee, a member. Many mornings I would drive Charlie to the train, Margaret to school, plan the meals, do the shopping, and off to Boston for the

45

day. I had begun to ask myself whether I would continue doing so many things in Reading or increase my activities in Boston.

Then to my surprise and delight, I was pregnant again. But also I was apprehensive.

Now I went to bed for five months. I could hear Margaret downstairs, telling her afternoon nurse as she was getting away with something outrageous, "Oh, no, Mother doesn't mind." I did mind, but I couldn't do anything about it. I had to keep calm and stay in bed. At Thanksgiving time, in 1930, Mother and Father were staying in Boston and came out to Reading to have Thanksgiving dinner with us. Margaret had sat on the bed beside me, and we had planned a delicious feast. When the day came, I got out of bed and went down to dinner. We had a happy day.

But on Friday, pains developed, and we called Dr. Howard Swain. "You'd best get in to the Boston Lying-in Hospital," he said. But how? There was no ambulance in Reading so they got the hearse. The basket was brought upstairs, and with a slight shudder, I laid myself down in it and off to Boston, Charlie riding with me. Dr. Swain was waiting to receive me when I arrived at Richardson House. That night my baby was born, a premature baby, 6½ months along, weighing 3½ pounds.

When I opened my eyes in the delivery room, I said, "Is it a boy?" "Yes," said a voice, "but it probably won't live."

Next morning Dr. Warren Sisson, the pediatrician, came to see me and carefully explained that with such an early baby, you couldn't tell what would happen. If he lived twenty-four hours, if he lived two weeks, still he wasn't finished—like a house, the wiring wasn't complete. You couldn't be sure he would be all right if he did live.

So we lived through the first twenty-four hours. Was he all right? Yes, he was still alive. And the next two weeks? Yes, he was still alive.

One day, about three weeks later, Dr. Sisson came rushing into my room. "Your baby has turned black," he said I wasn't spared any agony. But how I wanted Charlie's son to live!

By God's grace, and the baby's will to live, and the best

medical help in the world, he did live. We named him Herbert, for his grandfather, Dr. Herbert Howard, partly in grateful thanks to all the men in the medical profession who loved and admired Dr. Howard and helped this small scrap of humanity to survive. For some time I made the care of Herbert Graham Howard my major preoccupation. It was a long, slow pull, close to fifteen months, before my baby was out of the woods, and only then did I begin to resume outside activities.

The unhappy years were almost over!

During his days in the Senate, Charlie had been increasingly affiliated with the leaders of the Republican Party. I particularly remember a delightful evening when Leverett and Alice Saltonstall drove out to Reading to have dinner with us. It was late in the spring and warm. Leverett looked attractive in a dinner coat, informal shirt and black tie, white flannel trousers and patent leather pumps. One felt his charm, but at this time, early in his political career, he was far less handsome than he grew to be in his later years.

Leverett had chosen the most difficult field in which to try for success. His aristocratic name, and the fortune his family was known to possess were at that time liabilities, not assets, nor was he a fluent speaker.

Once, years later, I said to him, "I always like your speeches, Lev, because you use simple words. They are easy to understand."

"Well, Katherine," he said, "I use simple words because I can't pronounce the long ones!"—one of his typical understatements. Leverett never pretended to be anything other than what he was—a Saltonstall, and a Harvard graduate. His assets were his common sense, his friendly touch, and his integrity. Once, at a large and formal Middlesex Club dinner at the Statler Hotel, with head-table guests from Washington, as well as all of the Massachusetts political leaders, Leverett opened his remarks from the head table by saying, "When I was dressing to come here tonight, I got all mixed up with Alice's stockings hanging in the bathroom where I expected the towels to be." Everyone loved it.

Charlie always worked closely with Henry Shattuck, the leading Republican in the House of Representatives, and one of Boston's most respected and generous citizens. He devoted his life to public service. Before he became a Representative he had served on the Boston City Council. When he retired from politics, he became the longtime Treasurer of Harvard College. He and Charlie liked and respected each other and occasionally spent weekends together at the Pocanockett Club in Dover.

The friendships made in the Senate continued after Charlie became Commissioner of Administration and Finance. There was a pleasant reunion with the Saltonstalls and Bacons when we were invited by Governor and Mrs. Allen to attend Hoover's Inauguration in Washington in March of 1929. In the party were Gaspar Bacon, the President of the Senate; the Speaker of the House, Leverett Saltonstall, and their wives. Also in the party were Senator and Mrs. Eben Draper, the Eliot Wadsworths, and several others. We were to take the day train to Washington, traveling with the Governor in a private car.

When we boarded the train, the Governor and his wife, Eleanor, were in the drawing room of the private car. It was full of fresh flowers and large baskets of fruit, and boxes of candy. The door was open, and they were hospitably greeting their friends. All day long in their drawing room there was laughter and chatter and also a bridge game going. We visited back and forth, all except William Youngman, the Lieutenant Governor, who sat alone and aloof in the middle of the car, reading, with his hat on. His very nice wife was not with him.

I remember talking with Alice Saltonstall, young, blond haired, blue eyed, and so very natural and gracious. At lunch in the dining car, sitting with the Eben Drapers, I was surprised to see Mrs. Draper pick up her lamb chop and eat it in her fingers. But she was gay and fun. We arrived in Washington in the middle of the afternoon and were met by a fleet of Cadillacs, supplied by former Governor Fuller. At the hotel, various Congressmen and officials were there to greet us.

Hoover's Inaugural Day was damp and dreary. On that March morning of 1929, who could have foretold that the weather was an ominous forewarning of President Hoover's years in office, as the prosperity of 1929 turned into the worst depression of our history before his term of office ended.

Long after the Inaugural Ball which we attended Leverett told the following story: "Katherine and I were walking in together at the Inaugural Ball [the Massachusetts delegation marched in together as a body, and he and I were paired off]. We were greeted by tremendous applause. We smiled and bowed and acknowledged the applause, but it seemed to me it was more than we deserved. So, I looked over my shoulder and discovered that we were immediately followed by an Indian chief in full dress regalia. It was he they were applauding!"

We were also entertained at lunch on Capitol Hill by the Massachusetts Republican Senators and Congressmen. It was reported to me that someone there said, "Who would have imagined that Charlie Howard had a wife like that." I don't know what they meant, but I took it to be a compliment.

I saw less and less of Charlie after he became the Commissioner of Administration and Finance. It made no sense, and I remonstrated, "Charlie," I said, "let's buy a house in Boston. Then at least I will see you when you come home to get into your dinner jacket before you go out again!" It was now 1934 and the depression was deep. Houses on Commonwealth Avenue and Beacon Street were selling at ridiculously low prices, as families dismissed servants and moved to smaller and more manageable homes on Beacon Hill or out to the suburbs. Charlie and I would lunch together at the Union Club and then go looking. I was appalled at the heating arrangements in some of the houses. There could be one or two hot-air furnaces under the middle of the house. The anthracite coal would be dumped down a chute in the sidewalk, and then the choreman would have to shovel it into a wheelbarrow and wheel it to a bin by the furnace. Some houses had added elevators. Quite often they went straight up in the middle of the hall, a hideous anachronism. But as houses, they were beautiful with fine proportions, beautiful woodwork, Italian marble fireplaces. We didn't consider Beacon Hill. Back Bay was where we wanted to live. There were trees, and green front yards: on Commonwealth Avenue, the Mall; on Beacon Street, the River.

Before we took the plunge we had to be sure that Mother Howard was content to remain in Reading, with Jennie to care for her, and she was. This would mean that we would be responsible for two households, but Father's bequest made this possible.

We were finally attracted to 124 Beacon Street, which we bought from the John M. Elliots, who had renovated it only six years before. It had new electric wiring, gas stove, oil burner, and house telephones connecting the bedrooms and kitchen. It had an elevator which did not go up in the middle of the hall, but was discreetly placed. Nothing functional needed to be done.

It was a lot of house. Built in 1859–60, it was one of the earliest houses in the Back Bay. On the water side of Beacon Street, the sun pours in the windows at the front of the house, and from the rear, there is the view of the river, with Cambridge across the Charles River Basin. "124" is typical Back Bay: a reception room and dining room on the first floor, drawing room and library on the second, our bedroom and our son's on the third, our daughter's and the guest room on the fourth, and the maids' bedrooms, sitting room, and bath above; the laundry and kitchen were in the basement.

Charlie and I slept in our new house on our wedding anniversary, September 15, 1935. The next day the big move was made. Everything started auspiciously. The two maids I had engaged arrived. The groceries were delivered; we brought flowers from Marblehead, and the unpacking was begun. Peggy took Flash, the dog, to walk; Herbert got milk for the cat and her litter of kittens. Charlie came home early from the State House; Mother, who was visiting us, Peggy, and I changed for dinner and down we went to the dining room, lovely with silver tea chest paper, Waterford crystal wall brackets, candles and flowers on the table. All had gone well. This was my own home at last!

The day after was a different story. Both Mother and Peggy developed sore throats and fever and had to stay in bed. The maids walked off. I had a husband to feed and get off to work, two bed patients, a four-year-old looking tiny and forlorn who was missing Jennie and his grandmother.

"Thank God for the elevator," I said. I took trays upstairs. When I got back to the kitchen, the soapstone sink was stopped up and refused to drain. What a mess! Strange noises were coming from the elevator: there was Flash, our terrier, precariously poised on top of the elevator, inside the elevator shaft, barking his head off!

An S.O.S. to the employment agency, and to Otis elevator produced help. Flash was freed and never tried that trick again. The employment agency sent me an angel of an accommodator. She was competent. In no time at all the sink was drained, the dishes done, the house cleaned. When I thanked her for the wonders she had wrought, she said, "We State-of-Mainers learn to cope with anything."

VI

BEACON STREET

Charlie served as Commissioner of Administration and Finance under two Republican Governors, Fuller and Allen; and his reappointment by the latter placed him in office when Governor Ely, a Democrat, was inaugurated. I listened to Ely's Inaugural Address in my hospital room at Richardson House, as Herbert was being nursed into life. With a premature baby, and weeks of stay, which turned into months at the hospital, the bills were formidable. I was shocked when I heard Governor Ely proclaim: "And I shall remove from office the Commissioner of Administration and Finance, Charles P. Howard." My heart sank. How would we ever pay the bills? How would we live? However, Charlie continued in his office. By his ability and integrity and fairmindedness, he proved his worth. When Democratic Governor Ely was leaving office, Charlie's appointment was expiring. Governor Ely said: "I shall reappoint Charles P. Howard. In so doing, I shall be sure that honest government will continue in Massachusetts." Privately he added, "That's the worst thing I could do to James Michael Curley."

For Charlie, it was a difficult decision, whether to accept the appointment and serve under incoming Governor Curley, or whether to decline. Curley was anathema to Republicans. His terms as Mayor had been marked by scandal. Charlie's legal and financial friends from State Street implored him to continue in office to keep things honest on Beacon Hill. The power of Charlie's office, and his own stamina and integrity could pretty well assure this if he stayed on. After much cogitation, Charlie accepted.

Curley was a colorful figure. When he was elected, people optimistically said: "Curley did shady things on the way up. Now he's arrived at the top, he can afford to go straight. We think he will." People hoped that his great political gifts would be used for the good of the Commonwealth. He was handsome; he had charm; he was an orator. He could be a charming table companion and conversationalist.

Governor Curley's highminded period as Governor lasted about three months. Then the old Curley reasserted itself. An occasion arose when Charlie was tested to the limit. Governor Curley wanted to put sidewalks along roads and highways where no one lived and no one walked. The sidewalk granite was to come from the Westford quarries. Curley wanted the Westford granite without competitive bids. When Charlie would not agree, Curley threatened to remove him. It was a hard time to live through. At home, at night, I would look at Charlie and wonder how he could stand it. It was the talk of Boston's political circles. Charlie maintained that if he gave in on this contract, the whole basis of the businesslike management of the Commonwealth of Massachusetts would be wrecked. Purchases were made through the purchasing agent in his office according to specifications, and on the basis of awarding the bid to the lowest competitive bidder who complied with the specifications. If this principle were abandoned, the contractors would take over, and the size of the bribe could be the determining factor in who got the contract. Charlie would have no part of it. He did not yield. He was not removed.

The *Daily Item* of Wakefield, on December 17, 1937, wrote: "Last year Charles P. Howard refused to refund $20,000 imposed for delivery of inferior coal to the state, and blocked a payment of $150,000 extra on a road contract, so Governor James Michael Curley took this and other like incidents as an excuse to try to oust him, but it didn't work."

Charlie's reputation as a straight shooter and competent administrator in State affairs was reaching far beyond Boston. His reputation was known in Washington, where federal agencies to cope with the depression had been called into being by President Roosevelt. Charlie was asked to take on federal responsibilities. He accompanied Curley to Washington and to Hyde Park to confer with the President. Thus he became the Massachusetts coordinator and fiscal agent for the Civil Works Administration from 1933 to 1934; then the Emergency Relief Administration from 1934 to 1935; and the Works Project Administration (WPA) from 1935 to 1938. These were the federally funded agencies created to make jobs and provide relief and employment during the depression.

Governor Curley was succeeded by Governor Hurley. Still Charlie held office. At that time the appointment to the Chairmanship of the Commission on Administration and Finance was not coterminous with the Governor's term. The Governor served for two years and then sought reelection. The Commissioner's term was four years. The theory behind this was that the Commissioner would not be subject to pressure from the Governor, nor beholden to him for his position. In this way, the vast business of the Commonwealth would be removed from politics, and could be conducted strictly on merit.

More recently the Governor's term has been changed to four years and, like a Cabinet officer in Washington, the Commissioner of Administration and Finance is appointed by the Governor and serves for the length of the Governor's term or at the Governor's pleasure.

But Charlie Howard's position was for a term of years, regardless of the party in power. He was a well-known Republican. To remove him from office would be difficult, particularly when he had strong backing in the legislature where he had served. He was also popular with the press.

The time came, however, when his appointment was expiring. Democratic Governor Charles Hurley was delighted at the opportunity to get this capable, incorruptible, Republican Yankee out of his powerful position. And so his term ended. He was not reappointed.

On the morning of his last day at the State House, after Charlie left for his office, I went to the kitchen to plan the meals and make out the order list with our cook, Marie Surrette. Tonight's dinner must be especially good—all the things Charlie liked best. We sat down at the wooden table in the middle of the kitchen. But we hadn't gone very far when the wind was knocked out of my sails. "Mrs. Howard," said Marie, "I have to ask you for a raise." What a time to have this come! I thought. She didn't know that this was a traumatic day for Charlie and me. Well, I thought, I must keep this house on an even keel. I agreed to the raise.

When Charlie came home and I heard his key in the door, I came downstairs, as usual, to greet him with a welcoming kiss. The children came from their rooms where they had been studying. We sat down to a cheerful and delicious dinner with no reference to the rebuff from which he was smarting, nor to the dismay which we both felt.

It was dreadful for Charlie to wake up in the morning and not go to the State House. It was dreadful to be, instead of one of the most powerful men in the Commonwealth, a man without a job. His salary had been $7,500 a year (now it is $38,000). We should have to economize to make up for that. To be sure, he still had a law office and, in time, this was a godsend. But after twelve years being Commissioner of Administration and Finance, his clients were few, and politics was still in his blood.

Fortunately, Charlie was a nationally known expert on state administration. He had been elected National Vice-President of the Civil Service Assembly of the United States and Canada. He put out feelers, and was soon asked to make a survey of the state government of Wisconsin. When the time came for him to go, he was in bed with a bad cold, feeling physically and emotionally down and out. It was a struggle to get up out of bed, get dressed, and get on the train and go, but he did. When that was finished, Governor Vanderbilt of Rhode Island engaged him to make a survey of the State Government of Rhode Island, which he did with great success.

As spring approached in 1938, at the urging of many friends and civic leaders, Charlie decided to run for the Republican nomination for Lieutenant Governor of Massachusetts. Ever since our marriage I had known that he hoped one day to be Governor. I wasn't sure that we could afford it now, and I knew that in his position he had had to say no to many people. But he had strong backing and got off to a good start. Having served as Selectman, Town Counsel, and Moderator of Reading, having been twice elected to the

Massachusetts Senate, and having been Deputy Governor for twelve years, he was clearly the best qualified candidate. His home County of Middlesex was the center of Republican strength. Here he was handicapped when two other candidates from the same county, one from Belmont and one from Lowell, announced that they were running for the same office. There were two additional candidates, one from Milton, and Horace Cahill, from Braintree—five candidates in all for the Republican nomination for Lieutenant Governor! The gubernatorial candidates were Leverett Saltonstall and Richard Whitcomb.

We traveled all over the State, meeting the Republican leaders. There were long hours and late evenings. Quite often, on our way home after the last meeting, we would stop and Charlie would have ice cream with fudge sauce and marshmallow to renew his energy. He rarely took a drink—never at that time.

There is an intoxication about a campaign. The competition, the people you meet, the issues debated, all add up to a heady combination. You have superhuman energy and strength. And blessedly, Charlie could always sleep at once when he finally got to bed.

My part, like that of any candidate's wife, then, was just to go along, to meet people, remember who they were, take down names of those who wanted to help or would like to have literature sent to them to distribute. I was the one who listened to all the speeches and appraised them. Charlie would ask, "Was it a good speech? Did that point get across? Is that a good story to use again?" I got the audience reaction and we talked it over going home. I always could tell what the man in the street was thinking and feeling about things.

Edward Furber, Charlie's law associate, was working almost full time on the campaign, and Albert Leman, later Public Relations Director of the Department of Commerce under Sinclair Weeks, took over the publicity of Charlie's campaign, making a gift of his time and talents. It was a sixteen-hour day for both Charlie and me, and we were running on a small campaign fund.

The announcement of Charlie's candidacy and his subsequent campaign speeches made headlines all across the State. One of the most honest comments on his candidacy was a remark by a high official of the Democratic Party who said, "I've had many a knockdown, dragout political tussle with Charles P. Howard, but we still frequently lunch together. I'll say this much for him; he's a regular fellow. If he thinks something, he says it. If he gives his word, he keeps it."

Charlie spoke at rallies all across the State and the headlines played up the points he made.

The Springfield Union, March 23, 1938:

> "Calls on Voters to Drive Hurley Group out. Howard Makes Smashing Attack on Governor. Raps Callahan Reappointment."

Boston Evening Transcript, March 30, 1938:
"Howard Raps Move to Stop Salary Raises Finance Chairman Sees Morale of State Service Damaged"

Boston Herald, August 26, 1938:
"Howard Would Bar Gift Contracts if Elected as Lieutenant Governor"

and so on right up to Primary Day, September 20, 1938.

Charlie was endorsed by former Governor Fuller, still a powerful Republican figure. Each piece of his campaign literature carried the name of Henry Shattuck, 15 River Street, Boston. He supported Charlie, and showed it in lending his name to be used this way. According to law, all campaign literature must bear the name and address of a supporter.

Charlie had editorial support, and was referred to as the best-qualified candidate, as indeed he was. At this time there was no pre-primary convention. The voters made their choices in the September party primaries.

In the last two weeks of the campaign it was evident that Leverett Saltonstall would be the Republican candidate for Governor. He was clearly out ahead. His forces set about assuring that he would subsequently win the election. Charlie was told later that word went out in the last few days that Charlie Howard and Leverett Saltonstall would not make a balanced ticket. They were both Yankees, both Harvard men, both Protestants. A man with a different name and background would give the Republican ticket wider appeal. Even if Charlie were the better qualified candidate, Representative Cahill was the man to vote for.

Anyway, that was the winning ticket. Governor Saltonstall and Lieutenant Governor Cahill served three two-year terms. There is no doubt that Saltonstall was one of the best, and best-loved, governors in Massachusetts history. Lieutenant Governor Cahill never made it to the governor's office. Perhaps Charlie would have.

The defeat was a bitter disappointment to both of us. It was the first in Charlie's chosen field. We were both unhappy and felt we deserved a vacation.

I met him in the North Station. We boarded the luxurious train to Montreal in the early afternoon. The parlor car had fresh flowers in vases, radio music with earphones, excellent service. We settled in our chairs with our books, happy and content. It was raining. It kept on raining. At dusk we had come to White River Junction, where the train halted. After awhile Charlie went to inquire why we weren't proceeding. The conductor said that there was a washout up ahead. Wouldn't we step into the diner and have dinner, compliments of the railroad? Charlie declined.

"Get your things together," said Charlie. "We are leaving." We gathered up our bags and books, and stepped off the train into the wettest rain I had ever encountered. It was deep in the street and bouncing up about a foot after it hit the rainy surface. Somehow or other, Charlie commandeered a taxi. "We must get to the other side of the river," he said. The taxi drove us to the Hanover Inn. A good, hot dinner and a warm, dry bed were welcome. Next morning, the bridge we had crossed was not there. All the other people on our train were marooned in the second story of a hotel in White River Junction for over a week.

Flood conditions were developing all over New Hampshire. Charlie was up early and he and three other men at the Inn were able to hire a car and a brave driver to take us to Concord, New Hampshire, where he hoped to get a train to Boston. We went down one road only to find that the bridge was out. We turned back. Another road, the same result. Trying yet another one, our driver went to inquire at a general store. "Well," said the storekeeper, "a car just come through here from down below. You might try it." So we did. When we came to the bridge, it was deep under water. Our driver took it slowly. I opened the car window so we could climb out in case the bridge gave way beneath us, and we sank in the river. But we made it.

Finally we approached Concord. Charlie gave directions to the railroad station. A train was there, about to leave. The brakeman pulled the emergency cord to delay its departure. The men pressed five-dollar bills into the hands of the driver, and we scrambled aboard as the train pulled out. It was the last one to leave Concord for a week.

Back in Boston, Charlie went to his office to work and I went home to Reading. At six o'clock I got in the car to go to meet Charlie at the railroad station. Winds were blowing at hurricane force. As I went down Summer Avenue, huge elms toppled behind me. By the time Charlie's train came in, many of the streets were blocked by fallen trees. We took a circuitous route, and we had to abandon our car about a block from home and clamber over the fallen elms. Disaster had struck everywhere; high winds, high tides; trees and power lines were down, tremendous damage in all of Massachusetts, Rhode Island, Connecticut, and New Hampshire.

September had been full of action. Early in October we moved back to Boston. The campaign was over; now we could get back to normal life, I thought. Mother liked to stay with us into the fall to go to the Symphony concerts and to "buy a Boston hat." She would wear it in Boston with pleasure, and then when she returned to Winston-Salem, it never seemed quite right.

One evening, after a busy day, I was stretched out on the blue sofa in the library at "124" reading the mail and talking to Mother when Charlie came home from his law office. I handed him a letter and said, "Here is something I am not going to accept, you will be glad to see." Charlie was always saying to me, "Why do you serve on so many Boards? You do too much. You don't know how to say no. You are always taking on something more." The letter was from Mrs. Henry D. Tudor, President of the Women's Republican Club of Massachusetts, asking me to become a member of the Board of

Directors of the Club, and Program Chairman.

Charlie read it and said to me, "Why don't you give up something else and take this on? Mrs. Tudor and the Political Chairman were awfully good to me in the campaign. It would be nice if you could do it." I wrote Mrs. Tudor and accepted. This was the first step in my long involvement in State and National politics, and it was Charlie's campaign which had brought me to her attention.

Charlie resumed practicing law. An unexpected opportunity presented itself when the incumbent County Treasurer of Middlesex County died, and a vacancy existed. Charlie was appointed to fill the post. It was fortunate that we had kept the house and our voting residence in Reading. He was still Charles P. Howard of Reading. He was the popular Town Moderator. He owned the Victorian house on Summer Avenue and residential and business blocks downtown. He belonged to Middlesex County. Charlie now had a welcome salary and a position in which to exercise his political and financial talents, and I was entering a new field of endeavor, the Women's Republican Club of Massachusetts.

When I became a member of the Board of Directors of the Women's Republican Club of Massachusetts, it was a turning point in my career. I brought to the Club practical political experience as a longtime member and Vice Chairman of the Reading Republican Town Committee, and as a delegate to the Republican State Convention. I had worked hard in Charlie's two campaigns for State Senator, and I had been his silent partner in a statewide campaign where I had necessarily met the top Republican leadership. I did not, as Charlie suggested, "give up something else." I just added on the W.R.C., and it took precedence over the other volunteer activities I continued to enjoy.

My children were now fifteen and eight, at school all day. Charlie was busy as County Treasurer; I had a good housekeeper, and the Republican Club at 46 Beacon Street was just a short walking distance from "124."

It was a handsome club house, admirably suited for our uses. As one entered through the impressive doorway, the living room was on the right and the offices on the left. There was a large dining room on that floor for meals served every day and for political lunches or dinners. A handsome stairway led to the second floor and the ballroom where we held our political meetings, a "French" room for smaller gatherings and a large library. The house had belonged to the Eben Jordans and was bought for a moderate price, and much of the furniture was donated.

The Club was organized by women who had been leaders in the suffrage movement: Mrs. Charles Sumner Bird, Mrs. Robert Herrick and Mrs. George Richmond Fearing. These were *great* women. They cared desperately that women should have the vote, that they should exercise their franchise, and, now that they had it, that they should have equal representation on party committees, and that they should have equal protocol recognition at G.O.P. dinners and rallies.

Mrs. Charles Sumner Bird, the first President, said, "I felt, after the election that we should appeal more to the women of leisure and the antisuffragists who knew little about politics, and that we should keep on with our school of education and citizenship." She organized the Club on a county basis, with a member of the Board of Directors from each county. We had a membership of 2,000 to 3,000, a Board of Directors from all over the State, and a continuous program of activities, attracting both men and women to the Club.

When I first dropped into the Clubhouse to pick up some information, I was wearing a gray flannel pleated skirt, a flame-colored cashmere sweater, and a discreet string of cultured pearls. I stepped up to the desk of Miss Mary Smith, the Executive Secretary, and introduced myself. I had just driven in from Marblehead. She took one look at me and said, "My gosh, a member of the Board of Directors in a sweater!" She was used to the distinguished older ladies who had founded the Club and did not realize that they were now looking for someone young and energetic to carry on.

In my first job as Program Chairman, my committee and I had to plan programs for every Saturday afternoon, from fall to spring. I presided over them and introduced the speakers. At the beginning, I would write out my introductions, study them, and then speak from a note or two. It was good training.

The strictly political meetings were held on Thursday mornings. Mine ranged over many other areas. Samuel

Chamberlain had an exhibition of etchings and spoke; Dahl, the *Boston Herald* cartoonist, came and was very amusing; Dorothy Mayner, a black singer and a protegé of the Misses Curtis, sang for us before Koussevitsky discovered her for the Boston Symphony Orchestra. My success with the programs moved me up to the Vice-Presidency, and in 1941 I was asked to be President. I said I could not take it then. Peggy was to be a debutante that year, and I wanted to be free from major commitments to enjoy it with her. This was almost the last season that Boston girls took a whole year off to come out, with "small dances" or dinner dances or balls almost every Friday evening. The next year I accepted the nomination. When I became President, I took office with four dollars in the treasury.

I loved the job. It combined everything which appealed to me: first of all, a house, a Republican home, doors wide open to welcome people; activities of all kinds, political luncheons, dinners; a manager and a domestic staff and all the attendant problems; meetings to be held; contact with the political great of our State—and they were great: Governor Leverett Saltonstall, Senator Henry Cabot Lodge, Sinclair Weeks, Congressmen Christian Herter and Richard Wigglesworth; Wendell Willkie, candidate for President; Governor Bricker of Ohio, Vice-Presidential candidate; and many others. The Club was the center of Massachusetts Republican activities.

In addition to the Board of Directors, there was an advisory council of men: Sinclair Weeks, National Committeeman; George Rowell, Chairman of the State Committee; Francis Gray, Alexander Whiteside and others. They were good friends as well as advisors.

But when I took over as President, it was a job no one wanted. We were at war. President Franklin Roosevelt had widespread support. It was not patriotic to be partisan. Everyone wanted to be in a Red Cross uniform and "have a desk with two telephones." If a prominent woman was not doing full-time volunteer work for the Red Cross, she was working for British War Relief or some other Allied Country's War Relief. But I decided to do my war work through the Women's Republican Club. We set up Red Cross First Aid and Home Nursing courses in the Club house. With Mrs. Richard Sears' help, we put on dances in our beautiful ballroom for soldiers and sailors in Boston on furlough. The hostesses were chosen from our Junior Republican groups, which I had organized after I became President.

One evening Governor Robert Bradford came as guest speaker. He arrived late, took his seat beside me at the head table and said, "Katherine, tell me about the audience, and what they would be interested in." He had come straight from another meeting and had no prepared speech. "Well," I said, "they are business and professional women; they are intelligent; they are interested in your position on the sales tax. Don't feel you have to chat with me if you want to think about what you are going to say."

"Oh, that's no problem," he replied, "I have a little man at the back of my head who will work on the speech while we are talking." We chatted pleasantly all through dinner.

When I introduced him, and he launched into his address, it was one of the best outlined and coordinated speeches I have ever heard. The "little man" had done a good job.

I served as a Director and then as President from 1938 to 1945. They were happy and, I think, productive years. This was the beginning of my total commitment to the Republican Party.

On Sunday afternoon, December 7, 1941, Charlie and I were sitting in the library at Beacon Street. He was in his accustomed chair, reading, and I was on the floor, pasting clippings about Peggy's debut in a scrapbook. Herb, from his upstairs room, came into the library saying, "I heard on the radio that the Japanese have bombed Pearl Harbor!"

"That's ridiculous," said Charlie. "It couldn't possibly be so!" He went on to explain how impossible it was. The planes couldn't fly so far. Just then Marie Surrette, from the kitchen, arrived with the same news. We thought we'd better turn on the radio too. When the news was verified, my reaction was rather a personal one. Looking at the clippings, I thought, "If it's going to be war, I am so glad Peggy has had the best part of her debutante year." She would still have these memories.

As the war continued the next year, Charlie said that we had better get out of Boston in case of air raids. We rented 124 Beacon Street to the Canadian Enlistment Office with a

Major of the Black Watch Regiment in residence. We took Herbert out of Dexter School, and he went to the public school in Reading, where we spent the winter.

The United States Army began looking for men with administrative and executive experience for their Military Government when Europe was liberated. Charlie realized that his previous war experience and his governmental experience would be valuable. As France, Italy, and Austria were eventually liberated from the enemy, these officers were to move in and reestablish civil government. The top age limit was fifty-five years—Charlie was fifty-four. After consulting with his mother and me, Charlie enlisted. He passed all the tests and entered the United States Army again, as Major Howard.

The Boston Post, July 2, 1943, declared editorially:

Fine Work

In a day when there seems to be no limitation on public expenses and evergrowing tax burdens placed on the shoulders of everyone, the current report of Treasurer Charles P. Howard of Middlesex County certainly is refreshing.

As he prepares soon to go into the Army, he is able to point to a remarkable record for wartime economy in Middlesex County. The County debt today is $125,000. That's the lowest in 50 years.

Among his friends joining up with him were Lieutenant Colonel Henry Parkman, Jr., former State O.P.A. Director, and Captain Archibald Giroux, President of the Boston Stock Exchange. Charlie, Richard Eaton, Haven Parker, and Frederick Leviseur went off together to Fort Custer at Battle Creek, Michigan, to take basic training. They returned together to attend the Military Government School at Harvard, where they lived in Claverly Hall and had meals and classes in the Signet Club. They were allowed to invite their wives over for lunch on Saturday. Italy was the country they were studying, and Italian the language they were learning. At a Saturday lunch of baked beans and brown bread in Cambridge, I was amused to find these middle-aged men, all people of consequence in the community, worrying over whether they would pass their examinations next day, and, in particular, how they could remember the subjunctive of the Italian verbs written on the blackboards.

In November Charlie was sent for advanced training to the University of Virginia at Charlottesville. Herbert and I went there to spend Christmas with him. Traveling under wartime conditions, we took the day coach to New York, spent the night with friends there, traveled by day coach to Washington (parlor cars and sleeping cars were reserved for officers or government officials traveling on war-connected missions). In Washington we stayed with my sister-in-law. The next day, Christmas Eve, the Union Station was bursting with soldiers and sailors starting off for Christmas leave. Everyone was in holiday mood. When the train for Charlottesville pulled out, all seats were taken; the aisles were full. In friendly spirit, people took turns sitting and standing, sharing comforts and discomforts, and singing together the old and well-loved Christmas carols.

Charlie met us in Charlottesville, and we went about making our Christmas. We bought a little tree for our room. There were no decorations to be had. They were not being made or sold in this country, and certainly there were none from Germany or Japan, our enemies. But we bought cotton batting and other small objects to decorate the tree. H. G. hung up his stocking on his bedpost. He was very excited to be sleeping in a hotel bedroom all his own for the first time. We read the St. Luke's story: "There were in the fields shepherds abiding . . ." from the Gideon Bible in the hotel bureau drawer. Next day we had our stockings and presents and turkey dinner at the Charlottesville Inn. It was one of the most intimate Christmases ever.

In February Charlie received his orders for overseas duty. I met him in New York at our daughter Peggy's apartment for our last night together. He was happy and eager to be off. Neither of us realized that it would be three and a half years before he would return. Before he left, Charlie made out a power of attorney for "my beloved wife, Katherine G. Howard," giving me broad powers to deal with all his affairs and any emergency. So—off he went—with my love and my blessing.

I was on my own.

VII

ON MY OWN

It was lonely without Charlie. I missed putting my head on his shoulder at night and going to sleep in his arms. Night after night, I lay tense and unable to sleep, longing for Charlie, aching for his love and tenderness. I hated going to cocktail parties alone, sometimes being the "extra" woman invited for dinner.

It was doubly lonely, for not only was Charlie away, but Peggy was living in New York, and Herbert was at Milton Academy. We thought, with his father away, he needed the masculine direction which a good preparatory school would give him.

Soon after Charlie left, Mother Howard became ill and came to my house for good nursing care. Her doctor felt she should go to the Peter Bent Brigham Hospital, where, after seeming to make a good recovery, she died, March 1, 1944, the day Charlie landed in England. She was eighty-four years old. I have always felt that there were two contributing factors to her breakdown: first, she missed her own home and Jennie's care. Jennie had retired and gone back to Nova Scotia and Mother Howard had moved to the Women's Republican Club. But more importantly, she felt that she would not live to see Charlie come home. She had lost her will to live. The services were at the Episcopal Church in Reading, and she was buried beside her husband in the family plot there. My Red Cross cable to Charlie was not delivered. It was only from my letters, long delayed by wartime conditions, that he learned the sad news. He often said, "She seemed so well when I went. I would never have gone if I had ever dreamed that such a thing could happen."

At this time the Women's Republican Club kept me going. There was a "family" that needed me. There were meetings to be attended, speeches to be made, decisions to be arrived at and implemented. One of the older Directors, who was fond of me and loyal, but who did not always approve of my decisions, would say, "Mrs. Howard, if you do that, there will be repercussions." Yes, but not serious ones. The days were fine; yet I dreaded walking down the Hill in the dusk to an empty house and no husband. I was alone. Our wire-haired fox terrier was my only companion. His temperament was congenial to mine. The big event of his day was our walk up Beacon Street each evening before bedtime after I had written my daily letter to Charlie.

Now it was 1944, a Presidential election year. Because of my position as President of the Women's Republican Club, I was chosen as an Alternate Delegate-at-Large to the Republican National Convention, the first I ever attended.

Mrs. Louise Williams was National Committeewoman, Mrs. Peggy Green, State Vice-Chairman, and I was President of the Women's Republican Club. In the party structure we ranked in that order. Louise was an older woman. She was pretty and feminine, with every curl always in place, and a flowered hat crowning her costume. But she was peppery. She was insistent on the rights and perquisities of the position she held. If she arrived at a Republican meeting and found that the seating did not place her in the position of honor, she did not hesitate to scold the unfortunate club president or party official who had made the error.

Sinclair Weeks was Republican National Committeeman; George Rowell was Chairman of the Republican State Committee; and Charlie Nichols was Executive Secretary. Louise Williams referred to them as "the boys" and she did not hesitate to tell them off, either. Now she had decided to resign sometime in the near future, and she had told me that she would like to have me succeed her, but the decision was not hers. Who would succeed her?—Senator Leslie Cutler or Club President Katherine Howard?

Some time before, Charlie Nichols had said to me in an offhand manner, "You are being considered for the National Committee." There were two reasons, I think: one was that as President of the Women's Republican Club, I was known all over the state; and perhaps the second reason was that they knew and liked Charlie Howard and probably felt that he would keep me in line.

It was under these circumstances that I was elected Alternate Delegate-at-Large to the Republican National Convention of 1944. I was Alternate to Governor Leverett Saltonstall, the Chairman of the delegation.

As heir-apparent to Louise Williams, I was assigned to share a bedroom with her on the convention train and at the hotel in Chicago, where the convention was held.

On the train, the bedroom next to ours was occupied by Congressman Christian A. Herter and Francis C. Gray, a close friend of Leverett Saltonstall and Chris. Two more attractive men it would be hard to find. Francis had Yankee patrician looks; Chris Herter, a towering six feet four inches, had a soft, unforgettable voice and was described by my daughter as "the most beautiful man God ever made."

The Massachusetts delegation boarded the train at South Station, with picture taking, bands, and all the usual hoopla. As the afternoon progressed, there was much visiting back and forth between the delegates. Late in the afternoon Chris and Francis came and asked me to come to their compartment for a drink.

We had highballs and much congenial talk. When it came time for a refill, Chris said, "It's easy to see which glass is Kay's." To my embarrassment, bright red lipstick showed on the rim of the glass. Then it was suggested that dinner be served in their compartment and we all have it there together, a delightful idea, in which I concurred. But just as dinner arrived, some sixth sense warned me that Louise Williams would be furious at my desertion, and very reluctantly, I excused myself and rejoined her.

Charlie Nichols, the Executive Secretary, who had gone on ahead to get the lay of the land, met us at the train. When we arrived, he told the delegation, "It's all sewed up; Dewey's got it in the bag." However, there was much sentiment to place the name of Governor Saltonstall in nomination for the presidency. A meeting of the delegation was called for 9:00

P.M. in the Tropical Room. Governor Saltonstall presided, wearing a gray suit, dark blue polka dot tie, and an American Legion button in the buttonhole of his coat. Senator Weeks introduced Senator Ball of Minnesota, who spoke in favor of presenting the young, and then favorably known Governor of Minnesota, Harold Stassen, for the presidency. He said that we needed more vitality in the party and Stassen would bring it.

George Rowell moved that the delegation go on record as favoring Governor Dewey of New York for President. Saltonstall, presiding, put the question. Robert Bradford objected to the motion and said that he wanted to present the name of Governor Saltonstall.

Saltonstall then asked the secretary to take the chair. He said, "I believe the country is in a serious condition. I am grateful for Mr. Bradford's statement, and for the manner in which it was received, but I believe most people prefer to vote for Dewey, and I myself shall vote for Dewey."

I watched the play of the personalities. It was all new to me. I was more of an observer than a participant.

Next Sinclair Weeks rose and said, "I thought in February we should defeat the New Deal. I think so more than ever now. I was a Willkie man; now he is gone. I think there would be political advantage in a strong acclamation for Dewey."

Thomas Pappas, a delegate, asked, "Have you made up your minds?"

Saltonstall, who was presiding, said, "The chair would respectfully state 'yes'."

Several people spoke up for Saltonstall. Then Carroll Meins, always the practical politician said, "It is obvious that Dewey is going to be nominated, and it would be best to give Massachusetts' vote to him." It was so voted.

Next morning the Convention opened at 11:20. I was full of expectation. Here I was, alternate delegate to Governor Saltonstall, participating in a convention to select "the next President of the United States" as we always said.

It was my first convention. I went with high hopes of participating in something significant—of being a part of history. I ended by sitting long hours, singing the "Star-Spangled Banner," listening to interminable prayers and orations.

The heat of Chicago was appalling. There was no air-conditioning in Convention Hall. The sun beat down mercilessly; the wind blew like a blast from a furnace. There was no relief except in a few air-conditioned restaurants or bars.

Clare Booth Luce and former President Hoover were the featured speakers on one memorable evening. Hoover came to the podium amid tremendous applause and enthusiasm, but he could not respond. There was no smile, no welcoming wave. He was wooden and solemn. At the end of his address he introduced Clare Boothe Luce. It was the first time I had seen her. She wore a simple black jumper dress, with full, long blue chiffon sleeves, buttoned closely at the wrist. Her blond hair was parted in the middle and brought smoothly back to a simple knot at the rear. She was slender and radiant. She, at last, brought a smile to Hoover's lips.

We had all eagerly awaited her speech which had to do with war sacrifices . . . not "G. I. Joe" as the American soldier was called, but "J. I. Jim," the American soldier killed in the war. But she was trying too hard; she did not touch the heart. The speech did not catch on; the press received it coldly.

At last the day arrived for the nomination of the Republican candidate for President. Governor Saltonstall was asked to make a seconding speech for Dewey.

Leverett sent back word to me, his Alternate, to please sit in his seat, and cast Massachusetts' vote, when it came to the balloting. The delegates are seated at the front of the hall in a body, and the alernates are at the rear.

So I moved up to the number one seat in the Massachusetts delegation, on the aisle with the Massachusetts standard beside it. Leverett delivered his nominating speech with dignity and conviction. While he was speaking, Sinclair Weeks came and knelt beside me in the aisle and said, "Lev has certainly come a long way since we served together on the Board of Aldermen in Newton."

The speeches were over and the Presidential roll call began. Soon it was time for me to rise to my feet and say, "Massachusetts casts thirty-five votes for Thomas A. Dewey for President." Down in Florida Charlie's uncle heard the voice and said, "That must be Katherine."

I never dreamed that eight years later I would be reading the roll call myself.

After the Republican National Convention of 1944, I continued to serve as President of the Women's Republican Club. Louise Williams was still Republican National Committeewoman. Time was passing. Nothing was happening. So one day I telephoned to Sinclair at his office and asked for an appointment with him. I said that Louise Williams wanted to resign; that it had been suggested that I might succeed her; that the election of 1944 was now behind us; and where did we go from here? He listened with his usual quiet concentration. Then got up, walked across the room, rubbed the back of his head, looked out of the window and said, "I always liked Leslie Cutler, but I guess you would be a good national committeewoman." He picked up the telephone, called Charlie Nichols, Executive Secretary of the Republican State Committee and said, "We are going to elect Katherine Howard Republican National Committeewoman. Call a meeting of the Republican State Committee and line up the votes."

At the meeting, May 21, 1945, it was Sinclair himself who nominated me and without modesty I shall quote his conclusion:

> Katherine Howard has been very active in Republican affairs, both she and her husband, Colonel Howard. Each, as you know, has been extremely active, influential and helpful over a long period of years. Katherine Howard has been President of the Women's Republican Club for three years. The Club, previous to her taking office, was continually in the red. The members were being called upon to make up deficits. There was a mortgage and taxes due. That situation has changed and the Club has been in the black for three years running. When Mrs. Howard came in, there were eighteen junior members; this number has risen by several hundred. The Club membership has increased from 1800 to 2500. The saying is "uneasy is the head that wears the crown." The crown, in this case, has been worn, and worn easily, by Mrs. Howard. She is a real Republican, and an able Republican. I feel confident that she will prove herself a credit to Massachusetts as a member of the Republican National Committee.

The nomination was unanimous.

This was an example of the way Sinclair Weeks operated—a "boss" he was, but a boss in the best sense of the word. He was a boss because he was willing to give the time to finding candidates, then rallying support for them and raising money to help elect them. He had personal magnetism and they willingly followed his leadership.

Christian Herter is an example of one person he persuaded to enter the field of politics. Herter started as a State Representative, became Speaker of the House, Congressman, Governor of Massachusetts, and Secretary of State. Another was John Volpe. Weeks arranged for his appointment as a Vice-Chairman of the Republican State Committee, along with three others of different ethnic backgrounds, in order to give the Republican Party leadership from other than just Yankee Protestant voters. Volpe went on to become Governor of Massachusetts and Secretary of Transportation in Nixon's cabinet, and U. S. Ambassador to Italy.

My first visit to Weeks's office after my election was to inquire about my new job. "Sinclair," I said, "what does the National Committeewoman do? What are her duties?"

He thought a bit, then in that slow, deliberate way he said, "Katherine, I don't have the slightest idea."

"Well," said I, "if you think I'm just going to wear pretty hats and sit at head tables, you are very much mistaken."

As a matter of fact, each National Committeewoman must make her own way. Her effectiveness depends in large measure on her relations with the National Committeeman—on how much he includes her in policy and strategy meetings, how many duties and responsibilities he assigns her, how active she wants to be. As time went on, I became Sinclair's working partner.

One day Sinclair said, "Katherine, how is it that you were born and brought up in the South and you don't have a Southern accent?"

I smiled at him and said, "Well, Sinclair, I can turn it on anytime I want to." For some reason he thought this was vastly amusing and repeated it many times.

But my next meeting with him was one of indignation. I had received a brochure in the mail from the Massachusetts Republican Finance Committee, of which he was chairman, including my name as one of the members soliciting funds. I was furious, and I asked to see him. I said that I was not accustomed to having my name used without being consulted. I spoke at some length, and quite vehemently. He listened quietly. When I had finished, a slow smile spread over his face. "Katherine," he said, "your name is in very good company. You will be invited to attend the next meeting of the Finance Committee." I went away completely disarmed and full of respect for this man. It never diminished.

Sinclair's office was in the Statler Building at that time. There I would go, now that I had won my point, to meetings of the Finance Committee and sometimes to lunch alone with Sinclair as we talked over party matters. He would have his favorite lobster bisque sent in from the Statler dining room. As time went by, I was drawn more and more into closed meetings where policy was determined. I never knew him to act but from the highest principles. There was never a shady deal.

After I was admitted to the very innermost circle, Sinclair appointed me a member of the Massachusetts Policy Committee, which included the governor, our United States Senators, and the Republican members of Congress including Edith Nourse Rogers and Joseph W. Martin, Jr., Minority Leader of the House; the President of the Massachusetts Senate and the Speaker of the Massachusetts House of Representatives. This group met monthly with Sinclair presiding. It was useful in uniting National and State leaders, the Executive and the Legislative leaders, and the Party leaders.

Sinclair and I met the Republican Presidential nominees at the airport when they made visits to Massachusetts. He called me in for discussions with them. Frequently he, Carroll Meins, Charlie Nichols and I would meet at my house or his apartment to plan strategy. He was a challenging person to work with.

Another friend and companion in these days was Christian A. Herter, then Congressman from the Tenth Massachusetts District which comprised parts of Boston, Brookline, and Newton. After the Convention I did not see him until the day after the Presidential election in November 1944. Dewey had gone down to defeat. Franklin Roosevelt had been reelected again. I was just coming in from walking Flash when I heard the telephone ringing. To my surprise it was Chris.

He had been in Boston to vote. He asked what I thought about the election—and could we meet at the Ritz for lunch tomorrow to talk it over. In addition to talking about the disastrous election, we discussed Massachusetts politics. I could tell him what people were thinking and saying, and he could tell me about national legislation which I could put into my own language and incorporate into the speeches I was making to women's groups.

I worked out a series of talks called "Know Your Congressman." Using my artistic training, I made a series of large posters, large enough to be seen in a gathering of a hundred or more, one for each Republican Congressman: Herter, Wigglesworth, Angier Goodwin, Edith Nourse Rogers, and the rest. I made trips to Washington, had interviews with the Representatives in their offices, listened to them on the floor of the House, attended hearings over which they presided, and went to their homes in Washington. I submitted the posters to the congressmen for approval. I cut out pictures from magazines to illustrate points about their careers, pasted them on posters, and then I talked from the posters. I used these talks first at the Women's Republican Club; then when I was invited into a Congressman's district to speak, I would take the poster, tell about the committees he was on, the legislation he was sponsoring, and give a fresh, vivid account of his life. The Boston papers at that time gave very little coverage to our Congressmen.

Once, in a tight election, Edith Nourse Rogers called me up and asked me to speak to a group in Lexington, where there were many disaffected Republicans and Independents. I took the poster about Mrs. Rogers and was in the middle of my talk when she came in. She signalled me to continue. Apparently she was delighted with the speech and much more grateful to me than she needed to be when she got a big vote in that town and swept to victory in the district.

Congressman Herter came back to Boston frequently to meet with his constituents. We would lunch together, with our conversation ranging over state, national, and international politics. Who would have thought that this tall, handsome boy, born in Paris to aristocratic parents, who were both artists, would grow up to be one of America's leading statesmen? He told me that he came to this country as a boy of nine, already with trouble in those long, long legs. He had had excellent early academic training in the Ecole Alsacienne before he entered the Browning School in New York. He could take in the contents and meaning of a page at a glance. Having looked at a page of figures, he could remember it accurately.

When he graduated from Harvard, he was only twenty years old. "As I strolled across the Yard on Commencement day," he said, "I saw a friend and greeted him. I asked him what he was going to do." "The foreign service for me," the friend replied. It seemed to Herter that this was the field he would like to enter, and he celebrated his twenty-first birthday as an American attaché in Berlin, serving there until America entered the war. Leaving Germany, he was arrested in Mainz as a spy and had to use considerable diplomatic skill to escape summary execution by convincing his interrogators that he was, indeed, a member of the United States Embassy staff.

In 1918 he became Secretary of the American Commission to negotiate peace in Paris. From 1919 to 1924 he was Executive Secretary of Hoover's European Relief Council and then became Assistant to Secretary of Commerce Herbert Hoover.

There followed a period of about ten years when he was editor of *The Independent* and Associate Editor of *The Sportsman.*

It was from this background that Sinclair Weeks and other Republican leaders sought him out to run for the legislature, to which he was elected in 1931.

By the time I knew Chris in 1944, he was well established in the political field.

One day at lunch he told me of his projected trip abroad as a member of the House Committee on Foreign Affairs, and Chairman of the Select Committee on Foreign Aid. General Marshall, in an address at Harvard Commencement where he received an honorary degree, had proclaimed what came to be known as the Marshall Plan. The Senate was traditionally the branch of Congress concerned with foreign affairs. The House of Representatives, on the other hand, held the power of the purse, since money bills originated there. Chris explained to me that the Marshall Plan could never be implemented without the appropriation of large sums of money. No matter how much President Truman and Secretary of

consent, led to his asking me to serve on the committee in an active capacity, which I did. It became one of my major spheres of activity as National Committeewoman. In 1946 I suggested to him that I might set up a Women's Special Gifts Committee. He thought it was a good idea—told me to go ahead. I got together a representative group of women, some of whom had already solicited for the Red Cross and the United Fund. We worked all through the summer of 1946 and raised a surprisingly large sum of money, mostly from people of wealth.

The following year we determined to reach people all over the state, asking for donations of from one to five dollars. For the first time thousands of women were enlisted in what became known as the "neighbor-to-neighbor" plan. It was our theory that both the solicitors and the donors would have an increased interest in Republican issues and candidates because of their involvement as "askers" or "givers."

When Sinclair became Chairman of the National Republican Finance Committee, I asked why women could not be useful there. "It's all right with me, Katherine," he said, "if you can sell it to the other members of the Finance Committee. I will give you a spot on the program when next we meet."

Two months later when they were to meet in Cleveland, he asked me if I still wanted to come. Of course I did—even at my own expense.

So at the next meeting of the Republican National Finance Committee, made up of forty-eight men of financial power, one from each state, when my turn came, Sinclair introduced me and said I had a proposition to make. I knew I had to be concise. I said that in Massachusetts women had given more generously, had reached people hitherto not asked to give, and that through this work they became more interested in the party and more knowledgeable about Republican candidates and policies. I said that women owned a large proportion of the wealth in the United States, that they were accustomed to raising funds for public and private charities, why not for the Republican Party? It was unanimously voted.

Then it had to be sold to the Republican National Committeewomen who are, in the main, jealous of their prerogatives and don't want another woman in their state threatening their power and position. At a meeting of the Republican National Committee in Washington, I got the women members together in the evening, told them of the fact that another barrier against women's participation in the higher levels of party activity had been broken. Lest they all feel that they should be on the Finance Committee, I told them that I was not going to accept service on the Committee, that we each had enough to do as National Committeewomen, but that it would be a fine idea to have a nucleus of five women on this previously all-male committee. After some discussion, they accepted the idea. I asked them to send me names of women in their states who had had conspicuous success in raising money for public or private charities, and who could give generously. I would then submit the names to the Chairman. Weeks followed through and five women were appointed.

VIII

CHARLIE AT WAR

And what of Charlie? He sailed on the S.S. *Aquitania* on February 22, 1944, landed in Scotland the first of March, and proceeded to camp at Schrivenham in England. Frederick Leviseur was there too, and Alexander Williams, formerly music critic of *The Boston Herald*, and Donald Carlisle, famous for his books and cartoons about the Bedford hounds.

Charlie complained of the cold and dampness. Don Carlisle contracted pneumonia and came home to the United States; Alexander Williams, in his free time, explored the countryside on his bicycle. Charlie and Fred made friends in the nearby towns. Morale was at its lowest ebb when General Eisenhower appeared, gave the "at ease" command, and talked to the men about their mission and its importance. It was just the tonic they needed.

Fred said Charlie was "one of the bright boys" and he was transferred to London, where at St. Paul's School he began his high-level training for later service in Austria.

Charlie's letters contained descriptions of the V-bombs, of near misses to his apartment or office, of all-night watch on the roof for fire bombs. At the time when the buzz bombs were thickest, he wrote,

> Last night I was the Duty Officer, which meant I had to go on the roof whenever there was an alert. The night before, the officer had counted 162 buzz

bombs. I expected a rough night too. I made my inspections, instructed my staff what to do if a bomb hit any part of Headquarters, and went to bed in the basement. Immediately there was an alert. As I climbed up to the roof, three V-bombs went over, so low that they seemed to be just above the chimney pots, but they had lots of power and hit over a mile away. No more alerts all night.

He wrote of the men who were "up with the 'Larks' and to bed with the 'Wrens'."

He wrote of the thunder in the sky on June 6, 1944, as he saw wave after wave of aircraft over London, outward bound. He rightly guessed that the invasion of Europe had begun.

Now his letters began to speak of activities when off duty, at the Red Cross and the English-Speaking Union. More and more there were references to Miss Melissa Marston in connection with these two organizations. They went to lectures together and to the theatre. He visited her and her sister in the country. I pictured her as gray-haired and sedate. Evidently she pictured me the same way. Later, when I met her, she was young—a lady. I couldn't see how Charlie would like anyone with such enormous hips, for he liked his girls to be slender. Evidently she considered him rather her property. But her sister was wise enough to see, when later Charlie and I were there together, that we belonged to each other. I was not gray-haired or sedate, either! And I was slender.

Next Charlie was assigned to Eisenhower's SHAEF Headquarters at Rheims. On his uniform he always wore with pride the shoulder patch he received there, the shield with upturned sword. En route to Rheims, Charlie passed through Paris and bought a gift for me. At Rheims there was an artist who had sketched most of the colonels and generals, and Charlie decided to have his portrait done. He envisioned a dignified picture of himself as a Major in the U.S. Army. He wrote me to say he was sending it to me, and when it came, to get the children together and open it with them. In due course a package arrived from overseas. I asked Peggy and Herbert for Sunday dinner to see Daddy's picture. We gathered in the library, and with much anticipation unwrapped the package, brown paper, cardboard box, tissue paper, and then, not the picture at all but the sexiest looking black chiffon and black lace chemise you can imagine. The children couldn't picture this sort of thing from their middle-aged parents!

Several weeks later the picture did arrive. It was a pastel portrait of Charlie and a speaking image of him. While he was sitting for the picture, he could not refrain from telling jokes and stories. Some of them must have been quite racy. Instead of a dignified, wooden-looking Army officer, all uniform and decorations, it was Charlie himself with a gleam in his eye.

From his letters it was hard to tell where Charlie was, for because of censorship he could only speak of places in the most general terms. From a reference to Romeo and Juliet, I surmised that he had moved into Italy and was in Verona.

A little later his letter said,

Today I had to go to the other Headquarters, some distance from here. On the expert advice of some British officers who were in Rome with me, I did not move there. Their Headquarters are good, but their billets are very, very poor, so I shall commute by car. They are in a place which was for some time the home of the divine lady (obviously, Lady Hamilton) of whom you may have heard. The terrace and gardens are lovely and the view unbelievably so. Down there, away from the snowy peaks it was actually warm in the sun. But tonight the wind is blowing a gale off the snow, as usual, and the cold is bitter outdoors. Indoors, I am stoking the stove, and with a coat on, I am fairly comfortable. Once I get out of the army I am never going to a cold place again.

November 17, 1944:

My Honeybunch—Yesterday and Today I have worked as hard and as fast as a sprinter running on tiptoe, all day long. The first of the week I drew a final organization chart, showing the entire system of control and administration for the government of a certain country which we expect to conquer. It covered the control commission which we will set up, its entire staff, the national government for the country, and its state and local government.

The chart goes to the European Advisory Committee of which Winant is a member [Winant was U. S. Ambassador to Great Britain] which will decide on the organization actually to be used. Our ideas differ from the British in vital details. About the Russian ideas, we know only the position which they have taken in former cases. Then I had to draw up two memoranda explaining the reason for all the things in the chart, and another explaining the fundamental policy underlying the entire plan. It was quite a job. It had to be done fast, too.

On Christmas Eve of 1944 his thoughts turned homeward and he wrote:

Tis the night before Christmas and there certainly isn't even a mouse stirring here. The Italian waitresses at the mess have done their best. We have a good-sized Christmas tree with a few colored electric bulbs and decorations of strips of paper and bits of cotton all over the tree as snow. It looks quite nice. . . . Tomorrow, Christmas, I am to meet a colonel, newly assigned here, and give him some information. The afternoon I intend to take off and open the presents you all sent me. It will be great fun. I shall think about all the happy Christmases we have had together, especially when you and H.G. came to Charlottesville last year. Didn't we have fun? In case my Christmas seems a bit thin, think of those under the German steamroller in occupied countries. My Christmas will be nice. I hope next year to spend it with you.

Charlie was transferred to Caserta, Italy, Allied Headquarters, under the command of Field Marshal Alexander, where he was a member of the U. S. Group Control Council, readying plans for the occupation of Austria. The offices were in a magnificent palace surrounded by formal gardens, fountains, and waterfalls. Charlie and two other friends lived in a villa nearby. There he remained until June, 1945.

From Caserta, they finally moved into Austria, spending a few weeks in Salzburg before moving on to Vienna. In Salzburg he had a large office, only recently vacated by a retreating Nazi Gauleiter, who had left some of his possessions in the impressive office in a government building. Then finally into Vienna to stay until he came home.

Vienna was a ravaged city: houses without roofs or windows, rubble in the streets, heat nonexistent, glass for windows nonexistent, fuel nonexistent. The American officers had to scrounge for coal or gasoline. They worked in offices with no heat. Charlie wrote when he had been there for some time:

> November 25, 1945—Three months ago I came to Vienna. Things have certainly improved wonderfully since then. Although food is still short, there is no starvation. The people are still thin and white, but they look fairly well. Most of the shops which have roofs and windows are open, but they have very little merchandise. A large fraction of the rubble has been removed from the streets and from the bombed buildings, though much still remains. But heat is almost nonexistent.
>
> Recently I saw the first meat and fish ration a woman in the Russian section had received in seven months. It was a month's ration. It consisted of chopped meat, enough to fill about 2/3 of a cigarette package, and a trout-like fish about 8 inches long. Their regular ration is bread and dried peas, the latter full of worms.

Austria was governed by the Allied Quadripartite Council, and the country, like Vienna, was divided into four zones, British, French, American, and Russian.

Charlie served on the Council. He wrote:

> Executive Division USACA Section
> Hq—U.S. Forces in Austria
> November 2, 1945

Dearest Dear,

This is a great day for me. The organization plan which I drew late in August for the entire military government structure has finally been approved at the top and is being issued to replace the plan, which I drew, which was issued in early July. . . . They finally approved it, 13 pages of it, so I had about a 97 percent victory. But the battle involved an awful amount of grief in knocking down perfectly preposterous ideas.

Lots of love to the children.

Your lover, Charlie

November 17, 1945

John Dos Passos of *Life* was here a few days ago. He was turned over to me for background information on the situation in Austria before he interviewed the various generals. You may be interested to see what he says. . . . Last night I dreamed that I was home again. It certainly was wonderful to be there. At worst, I must be nearing the end of my absence. It looks as if I should be able to leave here in April, probably arriving late in May. Then we'll have a lovely summer.

November 25, 1945

Do you realize that next September we will have our 25th Anniversary? It does not seem possible, does it? I hope we will be together much more time during our second twenty-five years than in our first twenty-five years. With the children grown up, with no war to take me away, and with more money in the bank so I shall not have to work so hard, that should be possible. I think it would be nice if we went to the Ravine House for a fortnight to celebrate. I want to celebrate alone with you somewhere. We can celebrate with the children either before or after.

My love, Charlie

Charlie's letters, all through the spring and summer of 1946, were full of plans to come home. Perhaps he could leave in June and we would have the summer together. No, he couldn't come. There were continued postponements.

Charlie's thoughts were with us in spite of distance and other preoccupations. A letter to me said, "I have written Herbert what to do about his garden, if he has one. He should specialize on fall vegetables and plant them Memorial Day, or the first week in June. He could plant beans about June 15. He should not try to have too large a garden. What he has must be thoroughly hoed."

Another letter from Vienna at this same time, April 1946:

Today has been a heavenly day. The flowering shrubs are all coming out. The lilacs are showing and will be out in a day or so.

I spent most of the day at a meeting of the Quadripartite Political Affairs Meeting, negotiating the new control agreement. It was extremely interesting. The relations between the representatives of the powers are cordial, but each stands flatly for the views of his own government. We all had lunch together, then resumed the session. We meet again day after tomorrow. We sure did hang the Russian on his own logic on one vital point. He positively suffered, for he saw that we had him stuck on that vital point.

Lots of love to Peggy and Herbert. I love you very dearly, ever more so.

Charlie

May 6, 1946—Vienna
I was at a Quadripartite Committee meeting from 10 to 4 today. I talked to the Russians in German, the French in French, and the Englishmen in British. I swung the latter around to acceptance of our position on a long-disputed key clause. The Russian is wobbling. We hope he may come around at the next meeting on Friday. We reached agreement on a lot of clauses, so we do progress, if painfully.

Vienna—23 August 1945

The Allied Council meeting today was grueling. Most of it was devoted to Russian attempts, all of which were voted down. I don't see how General Kourassov stands the physical strain. All of us are "all in" at the end of the session. He keeps trying, fights hard for six or seven hours, and loses every point. Then probably Moscow gives him hell for not winning them all. I am always tired the day after a meeting. I should think he would have to spend the day in bed. . . .

I am too weary to write any more tonight. After the Council and Executive Committee meetings, I don't even read the paper. I just sit, eat a light supper and go to bed.

Lots and lots of love to Peggy and Herbert, and all my heart to my sweetheart.

Although Charlie had been away over two years, he was still an important figure in Republican politics. Robert Bradford, Lieutenant Governor of Massachusetts, wrote to him in late November 1945 about the growing Democratic strength in the state and saying:

It is high time you settled the affairs of Austria and came back to decide the fate of the Republican Party in Massachusetts or nationally. If, as I understand, you are now handling major policy questions for the Army, it should certainly be easy to do the same for the political front. The field of Lieutenant Governor is wide open, as it was the year you ran, and there are no announced candidates as yet.

I hope things are going well enough with you to have you come back and join us early next year. Sincerely, Bob.

We both wondered if Bradford was suggesting that Charlie come home and run for statewide office in the elections of 1946. But by the time he was free to leave Austria, the elections were long since over.

Bradford was elected Governor. Lodge was reelected to his former seat in the Senate.

Charlie was "frozen" in the job and there were no replacements. Important things must be finished before he left.

Much to his joy, he had been promoted to Lieutenant Colonel in December 1945. Also in that month he was decorated by General Mark Clark with the Bronze Star Medal.

Before he came home he was honored with the Legion of Merit, a decoration he had coveted. The citation read:

> Col. Chas P. Howard performed exceptionally meritorious services with Headquarters, U. S. Forces in Austria from May 1945 to August 1946. As Deputy Regional Military Government Officer, then Acting Chief of the Plans and Operations Division, and later as Deputy Chief of the Policy Branch, Executive Division, United States Allied Commission, Austria, he applied his broad practical experience in government planning and public administration to the problems of Austria with exceptionally keen insight, mature good judgment and unfailing industry. His efforts were a notable contribution to the accomplishments of this mission.

Many of the problems which have beset postwar Germany were avoided in Austria through the work of Charlie and others, officers of the Plans and Policy Division of the U. S. Commission in Austria. He could come home with a real feeling of satisfaction and accomplishment.

But coming home was a long, slow business. When he left Vienna October 13, 1946, he was put in charge of a train carrying U.S. personnel to Bremerhaven for return to the United States. It had to go through the Russian zone. The train was stopped by Russian guards. Everyone was questioned. The guards attempted to remove one passenger from the train. Charlie expostulated. Fortunately he spoke German as the Russian could too. The passenger was not removed. When they were finally given clearance and allowed to proceed, they had missed their "slot" on the railroad track and had to wait till the rails were clear again.

When they arrived at Bremerhaven, they found it to be a city with huge piles of rubble, and flimsy, unsupported walls which a strong wind might blow down and frequently did.

The Howard's house in Reading.

Above: Charles P. Howard being decorated by General Mark Clark.
Below: Governor and Mrs. Bricker, Governor and Mrs. Saltonstall, at
Republican Club of Massachusetts—Katherine G. Howard, President
(center).

Bomb-shattered Bremerhaven was filled with defeated, un-friendly people. It was a relief to board the *Lehigh Victory* and head for home. But the old Victory ship proved unseaworthy. They got as far as England, where it was evident that she was in no condition to cross the Atlantic. They had to wait for another ship to be sent from the United States. At last the *Delta Argentine* arrived, and they proceeded to the Azores. Misfortune plagued them again. Off Ponte del Garda, the boiler of that ship broke down. To make matters worse, they were confined to the ship. They saw the same old movies over and over again. Charlie, always a great reader, found Pres-cott's *History of Mexico* in the library and passed some of the time reading that. At last, from across the Atlantic again came a replacement for the boiler and they started home, a long tedious voyage from the sunny Azores to the gray, cold, North Atlantic and New York. It was over a month since they had left Vienna. Charlie's disgust and anger knew no bounds when he arrived at Camp Kilmer. There was a young lieutenant whom he had seen in Vienna just as he was leaving. "How did you get here?" Charlie asked.

"Oh," the lieutenant replied, "there was a plane coming over two days ago. There was an empty seat and they took me on."

As for me, I was jubilant when he finally left Vienna. At last he was coming home. He would be here to vote! But on election day he was still en route. Our friends planned wel-coming parties, but Charlie was stuck on a ship in the Azores. Surely he would be here for the Harvard-Yale game and the luncheon the Hodgkinsons were giving beforehand which would be a reunion with all of our best friends, and The Game, which Charlie loved. But no—arrival still in the future. At first I took the postponements with equanimity, but when the last one came and he was not going to be here for the family Thanksgiving party, it was beyond endurance. "Hope deferred had made my heart sick."

When Charlie finally landed, it was almost too good to be true. He telephoned me from Camp Kilmer. "Here I am at last, darling. I can get leave to go to New York late tomorrow afternoon and until midnight. Get a room and come on down to see your old man." "Of course, what joy!" I hung up. It was already evening. It was almost impossible to get a hotel room anywhere, but I set out to do it. I called all the hotels I knew in New York. "Absolutely nothing available," they said. Then I called the Boston managers of the Statler-Hilton Hotel and the Sheraton-Plaza Hotel, explained the situation, and asked if they could get a room for me. "Very sorry, Mrs. Howard, there just isn't a room to be had in New York." Oh dear, what could I do? I finally I called Charlie Nichols, Executive Secretary of the Republican State Committee. He could always do the impossible, and this time he did. In about an hour he called back. There would be a room in New York for the returning soldier. A reservation had been made for Colonel and Mrs. Charles P. Howard.

Next day I set out with a small bag to meet my husband. As the train sped from Boston to New York, I looked out the parlor car window at the passing scene, particularly at the shore line in Connecticut, the stretch I always liked the best. I wondered how it would be with us? A flood of thoughts went through my mind. Charlie gone so long, from August 1943 to late November, 1946, three years and three months of this time overseas. London, Paris, Rheims, Verona, Caserta, Salzburg and Vienna—Melissa Marston in England; his old sweetheart of World War I, Nanine Cornet, now Mme. Ake Falck, in Paris; Frau Karla Kruge, a widow, in Vienna. Always he had had feminine companionship in these cities. Whether it had been companionship or love I did not know. I thought of all he had experienced—the danger of V-bombs, cold, discomfort, danger—so far removed from home and its ties—but always the daily letter and the concern for me and the children. Yet three years and more is a long, long time. He had seen death and disaster in London, Italy, and Austria, had been part of great and historic things in planning for the present and future of Austria. He had experienced frustrations and triumphs. But surely must feel a great satisfaction.

As the wheels of the train clicked on the rails, I wondered how it would be with Charlie and me? The years—the years—the years. The women he had known—the men with whom I had worked and who were my friends—the events in Charlie's life—the events in my life. In spite of all the loving letters, and our strong commitment to each other, and to marriage itself, how would it be when we met? Charlie was an ardent and passionate man. Could I respond? Could I respond? Could I respond? The train sped me on. Could I respond? At last we pulled into New York. A taxi took me to the hotel. Charlie had arrived before me. As I entered the room, I saw at a glance that he was thin and tired and tense. There was even mud on his boots from Camp Kilmer. We kissed and embraced, and then to my surprise, he sat down and lit a cigarette. This was not my ardent Charlie. I was baffled. We talked. "How was your trip home?" "How are the children?" "When can you get to Boston?" All the while I was wondering why Charlie didn't pick me up in his arms and take me to bed. My reservations were gone. I wanted my husband. I wanted to be together as we always had been. It was I who seduced my husband.

Finally in early December he came back to Boston. He had written, "I don't want to be met at the station. I want you all to be at home in the living room, and I will come to you." He took the five o'clock train from New York. Jennie was back, keeping house for us. She was just as excited as we were at his return. But Herbert was worried. When his father went away, he was twelve and a half—now he was sixteen. Would his father realize that he was no longer a child? Peggy and I just felt eager anticipation. At last the door bell rang. Jennie flung it open. "Welcome home, Mr. Howard!" Charlie came rapidly up the steps to the living room on the second floor. The draperies were drawn; the fire was burning; it was cozy and beautiful. As he entered the room, he was buoyant and handsome, his uniform and boots all spit and polish. First, a kiss for me, then one for Peggy, and then, and then, a straight look at his manly son—a handshake, and, quick as a flash, he whipped out a package of cigarettes and offered Herbert one. They lit up. H. G. knew that everything was all right. The homecoming was happy. Presents, much animated talk, anecdotes, a happy family together again.

Then in the week following, I was heartsick; there was so much talk about "Karla" this, "Frau Kluge" that—"her maid sewed on my buttons and darned my hose." Frau Kluge and Charlie had been to church together (Charlie at church!) and to the opera—parties here and there—meager provisions of food and wine or liquor—but gaiety. It all got under my skin.

But he *was* home. We could take our trip, and start our life again. It was late in the season for Sea Island, Georgia, but all we wanted was to be together. We walked on the beach, and read, and talked and went to bed early and got up late. Charlie hired a car and driver to take us to Savannah, where I had not been since I left there as a child of seven. We drove on back roads lined with huge live oaks, gray moss hanging from the branches. When we came to Savannah, I remembered Bull Street and Christ Church where we went when we lived there. The driver found the Haskell-Pape School, now called the Pape School, where I got my first love of learning. He found the park where I played and Mother sketched, or I rode my tricycle while my nurse sat on the bench and talked with other nurses. It was still there.

When we came back to Boston, it was marvelous to be "Charlie and Kay" again. I appreciated him more than I ever had before. No more solitary entrances at cocktail parties, no more "extra woman" business at dinners, no more lonely evenings. Our finances were in good order, and I happily turned all that back to him, except for the household bills and my own accounts. Wonderful to be Mr. and Mrs. Charles P. Howard again. We might easily have lost each other; the State Department wanted him to stay on in Vienna, with a promotion, a villa, a car, and chauffeur, but Charlie wanted to come back to me. As for me, with a happy sigh of relief, I realized that I did not have to be on my own anymore!

IX

GETTING DEEPER INTO POLITICS

As Charlie and I took up our life together again we found the same community of interest we had always shared. Only gradually did the stories of his war experience come out, but he had kept in touch with Massachusetts politics and my increasing political activity through my daily letters to him. When he had gone away he had been in line for the Presidency of the Middlesex Club, then a powerful political organization; and Lieutenant Governor Bradford had suggested that he return if possible in 1945 and run for statewide office in 1946. But Charlie had fulfilled his mission and that opportunity no longer beckoned.

He returned with pleasure to his job as Treasurer of Middlesex County. During his absence, a loyal and competent supporter had served as his military substitute and had protected Charlie's interests at all time. His position was secure.

Charlie was warmly greeted at the Union Club Round Table for lunch, he reopened his law office, and Reading welcomed "Charlie" back as "Mr. Moderator."

He was active in the American Political Science Association, President of the Boston Branch of The Military Government Association, and later National President; and he was President of the Boston Chapter of the American Society for Public Administration.

As to the treasurership of Middlesex County, he liked to point out that the County had the same population as the kingdoms of Denmark and of Norway, and the budget was of equal proportions. Before going away Charlie had been able to borrow money at a phenomenally low rate of interest, and a few years after resuming his office he was able to report that

> Middlesex County paid $27,000 to extinguish the last cent of long term debt which it owed to anyone. The securities have long been rated AAA. Now there are none left to be rated.
>
> Middlesex County does not even owe a cent borrowed in anticipation of current revenue. On the contrary the County holds $850,000 in 60-day and 90-day certificates of deposit earning interest for the County. Middlesex is definitely solvent.

Charlie had returned in December 1946. With the advent of 1947, the Presidential election of 1948 began to loom on the horizon. The chief function of The National Committee is to put on the National Convention for the nomination of the President and Vice President. This entails frequent meetings, and having been elected in 1945, I now knew the members well. The Committee itself was tending more and more to be divided into pro-Taft and pro-Dewey groups, but I had friends in both groups, particularly among the women.

In 1947, a National Committee meeting was held in Kansas City to decide on the location of the 1948 Convention. Both Chicago and Philadelphia had issued invitations: the Taft group favored Chicago, and the Dewey group wanted Philadelphia. It was the first political skirmish of the coming campaign. Carroll Meins was representing Sinclair Weeks, who was in Europe. He and I were actively campaigning for Philadelphia. We agreed that at the reception held the first evening we would work separately soliciting votes. As we entered the large ballroom, a tray of drinks was passed. I took a tall glass, which was replenished from time to time, as I talked to various committee members. At the end of the evening, Carroll and I joined a small steering committee meeting in the California delegate's room. As I entered, the host said: "What would you like to drink, Katherine?" "Just what I've had all evening," I replied, "Ginger ale." "Thank God," said Carroll. "Every time you reached for a fresh glass I worried about you." Our efforts prevailed; Philadelphia really wanted us and Philadelphia was chosen.

Soon after this, I was asked by the Chairman of the Republican National Committee to serve on the Arrangements Committee, which "produces" the Convention; it chooses the Keynote Speaker, the Temporary Chairman and the Permanent Chairman of the Convention and decides on the allocation of tickets; it has political power to help or hinder the various candidates; and membership on it carries prestige as well as responsibility.

This meant trips to Philadelphia once a month from the fall of 1947 to the Convention itself in July 1948. Mason Owlett was the Pennsylvania National Committeeman and Frank Murdock, the local Chairman. Between them they made every meeting gay with social events as well as working sessions. I remember going to the Army-Pennsylvania football game in Philadelphia on a bright, sunny afternoon wearing a huge chrysanthemum; and I remember a dinner party given us by Joseph Pew, a small, courteous host, and a political powerhouse in Pennsylvania.

In addition to the usual problems to be solved by the Arrangements Committee, such as music, decorations, program, Keynote Speaker and other speakers, singers, etc., we had a wholly new problem, television. By 1948 it would be possible to telecast up and down the Eastern Seaboard, though there were not yet stations in the West. After much consideration, our Committee decided to use TV. When the time came, the overpowering heat made it necessary for Senators and Governors to remove their coats—there was no air-conditioning—and they were shown wilting and perspiring in their shirt sleeves. We were not sure that TV was an asset.

Before the Presidential Primaries in 1948, I was asked to serve as one of the Delegates-at-Large, along with the Senator, the Governor, the Lieutenant Governor, the Majority Leader of the House of Representatives, Joseph W. Martin, Jr., the National Committeeman, and the State Chairman. I prized the position, and I was pleased that they thought it important to have a woman in one of the slots.

After the Primary, the Massachusetts Delegates and Alternates met to choose the Chairman of the Delegation, and members of the various Committees. Senator Henry Cabot

Lodge and I were chosen for the Platform Committee. He became the Chairman and was ably assisted by General Robert Cutler, who scurried around with a clipboard, setting up meetings, taking notes, and being generally useful to Cabot.

I was assigned to the Subcommittee on Public Welfare. We held hearings, heard witnesses, including George Meaney, President of the A.F. of L., and Stassen, a highly respected ex-Governor of Minnesota, now pressing for the Presidency. Appearing before us he was overeager, and too willing to compromise. He had been a knight on a white charger, but then and there, for me, he ceased to be. After extensive hearings, the Subcommittee Chairmen under Lodge's leadership hammered out the final platform. He insisted it must be brief.

The National Committee met in Philadelphia a week before the Convention opened. Sinclair brought along his charming bride, Jane Tompkins Rankin Weeks, and they stayed with Sinclair's friend, John Hamilton, former Chairman of the Republican National Committee. Unfortunately Sinclair was stricken with a virus cold that kept him in bed all week.

I had been all over the place, meeting and talking with people, and it was not until near the end of the week that I received a message that Sinclair wanted to see me at the Hamilton's apartment. I found Jane and Mrs. Hamilton chatting in the living room. Jane said, "Go on into the bedroom. He's expecting you." I stepped into a pink and feminine room. Sinclair was sitting up in bed, propped up with pink pillows, and covered with pink sheets, blankets, and a pink blanket cover. It looked incongruous. "Katherine," he said, "I want to know what you think about the contesting Georgia delegations." I told him I had conferred with the delegation headed by W. R. Tucker and I felt the Party was lucky to have them. As we were talking, the Hawaiian delegation, attired in grass skirts and orchids, singing alohas, swept into the Hamiltons' living room, and then into Sinclair's bedroom. Sinclair called out in panic, "Janie, come here!" She came and sat on his bed. They were properly serenaded. That was the end of our conference on the Georgia contests.

There were two slates of delegates from Georgia, each claiming to be the legitimate one. The decision as to which group would be seated as voting delegates had to be decided by the National Committee. Having been born and brought up in the South, I was impressed by the caliber of the Tucker delegates, but John Hamilton had persuaded Sinclair to vote for the Foster delegation. I told him I was going to vote for the Tucker group, and did he mind? "Katherine," he said, "you have to vote your convictions."

My colleague from Michigan, Regina Hays, the first woman Secretary of the Republican National Committee, was not so fortunate. Her National Committeman did not approve of her independence in voting, and in his highhanded way saw to it that she was not to continue on the National Committee. She would serve through this Convention as Secretary, and thereafter her position would be vacant. Six months previously Sinclair Weeks had said to me, "Katherine, why shouldn't you be Secretary of the Republican National Committee?" It hadn't occurred to me, but it seemed a good idea. Why not?

When the word came that Regina Hays was finished as Secretary, I was about to go to a buffet luncheon for the women members of the Committee. As I was standing in line at the buffet table, I said to my friends as we mingled, "I'm in the running for the Secretary of the National Committee. I hope you will vote for me." Those to whom I spoke seemed to think it was a fine idea. No one else had given it a thought—everyone was concentrating on the struggle for the nomination for the Presidency.

The leading candidates were Senator Robert Taft, Governor Thomas A. Dewey, and Senator Arthur Vandenburg. Weeks and the majority of the Massachusetts delegation were for Vandenburg, but Charles B. Rugg, and some of the other Massachusetts delegates were for Dewey. Rugg had pledged his support to Dewey and was challenging Weeks's leadership of the party. The stakes were high, for everyone knew that this was a Republican year—Truman was in disrepute, the Republican Eightieth Congress had made a fine legislative record, the Republican nominee was sure to be elected. Weeks held firmly to Vandenburg until the word finally came that because of reasons of health he would not accept the nomination. Meanwhile, the tide was running strongly for Dewey.

On the last morning but one, it was evident that Dewey was in the lead. At lunch time I went to Sinclair's suite—Jane was sitting in the outer room—people were swirling in and out. A friend, greeting people there and answering the telephone, said to me, "Go on into the other room. Sinclair wants to see you." As I entered, Sinclair was sitting looking gloomy and stubborn. Tom Pappas and Max Rabb were standing looking out the window, their backs to the room. As I entered, Tom turned and said: "For God's sake, Katherine, see what you can do with this man—he's got to release the Massachusetts delegation so they can vote for Dewey this afternoon." There was further talk and discussion. I certainly can't claim credit—Sinclair hated to give up but his own good sense finally dictated his decision. Before the luncheon recess was over, word went out that Massachusetts would cast its votes for Dewey. Early that afternoon he was nominated.

When it was all settled, and Sinclair had had time to accept the inevitable, I called him late in the afternoon. "Sinclair," I said, "you suggested some time ago that it might be a good idea for me to be Secretary of the National Committee. What about it?"

"Heck, Katherine," he said, "I can't help you now. My name is anathema at Dewey Headquarters."

Always before he had taken the leadership in my behalf. Now, if I were to be Secretary, it would have to be without his help. I did not have long to wait.

Early next morning, about six o'clock, my telephone rang. "Dewey headquarters calling. There will be a breakfast meeting of a small number of members of the National Committee in Governor Dewey's suite. He would like to have you attend."

I accepted with alacrity, and was there at the appointed hour—7:30. About twenty people sat down to the usual political breakfast of grapefruit, scrambled eggs and bacon, rolls and coffee. Sinclair was not there. Governor Dewey looked dapper and immaculate, there was no trace of fatigue. After breakfast, in his carefully modulated voice, he announced that Representative Hugh Scott of Pennsylvania would be Chairman of the National Committee. At the same time he said that Herbert Brownell, his close associate in New York politics, would be campaign manager, and Mrs. Charles W. Weis, "Judy," National Committeewoman for New York, would be Co-chairman. They would have headquarters in Washington, and would run the campaign. When Judy was given this position of authority in a campaign, it was a first for women. Judy was a tall woman of fine figure and friendly manner, universally liked by men and women. When she was photographed with Governor Dewey, as she frequently was, she always slipped her shoes off, so that she would not tower above him. Governor Dewey was short, but well formed. His wife was of perfect proportions for him, just a little shorter, so that together they made a handsome couple. It was Mrs. Alice Longworth who made the devastating remark: "They look like a couple on top of a wedding cake."

Having disposed of the Chairman of the Republican National Committee, and the campaign managers, the Governor turned to the position of Secretary. Only one woman had held this office and she had stubbed her toe. They could, at this time, have restored the job to a man, but Dewey said he would like to confer with Mrs. Weis on this subject, and they withdrew for a few minutes. When they returned he asked the women members present to assemble down the hall in Mrs. Weis's room, and whomever they chose as Secretary of the Republican National Committee would be agreeable to him.

As we walked to Judy's room she whispered to me "It's going to be Consuelo Northrop Bailey, of Vermont." Before I could say anything, we were in Judy's room. It was a mess. The beds had not been made, the room was not picked up. We sat on the beds anyway, and Judy, presiding, said: "We are here to nominate a Secretary for the Republican National Committee." Quick as a flash, a good friend of mine, Inez Wing of Maine, said—"I nominate Katherine Howard." Instantaneously another seconded the motion. Judy must have been taken aback. She was the only one who knew it was to be Consuelo. "Are there any other nominations?" There were none. The vote was put, and I was unanimously nominated. Soon word came back from Dewey that the choice was agreeable to him. To my surprise, and gratification, I *was* the Secretary.

When I told Sinclair he said, "Katherine, that is the most bloodless election in the history of the National Committee."

I felt badly for Consuelo, who sent me an orchid with her congratulations. Happily she subsequently served two terms as Secretary.

For me it was all over but the speeches. On the night that

former President Hoover was to make an address, he was scheduled for a very late appearance. About eleven o'clock Charlie said he had had enough and was going on back to the hotel. H. G. wanted very much to hear Hoover, as I did. But speaking after midnight was not to Hoover's advantage, and his words were disappointing. When I returned to our suite I undressed in the dark; I had worn my diamond bracelet and I unclasped it and left it on the dressing table.

Charlie's trousers were gone when we awoke in the morning. He had laid them on a chair and hung his coat on the back. He couldn't believe his eyes. While we slept, a thief had come into the room and gone off with the trousers, wallet, keyrings and all. My bracelet was still on the dressing table.

Charlie said, "It's fortunate every Boston gentleman has his suits made with two pairs of trousers!"

Charlie and Herbert returned to Boston; the Weeks and I stayed over for the meeting of the Republican National Committee, where I was formally elected Secretary. *The New York Times*, Washington and Boston papers gave me attention in their front-page stories. Charlie met me at the train in Boston with a big armful of red roses and a welcoming kiss. "Darling," he said, "I'm proud of you!"

So now I was Secretary. Being an officer also made me a member of the Executive Committee. My relationship with the Chairman, Congressman Hugh Scott of Pennsylvania, was cordial. He was an urbane, genial gentleman, possessed of one of the finest collections of ancient Chinese art in this country. He made me welcome as one of the inner circle.

Now that I was Secretary everything that I said carried more significance. Invitations to speak poured in from all over the country, and press conferences were attended by the top reporters.

The Speakers' Bureau of the Republican National Committee sent me to Los Angeles, and arranged a press conference where I warned of overconfidence (everyone *knew* Dewey was going to be elected), praised the accomplishments of the Republican Eightieth Congress, and paid tribute to Governor Warren.

In the heat of an early October afternoon in Los Angeles, wearing my Boston fall clothes, I spoke to 500 women delegates from all over California. One of the guests came up to me at the end and said, "Oh, Mrs. Howard, I love to listen to you. I love your New England accent!" Just the week before, speaking to a campaign luncheon meeting in Maine, I had been told, "Oh, Mrs. Howard, it's such a pleasure to listen to you. I love your Southern accent!" Didn't they pay attention to *what* I said?

After my California speech, wilting in the heat, I had hoped for a bath and a nap. But no, my eager hosts must show me everything. Then we would have an early dinner and drive to Whittier to meet and listen to the newly elected young Congressman, Richard Nixon. He and his wife were going to meet their constituents in the schoolhouse in Whittier. So there we went. They *were* young, and friendly and unassuming. They were mingling with their friends and neighbors who had elected them. It was more informal than a P.T.A. meeting. Then Nixon was asked to tell them something about his work in Washington. He mounted the platform and told in straightforward and simple language about being assigned to the House Un-American Activities Committee, and some of their work in connection with communist conspirators. It was absorbing and shocking. He made the point that freshmen congressmen cannot pick their committees. They were appointed to them. This early assignment may have affected his future career.

As I spoke in San Francisco, Fresno, St. Paul, Minnesota, New York City, I found that the mood was everywhere the same. People were confident of victory for Dewey and the Republican Party. All the polls pointed in that direction. Even the Democrats were almost ready to concede the election.

The Republican strategy was geared to this—the election was in the bag—don't attack; don't alienate anyone; and you can't lose.

Then Truman set out on his "Give 'em Hell Campaign." He went to the Middle West. He went on the offensive. His colorful speeches and his game attitude caught people's fancy. But the polls did not reflect this.

On the last Thursday before the election Dewey came into Massachusetts. With some of the other party officials, I boarded the campaign train at Pittsfield and rode on to Boston with the Presidential Party.

At luncheon I was the guest of Becky McNabb, one of the oustanding women political leaders in New York State, who was Mrs. Dewey's aide on the train. By this time, Truman's speeches were making themselves felt. He was speaking six or seven times a day. He was giving them raw, red meat, and they liked it. Stanley High of the *Reader's Digest* was writing most of Dewey's speeches. They were beautiful odes to America. Dewey was on high ground—Truman playing gutter politics. I said to Becky—"Why doesn't the Governor light into Truman?" She said, "He desperately wants to. Night after night the policy group discuss it. As a former District Attorney, all Dewey's nature longs to attack, and night after night the policy group say: 'Don't get nasty, keep it cool, don't make any mistakes, and you can't lose'."

Senator Henry Cabot Lodge was on the train, and Walter Robb, Chairman of the Massachusetts Republican Finance Committee, Senator Saltonstall was there, and his able assistant Henry Minot. Minot had worn a battered, old and grease-stained hat with a hole in it which he tossed down on a train seat. As Walter Robb walked by he said, "I wish I had lived in Boston long enough to be able to wear a hat like that."

Came election night. Still confident, Charlie and I walked up Beacon Hill together after dinner, to Republican Headquarters. Knowing that after the victory I would be asked to say a few words at the victory celebration and on the radio, I had put together some notes to the effect that the people had chosen, the better man had won, we would unite, etc. When we arrived, people were beginning to gather for the celebration. Charlie and I stepped to an inner room where Charlie Nichols was receiving the returns by wire. I asked Charlie Nichols, "How's it going?" "The percentages are disturbing," he replied. From past records he knew how the percentage of votes should run for victory. Charlie and I went out and mingled with the party for about an hour. When we questioned Charlie Nichols again, he said, "Not good." Not long after, Charlie and I walked back down Beacon Hill to our house. "Wait till the farm states come in," said Charlie Howard, "it will be all right." But alas, the farm states were where Truman had been most effective. By early morning Truman had won.

There was havoc within the Republican party. The split between the followers of Taft, conservative middle westerners, and the more liberal eastern and far western group was deep and bitter.

A meeting of the Republican National Committee was called for January in Omaha, Nebraska. The purpose was to oust Hugh Scott, the chairman. Sinclair and some of his friends, former enthusiasts for Wendell Willkie, were against Hugh Scott. Now they were casting their lot against the wing of the party which they had supported and led. Weeks could not go to the meeting, but he did not give me his proxy. He knew I was going to vote for Scott.

This was a meeting never to be forgotten. I took the Twentieth Century train to Chicago, changed to the one which left for the West and as we pulled out, I went to the lounge car and sat down beside Doris Fleeson, the well-known syndicated columnist. There and then began a friendship which was true and lasting, although we were on opposite sides politically. We recognized this. It was something deeper than that which drew us together, perhaps a conviction that politics was the highest form of public service and that women were important and should be given their place in the sun.

As the train pulled into the first stop, some time later, Doris went off to file her story for the morning papers. When she returned she paused dramatically in the doorway, one arm upraised and resting on the door jamb. "Doris," asked one of the reporters, "what did you say?"

"I said," she replied, "that the built-up frustrations and bitterness of the Republican Party would make themselves felt in Omaha."

How right she was. The Taft group of Clarence Brown of Ohio, Congressman and National Committeeman; Mason Owlett of Pennsylvania, Walter Hallanan of West Virginia, and several others were out to take over control of the party.

It was snowing when we reached Omaha and it continued to snow. Soon, in the hotel, we were isolated. No traffic was moving. Helicopters were dropping food to the cattle and sheep on the ranges. We were shut off from the world except for the telephone and telegraph.

Inside, the atmosphere was as hot and rancorous as it was frozen outside. There was open warfare between the two wings of the Party. At the first morning meeting of the National Committee, I sat at the head table as the new Secretary and, as a matter of course, I started taking minutes of the proceedings. There was a paid secretary who had always done the minutes before, but he was so agitated at what was going on that, once he saw I was writing, he didn't bother. At the end of the meeting Scott asked me for a transcript of the minutes. Thank God, I had them. Immediately after the close of the session I had dictated them to Juanita Shields, the remarkable woman who had been secretary to chairmen Carroll Reece and Herbert Brownell. Then I corrected them, and she typed them, and in final form they were circulated to all members of the Committee.

Following the morning session there was a big luncheon meeting at which the Governor of Nebraska spoke. It was my first meeting with Val Peterson, with whom I was later to be closely associated. He told of the disaster to the state—trains were not running; roads were blocked; cattle were dying.

Came the final day. The crucial vote was taken and Hugh Scott was reelected. He emerged looking happy and triumphant—indeed yes, we had won.

Now the problem was to get out of Omaha, and home again. By now a few trains were running, but not many. A few roads were open but not many. Only a few cabs were running. I got packed and got my bags downstairs, but how to get to the station? The lobby of the hotel was filled with others in the same predicament. Finally a cab drew up; a bunch of newspapermen had gotten it somehow. One of them said, "Come on, Mrs. Howard, and go with us." We piled in, five newspapermen and I, sitting on top of one of them.

The railroad station presented a strange sight, almost deserted, but the train to Chicago, on which I had a roomette, was due to leave in a couple of hours. When I was finally aboard, I found my quarters were next to the National Committeeman from Ohio, Clarence Brown.

Next morning, while my roomette was being made up, I sat with Clarence in his roomette. "Katherine," he said, "your side won yesterday, but in six months we will throw Hugh Scott out." I was appalled. Scott had been fairly elected. Couldn't they accept the will of the majority?

Apparently not. When we reached Chicago, the very first

meeting of that hostile Taft group was held. They were losing no time in planning to upset the proceedings of the National Committee, just completed.

Sure enough, when Charlie and I were traveling in Austria seven months later, they carried out their threat. A telegram arrived for me announcing a meeting of the Republican National Committee. It was unprecedented to hold a meeting in the summer. But the Clarence Brown group had enough votes to force Scott's resignation. Their purpose now was to elect a new Chairman. Guy Gabrielson, a wealthy man and a prominent New York attorney who lived in New Jersey, was their choice. He had told many of us that he had made enough money, and he wanted to devote his time and talents to the Republican Party. He had much to offer. Gabrielson was elected; the Taft forces were back in the saddle. But I continued to be Secretary.

With the Convention of 1948 over, there were important things on the home front. In Massachusetts Sinclair Weeks was in difficulty. The Republicans wanted a scapegoat and he was it.

The speeches I made from time to time were aimed at restoring the morale of the Republicans. The unexpected defeat of 1948 had torn the Party asunder. There were bitter accusations by the "real Republicans," the followers of Taft, of the "me-too-ism" of the "Eastern Establishment," which, they said, caused the defeat. Twice Taft had been denied the presidential nomination. Twice the Party had been defeated under Dewey's leadership. The schism was wide and deep. After presidential defeats going all the way back to Hoover and the Great Depression of the thirties, suggestions were made that the Republican Party change its name. The G.O.P. was done for, they said.

In 1950 when Republican Governor Robert Bradford was defeated for reelection by Democrat Paul Dever, it was obvious to Sinclair Weeks and the Policy Committee that drastic action needed to be taken to widen the voter appeal of the Republican Party in Massachusetts. With the increasing number of Italian, French, Jewish, and Polish votes in the state, it was obvious that the Republican Party needed to broaden its base and draw them to its ranks as voters and officeholders. The day was over for an all Yankee slate.

The first move, spearheaded by Weeks and accepted by the Republican State Committee, was to name four "Deputy Chairmen" of the Massachusetts Republican State Committee with other than Yankee backgrounds. They were Robert Boudreau (French), James Gaffney (Irish), Mayor Olander of Northampton (Swedish) and John Volpe (Italian). But we still had to reckon with the voters in the Primary. The Democrats usually chose a predominately Irish Catholic ticket. The Republicans had customarily voted for Yankee names, and too often this had led to defeat. This being so, the Republican Policy Committee, headed by Weeks, and of which I was a member, considered having a Preprimary Convention. At a gathering with delegates chosen from all over the state, a slate more representative of ethnic backgrounds could be arrived at and even a woman might be put on the ticket, I thought.

One day in the spring of 1951, the telephone rang. It was Sinclair. "Katherine," he said, "about the Preprimary Assembly, we want to go ahead and explore it. I am appointing a committee to draw up plans, and Rules and Regulations, and procedures for it. The idea, as you know, is to have a Convention in the spring to draw up and nominate a slate of candidates for statewide office which will be the Republican slate at the Primary in September. I am naming former Governor Bradford, Jim Gaffney, and you. I want you to be Chairman." "Sinclair," I protested, "I can't possibly be Chairman of a committee with a former Governor on it." "Yes, you can," insisted Weeks. "I've talked to Bradford and he agrees. I want you to be chairman, because I know if you are, it will get done."

So I accepted.

I went to see Governor Bradford in his law office, and we made plans for the first meeting. James Gaffney was a fine, upstanding young man, a war veteran who had lost a leg in combat but was exceedingly active, and a lawyer by profession. He was a newcomer to politics, but interested and eager to serve. The three of us worked through the summer of 1951. We studied laws and precedents. With Bradford's political experience and fine legal mind, and Gaffney's ability to work on legal problems, and my keeping things going, and working with them, we made progress. We would meet with Sinclair occasionally, and when the comprehensive report on plans and procedures was finished, he was in accord with it. But now, to be implemented, it had to be accepted by the Massachusetts Republican State Committee. No one apparently had given that much thought, for according to the rules, no one can speak, or present a motion, except an elected member of the Committee. That ruled out Governor Bradford and Gaffney. There was no one to make the presentation and motion but me.

The night of the meeting arrived. I wished that Sinclair, a member of the State Committee, were there. But he did not come. I stood up and made the motion for the adoption of the report. I was Chairman of the Committee; I was a member of the State Committee; I had to do it.

Across the table sat Carroll Meins. Surely I could count on him. He and Sinclair, Charlie Nichols and I always worked together and agreed on things. But not tonight. Carroll rose to speak, and to my consternation, he ripped into the plan. Carroll was a former Chairman of the Republican State Committee. He spoke with authority. He carried great weight. He was unequivocably opposed to the Preprimary Convention plan. Next to him sat Philip Sherman. He was a forceful, jury-swaying lawyer. He used all his skilful, persuasive, and demagogic legal tactics to oppose my motion. It looked bad. Out in the hall I saw Fred Dearborn, later Counselor to Governor Christian Herter. He was in favor of the Preprimary Convention, but he had to stand there mute. He did not have the privilege of the floor. Next to me sat Beatrice Hancock Mullaney, an attorney from Fall River, and State Committeewoman from that area. This was the first she had heard of the proposed plan, but she was Catholic and Irish and came from a city made up of people of varied racial backgrounds. She could see value in the proposal. Beatrice rose to support me. She marshalled her words well. She was effective. I stood again to speak and to explain and to persuade. I became surprisingly cogent and eloquent. At the conclusion of my remarks the motion was put. As the Secretary read the roll call, and the yeas and nays were recorded, I held by breath—yes? no! yes? YES! The motion was carried! The State Committee had voted to adopt our plan for a Preprimary Assembly!

James Gaffney was made Chairman of a Committee on

Arrangements for the Convention, which was held in Worcester in June 1952. Nominated were: Christian A. Herter for Governor, Sumner Whittier for Lieutenant Governor, Mrs. Beatrice Hancock Mullaney for Secretary of State, Roy C. Papalia for State Treasurer, George Fingold for Attorney General, David Mintz for State Auditor, and Senator Henry Cabot Lodge was named for reelection as Senator. Fingold and Mintz were Jewish; Bea Mullaney—a woman—and Irish; Papalia, Italian; Herter and Whittier, Yankee. It was a well-balanced ticket and it was triumphant in November.

Later, a law was enacted to provide for Preprimary Conventions for both parties. In 1974 it was repealed.

X

THE FIGHT FOR THE TEXAS DELEGATES

Who would have thought that a casual glance at a small folder on a table in my sunny Beacon Street bedroom could affect the course of history? But so it was. One winter morning early in 1952 I was tidying up my room when my glance fell on

"Rules Adopted by
Republican National Convention
Philadelphia, Pennsylvania
1948"

These were the rules governing the procedures to be taken by the Republican National Committee in regard to the selection and certification of delegates to the Convention and other pertinent matters.

I must have laid it there when I returned from the Republican National Committee meeting in San Francisco in late January. There, as Secretary, I had issued the Call to the Convention as provided for in Rule 27 in that little folder. This morning it seemed to cry out to me for attention. I said to myself, "These are the Rules under which you will be operating as Secretary of the Republican National Committee, and, with luck, as Secretary of the Republican National Convention. You'd better find out what your duties and responsibilities will be." It all seemed remote and academic to me.

But I noticed the *"shall,"* and the responsibilities given to the *Secretary.*

A few weeks later I was at a luncheon given in my honor by the Women's Republican Club of Massachusetts. As the head-table guests were lining up to march in, a message was relayed to me—"Washington calling." It was Mr. Donald, the Executive Director for the upcoming Republican National Convention. For many years he had been the full-time employee of the Republican National Committee, charged with the responsibility of attending to all the details of putting on the Republican National Conventions under the direction of the Chairman and in cooperation with the secretary. A convinced and dedicated Taft man, he was an incorruptible Scotch Presbyterian who believed in honorable actions and fair play.

"Mrs. Howard," he said, while the head table waited to go in, "there is going to be a meeting of the Republican National Committee's Arrangements Committee in Washington in a few weeks. I think you should get the 'Proceedings of the Republican National Convention of 1928' and read it, because the action taken there is very pertinent to the question of contested delegates which is going to come up at the next meeting." Mr. Donald continued, "I don't want to see what happened to Mrs. Hays happen to you. If you get this book and study it, it will help you." I went to the library, got the book, and studied it over the weekend.

Early the following week I received a telephone call to come to Washington to a meeting of the Arrangements Committee of the Republican National Committee to talk about contested delegates. I took the "Federal Express," feeling queasy from an attack of intestinal flu. When the train pulled into Washington, I wondered if I had the strength to walk the length of the train to the station, but I did.

From there to the Mayflower Hotel where I had engaged a room and then to the meeting at the National Committee Headquarters. Guy Gabrielson, the Chairman, was there, and Ralph Gates, the General Counsel; Vice-Chairman Ezra Whitla of Idaho; and Werner Schroeder from Chicago, all lawyers; I was the only woman member, the Secretary of the Arrangements Committee.

It was May 27, 1952, the day of the Mineral Wells Republican State Convention in Texas. As we were meeting at National Committee Headquarters, telephone calls kept coming in from Henry Zweifel, Republican state chairman of Texas, and leader of the Taft forces there. There was a private line from him to National Committee Headquarters. It was evident that Guy Gabrielson and the other people at this meeting were working closely with Zweifel at Mineral Wells, where the notorious Convention to elect delegates to the Republican National Convention was being held.

At noon we all went to lunch together, but my stomach would not tolerate a martini which the others had, and I toyed with my food. I wanted to keep a clear head anyway. After lunch we returned to National Committee Headquarters and took up the question of how to deal with the delegate contests in Mississippi, Texas, and Georgia.

Gabrielson said, "Since the Texas delegates are district delegates, the contest should be referred to the State Committee of Texas and not come before the National Committee because only contests of Delegates-at-Large come to the National Committee at the Convention.

I made a mental note that this was the pertinent question in the 1928 Convention, and it was proved then that there were no district delegates from Texas as no District Conventions were held. They were therefore, according to Rule 2, Section G, all Delegates-at-Large. But at this time I was just listening and taking notes to follow up.

Mississippi was quickly disposed of by a telephone call to Perry Howard, National Committeeman and a Taft backer. Gates, the General Counsel, told him that he would present his faction's claim to the National Committee, Werner Schroeder would move that Perry Howard's group be seated, the National Committee in executive session would pass the motion on a voice vote, and Perry's delegation would be seated.

Then we came to Georgia. I remembered back to 1948 and Regina Hays's unfortunate experience in the Tucker-Foster delegation fight. Perhaps Mr. Donald telephoned me because he thought justice had not been done in that case. Now again the same Tucker and Foster groups were contesting. I was keeping quiet, listening and writing notes to myself: "Should I, as Secretary, certify the Tucker or Foster group?" "Should I, as Secretary, certify the Perry Howard group in

Mississippi or abide by the Supreme Court decision?" It was going to take a lot of studying of laws and precedents and briefs to make the just decisions.

Then Gabrielson turned to me and said, "Now, Katherine, about these contested delegates, Ralph Gates and Werner Schroeder *will make the decisions,* and then I'll direct Mr. Donald to send the notices out."

I could so easily have acceded. I could have let the men make the decisions and do the work. Again and again I was to find that they were willing to give you the title and emoluments, but they expected to run the show. But I *was* the Secretary of the Republican National Committee. I knew what my duties and responsibilities were, having studied that little white folder on my bedroom table. I expected to *be* the Secretary and do the job.

Before the moment passed, I heard myself saying, "Guy, I have the greatest respect for these gentlemen, and I'd be glad to have their help and advice, but according to the rules of the Republican National Committee, this is the responsibility of the Secretary. I am the Secretary. I'll be held responsible by the press and the public for these decisions. I intend to make the decisions according to the Rules of the Republican National Committee and the laws of the States, and I shall make them myself."

There was a pause. My voice had sounded rather dramatic, and with a smile I said, "That statement should have been accompanied by soft music!"

Guy smiled at me and said, "Of course, Katherine, you didn't let me finish."

My last note on that fateful day was, "Query: Will I be told to be more agreeable or I won't be elected Secretary of the Convention? What do I say then?"

Soon the meeting broke up and I went back to the Mayflower and to bed.

The telephone rang. It was Cabot Lodge calling from New York where he and Herbert Brownell were working on the Eisenhower campaign. Cabot had never paid much attention to me as a National Committeewoman. Now, he and Brownell found that I was in a position of power. Cabot wanted to know what "those hyenas" had been up to today. I told him that by the grace of God and some intestinal fortitude I had asserted the fact that I *was* the Secretary and I expected to exercise the functions of the office. The plan to bypass me had not worked. It was sprung on me unexpectedly, but I had found my voice in time. The next day, feeling better, perhaps because of my conflict with Guy, I returned to Boston. I was to come back to Washington before too long.

In the weeks preceding the Convention, the Secretary has an office at Republican Committee Headquarters in Washington. There, the heads of opposing delegations deposit their briefs with you and make their presentations. There you study the pertinent state laws, and Supreme Court decisions. I thanked my stars that I had learned to do this sort of thing at college.

Since I had insisted on my prerogatives, and had not "gone along," I was an outcast. In headquarters you were either for Taft or you were persona non grata. I had preserved my neutrality, in spite of all-out-for-Eisenhower Massachusetts. I *had* to. I had decisions to make, and they were going to be made by me in strict conformity with Rules and laws. I had to be neutral. I worked away all day long in my office, surrounded by hostility. I was avoided and disliked. I went back to the Mayflower at night, exhausted but determined. One evening I called up my old friend, Chris Herter. "Chris," I said, "I'm working at Republican National Committee headquarters. The atmosphere is dreadful."

"Come on over and have supper with 'Mac' [his wife] and me." He understood what I was going through. What a pleasure to relax in a friendly atmosphere at their beautiful house on O Street and to sit in their walled garden after dinner and talk of pleasant things. Next day I went back to work reassured and refreshed.

On the following weekend in Boston, Sinclair Weeks wanted to know how things were going. "Sinclair," I said, "it's an awful responsibility, and the atmosphere in that Headquarters is like the Kremlin. You wouldn't believe it. My tummy is all curled up with the hostility and the tension."

Next day he called up Charlie and said, "Why don't you take a week off and go down and keep Katherine company?"

What a relief! He was with me for dinner and the night and would go with me to the office and read the paper, and by his presence gave me the loving companionship and support I needed.

It had always followed "as the night, the day" that the

Secretary of the Republican National Committee was elected
Secretary of the Republican National Convention. Now word
came to me that I might be supplanted at the meeting of the
Arrangements Committee, early in June, or that they might
postpone election of the Convention Secretary until the Republican National Committee met just prior to the Convention in July. This was contrary to all precedents. But in this
way they could hold the threat of nonelection over me until I
had made the decisions on the Texas delegates. Rule their
way, like a good girl, and they would make me Secretary of
the Convention. Rule against them—I'd be out.

They should have known me better.

Being forewarned, I took action. The key to the situation
was the women's vote. At that time the National Committee
was made up of one man and one woman from each state. If
I could get all the women's votes and some of the men's, I
would be secure. I arrived in Chicago two days before the
meeting. With a list of the members of the Republican National Committee in hand, I telephoned the men on whom I
could count, and as the women arrived, I invited them to
supper with me the evening before the meeting. They all accepted except Rose Mayes, the Assistant Chairman—the top
woman of the Republican National Committee. To them I
stated my case. As far as the women were concerned, this was
not a Taft-Eisenhower fight. This was "the men" trying to do
a woman in. My predecessor had been disgraced and exiled
because of her independence four years ago. They weren't
about to have this happen again. For good measure, I threw
in the fact that I would not be a candidate for reelection. This
meant that they could all be nice to the outgoing girl, and
someone else could have her hour of glory at the next Convention.

All evening while we were dining, Rose Mayes drifted in
and out, taking word back to the Chairman and the male
officers as to how things were going. Before the evening was
over, all the women except Rose declared for me. When this
word went back, the officers who wanted to frighten me into
acquiescence, or replace me, knew it couldn't be done.

The old political adage is, "If you can't lick them, join
them." And so they did. In the report of the meeting of the
Arrangements Committee held next morning, it is amusing to

follow the capitulation of those who had been about to end my career.

When the Committee came to the selection of the Temporary Secretary of the Convention (the Permanent Secretary is elected at the Convention,) the senior member of the National Committee, Mrs. Tallman, placed my name in nomination. Seconding speeches came from women members from the North, South, East, and West.

Mrs. Tanner of Missouri said, "We agree that Katherine Howard is not only capable and qualified, but typifies everything that we can be proud of in a Republican National Committeewoman . . . besides, we all love her accent."

Mrs. Knowles of Montana seconded me by saying, "She has poise, charm, and, as Mrs. Tanner says, her accent would be a nice innovation at our Convention. And I am sure she would televise beautifully."

When Mrs. Donald of Nebraska, speaking for the Middle West, stressed the efficient way in which I had fulfilled my office, and when Mrs. Bailey of Vermont, speaking for the Northeast, joined in the seconding speeches, Guy Gabrielson threw in the sponge with the words, "Now you men aren't going to let the women beat you on all this." This brought laughter and loud shouts of "No." Ralph Cake of Oregon was recognized. "On behalf of all the men I want to say that we second the nomination of Mrs. Howard."

Mrs. Moulton followed up. "Let's have all the ladies stand." (They rose.) Mr. Gerald of South Carolina said, "How about the men standing?" There was applause as they stood. Guy said, "It looks to me as if Mrs. Howard is going to have some support," and I knew I had won the first round.

Then two of the officers who had been most opposed to me joined in. Carroll Reece of Tennessee, former Chairman of the Republican National Committee spoke up, "Mr. Chairman, I am going to insist on the opportunity to second Katherine Howard's nomination" and added, "I just want to say that she is a typical Southern belle."

Then Werner Shroeder chimed in. "I join in the nomination of Mrs. Howard. As a matter of fact, I am the original Katherine Howard person on this Committee. . . . Four years ago I talked to her, Herb Brownell and Russell Sprague, and I said, 'All the men on the Committee will be in favor of any

121

woman to be Secretary as long as that woman is Katherine Howard'."

Gabrielson now put the motion. "You have heard the nomination of Katherine Howard as Temporary Secretary of the Republican National Convention and you have heard it seconded almost unanimously. All in favor say 'Aye'—contrary . . ." There was applause as he said, "Katherine Howard is elected Temporary Secretary of the Convention. We will now listen to the Temporary Secretary-elect of the Convention."

This was a surprise. But I rose to my feet, thanked them all and said, "I sent a note to Guy with the message that I thought I should leave the room when my name came up, but he had the doors locked and wouldn't let me out. . . . I have never known whether my voice was Southern or New England, but whatever it is, I hope to make it clear and ringing when we have the call to victory this fall. I pledge to you that I will do the job honestly, sincerely, fairly, and I thank you from the bottom of my heart."

The meeting continued, but for the moment I could relax. First they had tried to bypass me, then they planned on supplanting me, or holding the threat of nonelection over me. Now these had failed.

Doris Fleeson wrote in her syndicated article, June 29, 1952: "The Taftites, intoxicated with their easy success, decided to make a clean sweep of things and depose Mrs. Howard as National Committee Secretary. . . . Her colleagues were swift to prove that they were proud of her and knew when to rebel."

After the meeting was over, Guy Gabrielson moved quickly. "I have the use of Walter Hallanan's private plane to fly back to Washington," he said. "Why don't you come along with me, and in the morning we will take up the Texas Delegates." I accepted.

Was he moving in on me quickly while I was still mellow from victory? As we flew out over the Chicago Lake Front, he asked, "Katherine, what do you want to get when we are elected?"

I said, "I really don't want anything. I just want to see us win."

He replied, "I think I would like to be Secretary of Commerce."

We had a pleasant time. I had won, and I thought he accepted the fact.

Next morning Charlie, who had come on to join me, and I were walking from the Mayflower to Republican National Committee Headquarters. Guy overtook us in his car and offered to pick us up. Charlie said, "I hope you don't mind if I come along with Katherine."

"Oh, no," said Guy, "we'd like to have you."

When we reached the National Committee offices, Guy said, "Now, Katherine, let's settle this Texas Delegate question."

"Fine," I said. "Please ask Mr. McCaffree (Director of Research) to bring down from the library the *Laws of the State of Texas* and the *Proceedings of the Republican National Convention of 1928*." We had before us the *Rules of the Republican National Committee* adopted in 1948 under which we were functioning. They clearly stated that in case of contested delegates elected in Congressional District Conventions, the contest should be referred to the State Convention for decision, and if there should not be a State Convention before the National Convention, the State Committee would decide.

In the case of Delegates-at-Large, the contest would be referred to the National Committee meeting just before the National Convention, and an appeal could be taken from their decision to the Credentials Committee of the National Convention.

The question before us, therefore, was whether the delegates from Texas were district Delegates or Delegates-at-Large. If they were District Delegates, as Gabrielson had declared at our first meeting, May 27, in Washington, and as Taft's Campaign managers contended, the contest would be referred to the Texas Republican State Committee, controlled by Taft advocate Henry Zweifel, and the decision would be to throw out the Eisenhower delegates and send a full Taft slate to Chicago. This would have given Taft the delegates he needed to be nominated and would have deprived the Eisenhower forces of what became the winning issue, the moral issue.

Guy and I sat there in his office, arguing it back and forth. He maintained that thirty-two were District Delegates because they had been elected in caucuses held in corners at the Republican State Convention in Mineral Wells. It was very important to Guy to win this argument. He must have thought it was going to be easy—he was a trained and highly successful lawyer; I was just a woman. He didn't even call in his General Counsel, Ralph Gates; there were just he and I, with Charlie as a silent witness.

First I pointed out that, according to the rules, District Delegates were those elected in District conventions and in Texas no District conventions had been held.

"But," said Guy, "the Districts caucused at the State Convention; therefore, they are District Delegates." I stressed that this was contrary to the rules of the Republican National Committee.

It was fortunate that Mr. Donald had told me to read the *Proceedings of the Republican National Convention of 1928*. From Texas that year there was a slate of "District Delegates" and a slate of Delegates-at-Large, elected at the Republican State Convention. When Guy and I reviewed those proceedings, it was inescapable that the same question as to District Delegates and Delegates-at-Large had arisen in 1928.

Then Mrs. Mabel Walker Willebrandt, Delegate from California, Chairman of the Committee on Credentials, and at that time assistant Attorney General of the United States, had presented the report of the Committee, which was in favor of seating the slate elected as Delegates-at-Large.

She said, "All Delegates elected at a State Convention had to be ruled Delegates-at-Large, since the Rules provided that District Delegates are those elected in Congressional District Conventions." No District Conventions had been held in Texas in 1928 or now in 1952. The rules and laws had not changed.

The crucial political point was—Would the Texas question be settled in Texas, or would it come to the National Committee and Convention? The Taft forces wanted the former; the Eisenhower forces wanted the latter. As for me, it was my responsibility to make the decision in accordance with the Rules, regardless of what either side wanted, and I had to make my decision stick.

In that quiet office, Guy and I argued it out. Charlie sat by. Both Charlie and Gabrielson were Harvard Law School graduates and respected each other.

Finally Guy, the lawyer, had to agree with what was the last thing that Guy, the politician, had wanted. The facts were there before him. He leaned back in his chair, "All right, Katherine," he said, "You may tell Mr. Donald to certify the contested Texas Delegates as Delegates-at-Large. Tell him to prepare the documents and the letters for your signature." I remembered that at the first conference he had said, "Ralph Gates and Werner Shroeder will make the decisions, and *I'll* tell Mr. Donald to send out the notices." It was a considerable victory.

Charlie and I rose and said good-bye and I bounded up the stairs to tell Mr. Donald the news. He was clearly relieved. He wanted Taft to win, but he wanted honesty and justice to prevail. He set to work to prepare the documents and letters to go out over my signature.

But the fight wasn't over yet. Ralph Gates, the General Counsel, had to sign the certification. When I handed it to him for signature, he put it in his pocket and walked off, saying he had to go to a meeting. I didn't know when I would get it back. As he started for the door with that important document in his pocket, I said, "I'll come along with you, Ralph, and bring it back." With no comment he walked out. Following him, I just barely made it to the elevator before the door shut. It was the same with the taxicab. In I jumped. The last thing in the world he wanted was for me to come along. It was almost like cops and robbers. When he arrived at his destination, pursued by me, we walked into a room filled with lists of delegates and charts, the strategy room of the Taft inner circle. Reece, Hallanan, and Bud Kelland were there counting up sure delegates, the doubtful ones, and who and what could influence them. They couldn't have been more astonished when I walked in after Gates. This was the end of the road for him. He fished the document out of his pocket, signed it rapidly, and handed it to me without a word, and I departed. That night Charlie, with a hug and a kiss, told me he was proud I had been able to pull it off, and I told him how much his presence had meant.

Even after this, there were more and more delays. Guy

controlled the staff at National Committee Headquarters, and there were delaying tactics; it took an almost superhuman effort to get final clearance for the letters and notifications to be mailed and actually to get them into the mailbox.

Meanwhile, the nation, shocked by proceedings at Mineral Wells, were wondering about the Texas Delegates. They may have been baffled about the distinction between District Delegates or Delegates-at-Large, but they were keenly interested in who was making the decision and what it would be.

William Knighton, Jr., of the Washington Bureau of *The Baltimore Sun,* headlined an article:

> Washington, June 17. A slender, comely, middle-aged woman with dancing blue eyes, who is in politics because she "loves it" and because she feared a job in a museum would give her claustrophobia, is administering the rules of the Republican Party relating to the controversial subject of delegates' contests. . . .
>
> The procedure for dealing with contests over delegates and alternates is specified in Rule 4 of the 1948 National Convention.
>
> . . . Mrs. Howard stated that the decisions had been made solely on the basis of the rules as adopted by the National Convention held in Philadelphia, Pennsylvania, in 1948, and upon the election laws of the various states.

I appreciated the compliments of the press, but what really mattered to me was the acknowledgment by Gabrielson that the Texas Delegates were "at large," and the certification angrily signed by Gates.

Now I had to think about other things. What to wear? For the first time, a National Convention was to have national television coverage. I got in touch with television studios in New York. They advised no black and white—soft shades of blue—so I started getting my wardrobe together. Then there was the question of glasses. Could I wear contact lenses? The answer was no. Because I wore bifocals, I would have to appear in my glasses.

With all the decisions made, at last came the time that I could declare my support for Eisenhower. Two days before my announcement, Sinclair Weeks, in a dramatic statement, had declared his intention to vote for Eisenhower, and called on Taft to withdraw in favor of Eisenhower. This, naturally, was front page news across the country. My announcement was newsworthy, too, because of my position as National Secretary. I said, "After careful consideration of the qualities of the two capable men who are leading candidates for the Republican nomination for President, I have decided to support General Eisenhower. I believe he is the greatest leader to appear in public life in the present generation, and that he alone can unify the country in this time of world crisis. . . . I urge the men and women of America to support and work for the nomination and election of Eisenhower for President." The date was June 26.

Guy Gabrielson bitterly resented my endorsement of Eisenhower. He had all the rest of the National Committee officers working for Taft, but he didn't have me.

Max Rabb called me up from the Brown Palace in Denver to say that General Eisenhower was very much pleased and that my announcement had come at a time when morale was low at Headquarters.

So the first six months of 1952 went by. The year had started with the call to the Convention issued at the National Committee Meeting in January. There had been the effort to bypass me, or bulldoze me into acquiescence, my dogged resistance, and my ultimate success in forcing an honest decision in regard to the Texas delegates. This decision brought the Texas question to the National Convention and on it the nomination might depend. The issue could so easily have been buried in the murky depths of the Zweifel-dominated Texas Republican State Committee.

XI

"MASSACHUSETTS, THERE SHE STANDS"

When Charlie and I stepped into the lobby of the Conrad Hilton Hotel on Sunday, June 29, 1952, it was already a seething mass of people. The National Committee was arriving. Advance groups of Taft and Eisenhower men and women were setting up headquarters and placing signs saying, "Win With Ike" or "Taft." This was to be the first Convention which would be carried on nationwide television, and blessedly the first one to be air-conditioned.

The TV personnel had arrived, hoping to televise the National Committee proceedings, which would begin on Tuesday morning.

The press was deeply agitated over the shameful procedures at the Mineral Wells Convention. Would the Taft-controlled National Committee rubber stamp what the Taft-controlled State Convention had perpetrated at Mineral Wells? Would the Convention officials, all of whom, except me, were Taft-oriented, be able to steam-roller the Convention in such a way as to insure a Taft victory? The Taft forces were supremely confident. They estimated that they had 585 votes of 604 needed for nomination. The Eisenhower forces could count only 400. At the outset, it looked as if Taft had it sewed up.

Charlie and I went to our Suite #2319-A and #2320-A, bedroom and living room. Our children had rooms nearby and joined us for breakfast each morning in our suite. Guy Gabrielson's "Presidential" Suite was just down the hall. It was planned this way so that we would be near and could easily confer. We never did.

Before the curtain goes up on the National Committee mettings, it is necessary to review the issues raised by the Mineral Wells Convention. The Taft forces claimed that it was Democrats who invaded the caucuses in Texas, and it was Democrats who voted for Eisenhower in Texas, not real Republicans. The facts are these: Henry Zweifel, Republican National Committeeman from Texas and the leader of the Taft forces, invited "unhappy" and "restless" Democrats to join the Republican Party. He said, "Now it has long been apparent that many voters have become sick and tired of the New Deal and would like to join up with the Republican Party." On February 16, 1952, at the Texas Republican State Executive meeting, L. J. Benchenstein laid down the sole requirement for participation by Texas voters in Republican precinct conventions: Each voter must sign a declaration stating, "I am a Republican and desire to participate in Republican Party activities in the year 1952."

Precinct conventions were held May 3 in Texas and duly qualified Texas voters voted two to one for Eisenhower delegates to go to the County Convention. Every one of the voters signed the prescribed declaration. It should be noted that this declaration was originally drawn up and promulgated by Henry Zweifel.

These delegates, elected in Republican Precinct Conventions, attended County Conventions on May 6, where they elected delegates to the State Convention at Mineral Wells May 27, and the count showed Eisenhower delegates 722, Taft delegates 262.

At the Mineral Wells State Convention, 500 of the 722 Eisenhower delegates were thrown out by the Zweifel-dominated State Committee. In their places were seated 500 Taft delegates, chosen by minorities who had bolted conventions. (Not one single contested Eisenhower delegate was seated.)

Joe Ingraham, Chairman of the Harris County (Houston) Republican Committee and an original Taft supporter, stated in writing on June 10, 1952, "The campaign for Taft was a negative one. Their entire efforts were directed to getting people to agree to bolt their Precinct Conventions or their County Conventions and getting members of the State Executive Committee to agree to seat the Taft Delegates regardless of the merits of the case." He was shocked. He now shifted his allegiance to Eisenhower.

When the 500 Eisenhower delegates were thrown out by the Zweifel group at Mineral Wells, they held their own Convention and named what became known as the Jack Porter slate. Each Convention named its own slate of delegates to the National Convention.

It had not been my duty, as Secretary, to pass judgment on which slate was the right slate. It was my job to declare that a contest existed and that as the delegates had not been elected in District Conventions, they were Delegates-at-Large and as such, the contest would be settled by the National Committee and the national Convention. If I had not maintained my position, won out over opposition and made it stick, the winning issue would never have reached Chicago.

Paul T. David, Malcolm Moos and Ralph M. Goldberg, writing in "The National Story" say:

> Late in May came the Texas affair. What was thought to be another routine exercise by party professionals was challenged by an uprising that had the muzzle velocity of a Texas twister. . . . Probably no single factor in the entire preconvention struggle had a greater bearing on the outcome than the Texas controversy. . . . Eager for an issue that would halt or slow down the momentum of the Taft campaign, Eisenhower strategists made the most of the Texas incident.

Indeed, General Eisenhower himself said in Dallas on June 21, "Backers of Robert Taft were guilty of a betrayal of the whole Republican Party and its principles when they deliberately and ruthlessly disfranchised the majority of voters that voted for another candidate at the precinct and county conventions." Making campaign stops on his way to the Convention, he lashed into the Texas business and said at one stop: "I am not going to stand by and see a few arrogant politicians brazenly disregard the will of the people." And at another on July 4, "This is a struggle in which all of us should unite against a little group of willful men who want to capture control of the Republican Party for their own selfish purposes."

On Monday, June 30, Taft arrived in Chicago and took up residence in the Conrad Hilton Hotel. Of course there was a tremendous reception for him, and the hotel was jam-packed with people. Taft enthusiasm was running high.

My office, as Secretary of the Convention, was Room 808. There, Daniel Needham, Jr., my legal secretary, and Mrs. Marjorie Orpin, my personal secretary, set up our Headquarters. We learned that it was impossible to get anywhere on the regular elevators and soon took to riding the freight ones, or walking back stairs, when possible.

Meanwhile, Congressman John Heselton, Massachusetts member of the Credentials Committee, was feverishly working on the upcoming contests. He was Chief Counsel for the Eisenhower forces on the contested delegates from Florida, Georgia, Louisiana, Mississippi, and Texas. Volunteer lawyers from all over the country met on the eleventh floor where Sinclair Weeks had set up a suite of rooms for them to examine the claims of the contested delegates. Among them were his personal attorney, General Ralph Boyd, Charlie Howard, General Robert Cutler, William Rogers from New York, and Ben Guill, former Congressman from Texas.

On Tuesday, July 1, the National Committee meetings started. When we arrived at the North Ballroom, the television men, on their own initiative, were already setting up their cameras. Guy Gabrielson was furious about this. The Taft people did not want national publicity. The Eisenhower people wanted the nation to know the full story of what went on in Texas and Louisiana. This was the week before the Convention opened, and the elected delegates were still at home, but following every move in Chicago. The chief issue now was not "Can Taft Win?" or "Win With Ike," but "The Texas Steal." The first vote, and the first test, was on whether the meetings would be televised or not. It was indicative of all the National Committee votes to follow—fifty-nine against TV coverage, and forty-one for it. In almost all the votes to follow the ratio was sixty for the Taft side and forty for the Eisenhower side.

At this National Committee meeting, the contested delegate fights would be presented and passed upon by the National Committee. George Hansen, Chairman on Contests, had the floor. He said, "The purpose of this report is to review all the contests. . . . which were filed with Mrs. Charles P. Howard, Secretary of the Republican National Committee. . . . The various contests will be considered by the Republican National Committee, sitting as a Committee of the Whole in which the Contest Committee will be merged. In considering these contests they should be called alphabetically."

Hansen reviewed for the Committee the dates on which slates from the various states had been filed with the Secretary, and on what date the Secretary had notified the contesting groups that a contest existed, and the credentials of each one would be submitted to the Republican National Committee for decision.

In making these decisions as to whether or not contests existed, I had to ascertain whether

(1) The delegations were chosen in accordance with the "Call" from the National Committee, issued by the Secretary, from the meeting of the Republican National Committee held in San Francisco in January 1952.

(2) Whether the delegates were chosen in accordance with the rules of the Republican National Committee of 1948.

(3) Whether they were chosen in accordance with the State laws governing the selection of delegates and alternates.

I also studied the files from previous years, and talked with the lawyers representing the various factions.

George Hansen proceeded with his review of contests: Florida, and then Georgia, and Louisiana. There John Minor Wisdom had headed up an Eisenhower uprising against John Jackson, who was one of the old-fashioned Southern National Committeemen who thought they could "deliver" delegates as they had in the past. But Ike had stirred a new spirit in the South.

Hansen continued his report, coming now to the Texas delegates. He said, "The Zweifel group filed with the Secretary, Mrs. Howard, six Delegates-at-Large and thirty-two *District* delegates." I was amazed. This contest would not have been certified to the National Committee if they had been "District" Delegates. Hansen, National Committeeman from Utah, was pro-Taft. He seemed to be consciously or uncon-

133

sciously giving his sanction to the original Taft contention that they were *District* Delegates. Having concluded his review of the contests, Hansen announced that they could then go from the National Committee to the Credentials Committee and to the Convention. That is exactly what happened.

When the session was over, we streamed out of the room, whose doors had been locked. There was the television in place, just outside the door, and it caught the members of the National Committee as they emerged and some made statements. It was all one could do to force one's way through the crowds.

The day before, from Eisenhower Headquarters in Denver, a broadside had been sent to all convention delegates and alternates which contained copies of twenty letters and telegrams from Eisenhower voters in Texas supporting the Eisenhower charge that the voters were disfranchised by the Taft steamroller. Senator Carlson from Eisenhower Preconvention Headquarters at the Conrad Hilton, made public excerpts from Texas Republican leaders, business and professional men, and housewives, supporting their statements. Ben Guill, former Republican Member of Congress from Texas, said, "Among those of us refused seats at Mineral Wells were Jack Porter, Republican nominee for the U. S. Senate in 1948 (defeated by Lyndon Johnson); Alvin Lane, Republican nominee for Governor in 1948; Ralph Currie, Republican nominee for Governor in 1950; Joe Jackson, Republican nominee for Congress in 1951." These were some of those whom the Taft forces claimed were not "real Republicans," because they voted for Eisenhower in the Precinct and County Conventions!

One night, after midnight, my telephone rang. It was General Clay, asking me to come to a secret meeting in his room. Charlie was with me, and when we arrived, guards carefully scrutinized our credentials. Cabot Lodge was there, Eisenhower's Campaign Manager; and Sherman Adams, Floor Manager for the Eisenhower forces for the Convention; and Sinclair Weeks, leader for Eisenhower in the National Committee. General Clay asked me to tell him all about the Texas case, from the beginning right up to the present moment. Of course, it was all at my fingertips. I cited rules, laws, Supreme Court decisions, the Convention of 1928 and its bearing on the case, the whole astounding story. When I had finished, Cabot Lodge took from his pocket an Eisenhower pin, and pinned it on my dress. It was a gold bar from which hung three hearts, and on the hearts, I K E. I wore it constantly and cherished it. When our session was over and I had answered whatever questions the General had, we left as quietly and secretly as we had come.

The next day, July 2, we took up the Georgia case. This was an old, old story for the National Committee, which had debated it in 1944 and 1948. The Tucker group were the ones who had received the call to the convention which we issued in January; they had regularly held meetings. The Foster group, who opposed them, based their claim on a court decision, and the case would not be tried until after the election. But when the roll call vote came, it was again a clear Taft victory, being sixty-two to forty-one to seat the Foster group. *The Chicago Tribune,* pro-Taft all the way, came out with a two-inch headline:

17 GEORGIA VOTES FOR TAFT
TAFT EXPECTS NOMINATION ON FIRST BALLOT.

The article continued: "Ike forces falter in three states."

The three states they referred to were Pennsylvania, Michigan, and New York. Arthur Summerfield of Michigan and Governor Fine of Pennsylvania were flirting with both the Taft and Eisenhower forces, Governor Fine saying, "I don't intend to be on the losing side." At this point, Taft was the leader with all the contested votes going his way, and all the men who would be presiding at the Convention being pro-Taft. On Thursday a telegram arrived at the National Committee Meeting from former President Hoover suggesting that one person each from the Taft and Eisenhower camps meet with him to review the Texas situation and make a recommendation. Replying for the Eisenhower forces, Campaign Manager Lodge said, "It indicated a 'smoke-filled room' approach and that the Eisenhower group wanted the Convention to decide."

Next Gabrielson read a letter from Taft proposing a compromise of twenty-two delegates for Taft and sixteen for Eisenhower. Lodge, learning of the letter prior to the Committee meeting, said he regarded it as a sign of panic and firmly stated that "There will be no compromise." Sinclair

Weeks said, "The Taft compromise is 'studiously deceptive' since General Eisenhower is a three to one favorite in Texas and is entitled to all the delegates."

Taft was in Chicago, directing the strategy and feeling more confident each day, as with monotonous regularity, the National Committee voted to seat his delegates. Ike and Mamie had left the Brown Palace Hotel in Denver and were proceeding by train to Chicago, making whistle-stop speeches along the way, and a major address on nationwide TV at Ames, Iowa, on July 4. In this speech Ike denounced "the Texas Steal," and stressed the moral issue.

In the gold-curtained North Ballroom in a tense, court-room atmosphere, the Taft and Eisenhower factions presented their cases with expert lawyers and with witnesses. Each side had ninety minutes; then the meeting was thrown open to questions by National Committee members. Guy Gabrielson sternly wielded his gavel during the sharp exchanges between the Eisenhower and Taft proponents. Everyone knew that the decision on the Texas delegates could affect the choice of the Republican nominee.

In the question period Sinclair Weeks rose to move that the Jack Porter Eisenhower delegates be declared the rightful slate for Texas—thirty-eight delegates in all. At first Gabrielson refused to recognize Sinclair, simply ignored him; Weeks made it a point of personal privilege, citing his long service as a National Committeeman, and as Chairman of the Republican National Finance Committee. He was finally recognized and put his motion in a masterful way.

The vote, however, followed the usual pattern: for the Porter-Eisenhower slate, forty-three votes; for the Taft-Zweifel group, fifty-eight. Sinclair's motion was defeated, as he and Lodge expected it would be. The Taft forces had won every vote in the National Committee; now the contests were certified and passed on to the Credentials Committee, whose critical hearings would begin next week.

On Saturday, Ike and Mamie arrived. The hotel was bursting its seams. Chants of "We Want Ike," "Win With Ike" filled the air. Caucuses were held; everything was at a feverish pitch of excitement; Taft had won a lot; but at what a price. The country was aroused on "The Moral Issue."

On Monday morning, July 7, 1952, the curtain was about to go up on the Republican National Convention. This was the first convention where the action took place before the eyes of a watching nation. All over the country people sat glued to their television sets. There would be plenty to see and hear and be involved in. When I arrived at Convention Hall, the approaches were crowded, the sidewalks jammed, and delegates had difficulty getting through to their seats. However, it was strangely quiet on the platform. Guy Gabrielson, who was to preside that morning, was nowhere in sight. But Mr. Donald was there. I found the table on the platform, which was my station, and then Mr. Donald came over to me and said, "Mrs. Howard, the Convention is about to open, and before it does, you and Mr. Gabrielson have got to get together before you are up there, in front of television. You haven't seen each other; you haven't spoken to each other; and you haven't gone over your lines. You ought to get together before the Convention starts." In the beginning, a Convention is like a play. You have certain things that you have to do, lines that you have to say, and a script to follow.

"I'd be happy to see Mr. Gabrielson," I said. "Where is he?"

"He's in his office behind the platform."

This was the first time I knew that he had an office there. Evidently Guy was so angry with me that he was avoiding me. Following Mr. Donald's advice, I went to Guy's office and knocked on the door. No one answered. I tried the door and it was locked. I waited a few minutes and then I wrote a note and slipped it under the door. It said, "Guy, Mr. Donald says that we ought to get together to go over our lines before the Convention opens. I am here to see you at your convenience."

In a few minutes someone unlocked the door, and I went in. There were Gabrielson, Tom Coleman, Taft's floor manager; Ralph Gates, Carroll Reece, Senator Knowland, and Cabot Lodge, the only Eisenhower representative. It was the first and only time I had ever seen Lodge when he was not sartorially perfect. He had on a white suit, and it was rumpled. He needed a shave. He must have been up all night. It surprised me to see Senator Knowland there, and I realized that I was in the midst of an intense and heated argument. I

137

heard Guy say, "Why should we take the Texas fight before the Republican Convention? Why should we wash the Republican Party's dirty linen before the eyes of all the American people? Why don't we just sit back here and settle this thing, accept the compromise, settle it here and that will be that."

Cabot replied, "I will not be a party to any backroom deal where we sit and dispose of the Delegates who have been elected by the votes of the people." He said, "We will take it before the American people. We'll fight it out in public, before the eyes of all the people, and we will come to a fair decision."

I was proud of Cabot Lodge.

That ended the conference.

One hour late, at 12:30, Chairman Gabrielson banged his gavel and declared: "The twenty-fifth Convention of the Republican Party will now come to order." Then followed the Presentation of Colors, the Pledge of Allegiance, the National Anthem, the Invocation and the address of the Chairman of the Republican National Committee, Guy Gabrielson.

At the conclusion of his longish speech, he requested that the aisles be cleared and then he said:

"I want to present to this Convention at this time the Secretary of the National Committee, Mrs. Charles P. Howard. The Secretary of the National Committee will read the Call for the Convention."

I had left my table, and walked forward to the podium. I was sure and calm as I stood beside him and looked out over that vast amphitheatre crowded to the rafters and started to read the Call which, of course, was quickly terminated by a vote "that further reading be dispensed with."

All this time I was standing by Guy and we were perfectly friendly in playing our parts. I don't think we ever did have an opportunity to "go over our lines," for as we stood in front of the microphones, just prior to his announcing that I would read the temporary roll of delegates, he pointed to the page in front of me and said in a natural voice, not meant to be heard, "You begin here." I replied, "No, dear, it says to start *here*." We were both surprised that the microphone picked it up and it went out over the air waves. It was even more surprising that I inserted that "dear."

Bob Considine, in a syndicated article in the *New York Journal American*, described the opening session:

> The gentler Republican sex appeared for the first time on the platform immediately after Gabrielson finished his opening remarks. She was Mrs. Charles P. Howard, Secretary of the Republican National Committee, a fine, trim clubwoman tastily done in a blue job.
>
> Mrs. Howard attended to such parliamentary rigmarole as announcing the various Convention officials selected earlier by the Arrangements Committee of the National group.

Katherine Kennedy Brown of Ohio moved the election to these offices. The list included Walter Hallanan of West Virginia, an all-out-for-Taft man, as Temporary Chairman.

But now the great fight was to begin. Here, in the first session of the Convention, the lid blew off.

A "Fair Play" Amendment had been worked out at the Republican Governor's Conference in Houston on June 30, the same day that the National Committee in Chicago began its hearings on the contested delegates. As the governors met, they realized that the Taft-controlled National Committee would decide most of the contests in favor of Taft and that the machinery of the Convention would be in the hands of Taft-oriented men, Gabrielson and Hallanan, at the time that the seating of contested delegates would be decided. One of the first motions to come before the Convention would be to adopt the procedures which governed the Convention of 1948. Under these Rules, the delegates on the Temporary Roll, who were now pledged to Taft by the decisions of the National Committee, could vote on the contests. They could not vote on their own contest, but the Georgia Delegates and the Louisiana Delegates could vote to seat the Taft Texas Delegates; Louisiana and Texas Delegates could vote to seat the Georgia Taft Delegates; and the Texas and Georgia Delegates could vote to seat the Taft delegates from Louisiana. There were sixty-eight contested Delegates and all those for Taft would have been seated under this procedure.

At this point Gabrielson introduced Bricker of Ohio, who presented the "Taft" view of how this Convention should be run and asked for the adoption of the 1948 rules.

There was an eruption of cheers and howls. Cabot Lodge had previously advised Gabrielson that Governor Arthur Langlie of Washington wished to present an amendment, and Langlie now came to the platform and handed me the "Fair Play" Amendment which I was to read. Gabrielson recognized Governor Langlie, who moved that "No person on the temporary roll whose right to be a delegate or alternate is being contested shall be entitled to vote in the Convention or any Committee until, by vote of the Convention, the contest has been finally decided and such person has been permanently seated."

The Convention was in an uproar. Eisenhower delegates roared approval and waved banners. The aisles were crowded. Now General Counsel Ralph Gates appeared on the platform. Chairman Gabrielson told me that he was going to ask me to read the amendment. I stepped to the podium. Behind me Senator Lodge, his brother, Governor John Lodge of Connecticut, Governor Langlie, Governor Dan Thornton and Governor Driscoll were in a violent argument with Gabrielson and Gates.

The aisles were crowded. The Chairman shouted, "We are waiting for the aisles to be cleared to carry on the business of this Convention."

When order was restored, he said, "So that you may fully understand the motion, I am asking the Temporary Secretary to read to you the substitute resolution offered by Governor Langlie." I had been studying it while the wrangling had been going on behind me. Now in a moment of quiet Gabrielson said, "Mrs. Howard, will you read the resolution as amended." As I was reading it, out of the corner of my eye I could see the great hulk of Congressman Clarence Brown on the floor of the Convention making his way to the front steps which led up to the platform.

This is where and how the fatal Taft mistake was made. Tom Coleman, floor manager for Taft, had wanted to compromise on the Langlie Amendment. When Ike's people would not compromise, the Taft people had planned to ask for "a point of order." This would not have been subject to a roll call. It would have been accepted or rejected by the whole Convention by a voice vote. Many would not have understood what it was all about, and the Chairman might have rammed it through. By some failure of communication, Brown did not get the word. Up he came to the platform to present the Brown Amendment to Governor Langlie's substitute motion. The hubbub broke out again. Gabrielson banged and banged and directed the police and fire officers to clear the aisles. He said, "Every person having business before this body is going to be heard under proper circumstances and conditions if we have to stay here a week to get this straightened out. Mr. Clarence Brown of Ohio has the floor."

The essence of his amendment was to exempt seven Louisiana Delegates from the dispute, but his amendment would have to be subject to a roll call vote. This would reveal the relative Taft-Eisenhower strength at the very beginning of the Convention.

The Chairman said that one hour would be allotted to each side to present its case, and applause would be deducted from each side's time.

The Eisenhower people were prepared. They chose Governor Langlie, handsome Governor Lodge of Connecticut, Mrs. Murdock, National Committeewoman from Pennsylvania; and Congressman Christian Herter of Massachusetts, tall, good looking and persuasive. They looked fresh and honest and believable. The Taft people paraded the same old faces, Senator Bricker, Congressman Brown, and Judge Dawson of Kentucky, and Senator Brooks of Illinois.

Congressman Herter summed up for the Eisenhower-Langlie Amendment, and ended by making it crystal clear: "Vote NO on the Brown Amendment; vote YES on the Langlie Amendment." All over the floor standards were up with the same message, "Vote NO for the Brown Amendment; vote YES for the Langlie Amendment."

I called on an Assistant Secretary to read the roll call. Every delegate and guest in that vast amphitheatre knew this was a make-or-break vote.

During the reading I looked up at Charlie, sitting in a box to my left, and at my children, Margaret and Herbert. Then down to the front row just below the podium where sat Floor Manager for Eisenhower, Sherman Adams; and Sinclair

Weeks. The clerk's voice went on; the Eisenhower total was mounting. Taft's preconvention claims rose to plague him. Unbelievably, on the first roll call of the Convention, Eisenhower received 100 more votes than Taft! The Brown Amendment was defeated—548 YES Taft votes; 658 Eisenhower NO votes. Eisenhower had won the first round! It was a stunning blow to the Taft forces. One of their group then quickly moved that the Langlie Amendment be unanimously approved by the Convention. They couldn't risk another roll call defeat.

The Eisenhower people were jubilant. Cabot Lodge said, "This is it. We have defeated the Taft forces on the ground of their own choosing."

It was a tremendous victory—Eisenhower forces with 100 more votes than Taft!

The next round followed immediately, but first Chairman Gabrielson said, "Will the people who are parading at the back of the hall kindly refrain from doing so? We have committees to appoint this afternoon to get this Convention under way. You will have all the time you want for demonstrations later." Resolutions for the appointment of Committees on Credentials, Resolutions, Rules and Orders, Permanent Organization were made, sent to the Secretary's desk and read by me.

And so, at 5:15 P.M., we recessed until the evening session, called for 8:30. Back to the hotel with Charlie and the family for a good hot bath, a change of clothes, and dinner.

Guy Gabrielson called the evening session to order at 9:00 o'clock, instead of 8:30 as announced. After the usual Presentation of Colors, National Anthem, Pledge of Allegiance, Invocation, and Music, the Chairman of the Republican National Committee introduced the Temporary Chairman of the Convention, Walter Hallanan, and turned over to him the duties of the presiding official. This evening session was to have been a big plus for the Taft forces with Hallanan in the Chair and with General Douglas MacArthur as keynote speaker. The feeling was that he might stampede the Convention into votes either for himself or for Taft, but the intensity of the struggle was such that he made little impression.

Next morning when the Convention was resumed, the real action took place at the Credentials Committee Hearing on the Contested Delegates. Pro-Taft Ross Rizley was elected

Chairman and the hearings, which began at 10:00 A.M. Tuesday morning, started with the Georgia contest. They were held in the Congress Hotel and were televised. The Committee struggled many hours over Georgia and finally voted to sustain the National Committee vote to seat the Taft delegates. The vote was thirty to twenty-one. This must have been balm to Senator Taft.

Lodge immediately stated to the press, "The Georgia contest will now go to the floor of the Convention. I am confident that the delegates, when they hear the presentation of the contest, will vote to seat the legally elected delegates from Georgia. The Convention is a people's convention and we have always had complete confidence in the judgment of the delegates."

Tuesday afternoon the Credentials Committee resumed hearings, proceeding to the Louisiana contests, and sat until 2:30 A.M Wednesday morning. After a short break for some sleep, they reconvened at 10:00 A.M. Wednesday. The Convention itself was just ho-humming along, because no votes could be taken until the contests were settled and the Permanent Roll established.

And while the music and speeches went on in Convention Hall and the contests were being heard by the Credentials Committee, the Eisenhower strategists were working to corral the votes of Minnesota, California, Pennsylviania, Michigan, and Maryland. Governor Fine of Pennsylvania, Arthur Summerfield of Michigan, former Governor Stassen of Minnesota, Governor McKeldin of Maryland, and Governor Warren of California were the key figures who were being sought out in private meetings and conferences. The votes of these states were essential to victory.

On Wednesday, the Credentials Committee voted to seat the pro-Ike Louisiana delegates, and proceeded to the key Texas contest; here they voted twenty-seven to twenty-four to accept the compromise solution which had been offered by Taft—twenty-two Delegates for Taft, sixteen for Einsenhower—and accepted at the National Committee hearings. It was 4:00 P.M. on Wednesday when their sessions ended and, of course, the result was a setback to Einsenhower. The report of the Credentials Committee was not to be tamely accepted. The issue was going to be presented to all the Delegates and to the nationwide television audience. The Delegates themselves were going to decide.

The evening meeting on Wednesday was to have begun at 5:30 but was delayed until 7:30 to give the Credentials Committee more time for its report. Soon Congressman Joseph Martin, Republican Leader of the House of Representatives, was to take over as Permanent Chairman, and I was to become Permanent Secretary of this Convention. Joe Martin was respected for his fairness. He had been Permanent Chairman of the last three Republican Conventions and Speaker of the House in 1946–48. "He made thousands of rulings without so much as one ever being appealed or questioned," said Walter Hallanan in introducing him.

According to Convention protocol, this is the time when the Premanent Chairman makes his address. Joe Martin did. It was interminable! Everyone was restless, wanting to get on to the reports from the Credentials Committee. But Joe talked on and on, covering every imaginable topic and issue. Most of them were serious, but he received applause when he said, "Once upon a time Americans lived on hamburgers when they were broke. Now they go broke if they try living on hamburgers." But in the main, the delegates were not listening. Walter Hallanan banged his gavel and said, "Ladies and gentlemen, it is due Joe Martin at this Convention that we give him our attention. We will not proceed until there is quiet in the hall." At last Joe's address got up to the atomic age, and the fact that travel in space was on the verge of reality. He ended by saying, "It is up to us to carry the banner of Americanism to victory at the polls next November fourth," a typical ending to a political speech. Now we could get down to business.

The Chair, still Walter Hallanan, recognized Mr. Ross Rizley of Oklahoma to present the report of the Committee on Credentials. He said that the contests would be taken up alphabetically, beginning with Florida. Pro-Eisenhower State Senator Donald Eastvold of Washington had been chosen to present the Minority Report. "But as to Florida," he said, "although we would like to have supported these delegates who represented the candidate of our choice, we sincerely felt that on the merits of the case the delegation which did not represent the candidate of our choice was entitled to be seated." He seconded Ross Rizley's motion. This was a master stroke, clearly showing impartiality and fairness on the Eisenhower side. Speakers for the Minority Report, including Warren Burger of Minnesota, made the opening statement. Then came the opposition, those in favor of seating the pro-Taft Georgia Delegation, of whom the most persuasive speaker was Senator Everett Dirksen. His words at that Convention will never be forgotten by anyone there. Beginning with a low and melodious voice he said, "Come, let us reason together." I sat there listening to him and watching him. He had the audience in the palm of his hand. They went up and down with him, following where he led, hanging on every breath. I thought he could take them anywhere, and he did. With a dramatic rise in his voice, with his arm at full length, finger pointing at Dewey in the New York delegation, he declaimed, "We were with you in 1944; we followed you in 1948; and you led us down the path to *defeat!*" I thought this would be the end of Dirksen; it was in such bad taste.

The whole Convention exploded. Some were booing Dirksen. Some were booing Dewey. I could see the New York and Michigan delegations shouting and booing and pouring into the aisles. Dewey was born in Michigan, and his father and grandfather had been Republican leaders. Michigan considered him their native son, and to the New York delegation he was Governor Dewey and twice a Presidential candidate from their state. The tumult and tension were such that one Michigan delegate collapsed, had to have medical attention and be carried from the hall. The boos and shouts rose to a crescendo. It was a wild scene.

The gavel banged and banged and banged. Hallanan implored, "Ladies and gentlemen, be in order. The Sergeant-at-Arms will take care of the disorder in that part of the hall."

Resuming where he left off, Senator Dirksen made a plea for the delegates to accept the judgment of the Credentials Committee and the National Committee and to vote NO on the substitute motion.

Now it was Senator Eastvold's turn to rebut Senator Dirksen. He was thirty-two years old. He said, "I am a young man from the State of Washington, and I feel I am in pretty high company tonight." He continued, "The National Committee and the Credentials Committee are not on trial tonight, but their decisions are." He presented a masterful summary of the issues at stake in the contest over the Georgia delegates. It was factual. It was simply and earnestly presented. He gave clearly understandable reasons why the Tucker (Eisenhower) group should be seated.

Then Senator Saltonstall was recognized. "Mr. Chariman," he said, "I have been authorized by the majority of the Massachusetts delegation to request a roll call of the states on this question." To refute the charge that Eisenhower was nominated by the Eastern Establishment, seconds to the motion came from delegates from Oregon, Washington, and Missouri, as well as from Connecticut, New Hampshire, and New Jersey.

This was the second crucial roll call. The vote on the Minority Report to seat the Eisenhower Delegates from Georgia was 607 to 531, another terrible setback for Taft, another victory for Eisenhower. For Eastvold against Senator Dirksen, it was David over Goliath.

We were all aware of the turning tide. The seating of the Louisiana pro-Eisenhower delegation, and of the Perry Howard pro-Taft Delegates from Mississippi was accepted on a voice vote.

Now we came to the Texas contest. Chairman Ross Rizley of the Credentials Committee, speaking for the majority of that Committee, moved that the names of the delegates on the temporary roll (the Taft group) be placed on the Permanent Roll for the State of Texas.

Again Donald Eastvold was recognized to present the Minority Report, signed by twenty-four members of the Credentials Committee, representing all sections of the United States. He was followed by several others including John Minor Wisdom of Louisiana, who concluded by saying, "May I remind you that there are more eyes on this Convention than the eyes of Texas. They are the eyes of 160 million Americans who look to you to uphold the integrity and morality of the Republican Party."

The Taft opposition to the Minority Report was made by Mr. Vernon Romney of Utah and Mr. Eugene Worrell of Virginia.

Governor Dan Thornton summed up for the Eisenhower side, "We who have backed the Minority Report submit it to the jury of this Convention. We maintain that the members of this Convention are the bosses of this Convention, and not the

146

Committees that are meeting in smoke-filled rooms.

"You are the ones to decide the fate of this party. Good night, and God bless you!"

Senator Saltonstall rose to request a roll call vote.

But a great surprise was in store.

Mr. Palmer from Iowa, spokesman for the Taft forces, moved that the Convention unanimously support the substitute motion to accept the Minority Report in regard to the Texas delegation. It was accepted on a voice vote. Then Ross Rizley moved that the Majority Report as amended be accepted. Thirty-eight Texas Delegates of the Porter-Eisenhower faction took their seats. The long Texas contest was ended.

Many people were taken by surprise. What had led the Taft forces to concede on the Texas Delegates question without bringing it to a vote? Of course the reason was that they could not afford another roll call defeat. The tide was running against them, and even Hoover's statement which every delegate and alternate had found on his chair as he arrived earlier in the evening did not stay the tide. It said, "My conscience demands that I speak out. I favor Senator Taft, whom I have known since he was associated with me in World War I."

The Permanent Roll was adopted and at quarter of two on Thursday morning the Convention recessed until noon on Thursday. We had been in session since 7:30 Wednesday evening.

In Marblehead I belonged to a summer luncheon group. We called ourselves "The Tired Mothers." Next morning a telegram arrived from Mrs. Frank G. Allen. "We're getting tireder and tireder. Wish you would send the Convention home earlier."

As I sat on the platform, participated in the proceedings, received the motions, kept track of the roll calls, I was turning over in my mind whether or not I would read the roll call for the nomination of the President. No woman in either party ever had. I consulted Mr. Donald about it. He was doubtful. I talked with Charlie about it. Finally I said to Charlie and Mr. Donald, "If I feel I can do it, and do it well, then I shall. If I don't feel I can do justice to it and to the occasion, I won't." By now I was quite at home on the platform and in the procedures.

147

Thursday morning arrived.

Now at last Joe Martin was escorted to the platform to preside as Permanent Chairman. The Committee on Resolutions read the Party Platform and it was accepted without debate. There were more speeches—too many and too long. In a recess after luncheon I went to the Convention Hall and asked a young Republican from Harvard to station himself in the gallery to see how I came across. But, as I stepped to the podium, the microphones were way below my throat. Instinctively I reached out to adjust them. *"Don't touch those microphones!"* ordered George Murphy, a delegate from California in charge of radio and television. *"Don't touch those microphones;* they are adjusted to Joe Martin!" Joe was five feet, four inches tall, and I am five seven and one-half inches, and with high heels, even taller. Underneath the podium was a box to stand on. My next thought was to turn the box around so that Joe Martin could stand on that, and I could stand on the floor, But no, the box was screwed to the floor, and it covered all the standing space beneath the podium. It had to be all the way up or all the way down. What to do? I remembered Judy Weis, Republican National Committeewoman from New York, who always took her shoes off when she had a newspaper picture taken with Governor Dewey, to equalize their heights. I looked out over the audience; there was a wall all around the platfrom; no one could possibly see my feet so I decided that the simplest solution to the problem was to slip off my shoes, and all would be well! The young Republican heard me "loud and clear," and I decided to read the roll call for the nomination of the President.

Throughout the week I had worn various blue outfits; on the first day, a Prussian blue silk dress and jacket with ice-blue applications on the lapels, and matching maline wound around my navy blue hat. The press called it not ice-blue but "Ike-blue." Then I had a very pretty light blue two-piece silk outfit, and a tiny matching hat; and a red and white striped silk dress with navy blue taffeta coat. Tonight I was wearing a dusty pink two-piece outfit, with satin binding on the lapels and high-heeled beige slippers. I decided that I would slip them off, read the roll call, and no one would know. But I had reckoned without television; and I did not realize that TV cameras were also *behind* me. Guy Gabrielson had made no objection when I told him that I wished to read the roll call for the nomination. After all, it was my prerogative.

At last we were coming to what the Convention was all about. What a night! I got my cue when Joe Martin said, "We shall now proceed to the calling of the roll for the nominations for the President of the United States. The roll will be called by the Secretary of the Convention, Mrs. Howard." I left my desk and walked toward the podium and, as I stepped up to it, slipped off my shoes. No one saw it but Guy Gabrielson, sitting on the platform, and a backward glance showed his eyes almost popping out. Following Convention procedure, I called the roll of the states in alphabetical order. Alabama, the first state, said, "Alabama passes to the state of Illinois for the purpose of nominating Senator Taft. There was tremendous applause. On to California's Senator Knowland, who stated that California "reserved the right to nominate Governor Warren." Unconscious of the TV behind me, I continued the roll, coming to Governor Theodore McKeldin, who announced amid tremendous applause, that Maryland was prepared to nominate General Eisenhower. Governor Anderson of Minnesota placed the name of former Governor Harold Stassen in nomination, and Oklahoma followed suit with the name of General Douglas MacArthur. As I read the last name on the roll, the Virgin Islands, my job was done for that night. I slipped my feet into my shoes and walked back to my desk.

Joe Martin declared, "We are now ready to proceed with the duty of nominating a President of the United States." Senator Dirksen led off with a nominating speech for Taft, followed by Senator William Knowland's speech for Governor Warren of California, and then, Governor Theodore McKeldin's dramatic nomination of General Dwight Eisenhower. He was an orator, as was Dirksen. Mrs. Edward Howard, a woman delegate from Minnesota, placed in nomination Governor Harold Stassen for President, and last of all, General Douglas MacArthur was nominated. At the end of each speech, the cheering delegates, carrying banners and state standards, fell in behind the bands; balloons were released, and enthusiasm rose to a peak. For Taft and Eisenhower the demonstrations were spontaneous and contagious. For Warren, the band and organ played "California Here I come" and Nixon was prominent among those parading. It was 2:30 A.M. when General Douglas MacArthur's rather colorless demonstration was ended and the Convention adjourned. As Charlie and I drove home after the long evening session, I did not bother to mention my shoes.

The following morning at breakfast in our suite, Sam Potter, my son's friend and our guest at the Convention, said, "Mrs. Howard, you were observed last night with your shoes off." "What!" exclaimed my husband, who could not have been more horrified. Sam, as an editor of the *Harvard Crimson*, had learned the news from members of the press. I was chagrined. In those days ladies did not take their shoes off in public!

The Convention was due to open that morning at 10:00 A.M and, of course, I was there beforehand. But like most of the sessions of that Convention, it was an hour and a half late in beginning. To pass the time away, I went into the make-up studio. While there, a newspaper reporter, with elaborate casualness, strolled to the water cooler, filled a cup and turning to me said, "Why did you take your shoes off last night?" I told him the simple reason, but it was a day before the story swept the country.

Now we came to the climactic day of this Convention. No woman before had ever read the roll call for the nomination of the President. Again I stood by Joe Martin as he said, "The Secretary of the Convention will call the roll. Now the first ballot is for the nomination for President of the United States." Again I read, state by state, announcing how many votes each state had, and the Chairman of the delegation would rise and announce the number of votes for each candidate.

Alabama led off with 9 votes for Senator Taft, 5 votes for General Eisenhower; California gave all of its 70 votes to Governor Warren. Leverett Saltonstall of Massachusetts announced 34 votes for Eisenhower, 4 for Taft; and Governor Dewey followed with 4 votes for Taft and 92 votes for General Eisenhower. Ohio cast all 56 votes for Taft. Several states called for the polling of the entire delegation. At midpoint of the roll call Eisenhower was 256, Taft 228, Warren 71, Stassen 20, MacArthur 1.

But after the Pennsylvania vote, 2 for MacArthur, 15 for Taft and 53 for Eisenhower, it was clear that Eisenhower was approaching the 604 votes needed to win on the first ballot. Feeling in the hall was intense. It was now or never for several delegations to get on the winning side.

Over to the left of the hall there was agitation in the Minnesota delegation. The Minnesota standard was signalling for the Chairman's attention. Martin rapped the Convention to order and recognized Senator Thye, who said, "Minnesota wishes to change its votes to Eisenhower." "What is the vote from Minnesota?" asked Joe Martin. Senator Thye: "Twenty-eight votes for General Eisenhower." The Convention was electrified and there was wild applause. Eisenhower now had 614 votes, more than he needed for nomination. Taft had 500.

Standards all over the hall were signalling, each state wanting to be ahead of the others in getting on the bandwagon. I stood by Joe Martin watching the mounting enthusiasm, as the states vied for recognition. It was hard for Joe to determine the order, but he had had long experience and was unshakable. And he was respected. Texas followed next—Kansas, Pennsylvania "70 unanimous votes for General Eisenhower." With each announcement the pitch of excitement grew higher: New Jersey, unanimous also; and Delaware and Massachusetts, Virginia and Idaho and North Carolina and Nebraska.

Meanwhile the tally clerks were frantically tallying, as delegations changed their votes. Chairman Martin announced: "The tally clerks report the vote as follows: '4 for General MacArthur, 77 for Governor Warren, 280 for Taft, 845 for General Eisenhower'."

I looked up at Charlie; our eyes met in joyous exultation.

But on the platform, Bricker was downcast; Werner Shroeder was unashamedly weeping, and David Ingalls was trying to keep the tears back by blowing his nose vigorously.

As soon as the news was flashed on the television screen in General Eisenhower's suite in the Palmer House, he strode across the street to the Conrad Hilton Hotel to visit Taft. Eisenhower's instinct for doing the courteous and kindly act was infallible. Taft responded in like manner, pledging his support.

Back on the platform at the Convention Senator Bricker of Ohio, representing Senator Taft, moved that Eisenhower's nomination be made unanimous. Charlie and I joined in the jubilation and then, happily exhausted, went to lunch. As we sat there, Congressman Bender of Ohio, one of the most exuberant of the Taft supporters, came by. He was crestfallen. He stopped by our table and said to me, "Mrs. Howard, you have won, but in victory you should remember to walk humbly."

During this period several party leaders were meeting with Eisenhower to decide on the nominee for the Vice-Presidency. Charlie and I discussed various possibilities.

"Certainly Cabot Lodge deserves it," I said.

"But we couldn't have the two top candidates from the East Coast," Charlie replied. "It will have to be someone from the Middle West or West."

We speculated further. "Governor Warren of California would have been a good choice," said Charlie, "but since he never released his delegates to vote for Ike, he won't be considered." And we were surprised when thirty-nine-year-old Senator Richard Nixon was chosen.

At the afternoon session of the Convention Senator Knowland nominated Senator Nixon, and he was named by acclamation. He and Mrs. Nixon were escorted to the platform amid tremendous applause.

Now again I was at the podium, reading the many resolutions sent to the Secretary's desk.

At last General and Mrs. Eisenhower came to the crowded platform. I stepped aside to yield my place to Senator Henry Cabot Lodge, the victorious campaign manager. As General Eisenhower spoke, he was all that I had hoped and believed. My cup was running over.

Senator Nixon spoke next, and at 8:20 we adjourned *sine die*.

As I stood on the platform, hardly believing it was all over, and victoriously, Eddie Folliard of the *Washington Post* came up to me. "Mrs. Howard," he said, "I have been delegated by the press to ask you to continue as Secretary. You are the best Secretary the press ever dealt with." I was pleased. But I had given my word to "the girls." I could not go back on it.

As I packed up to leave Chicago after the tremendous Eisenhower victory, I felt that I could not go without saying good-bye to Guy Gabrielson. For several years, up to the months preceding the Convention, we had been good friends and associates. We had worked closely together. But in due course he had been for Taft; I, for Eisenhower. I did not approve of his pre-Convention activities, but now it was all over. It seemed only courteous to say good-bye.

So I walked down the hotel corridor that Saturday morning, from my suite #2319A and 2320 to Guy's Presidential suite. So recently it had been the center of activity for kingmakers, for press, for all those who wanted to be near or at the seat of power. I rang the bell. A wait. Then Guy himself answered the door. He looked distraught. Gone were the secretaries, the assistants, the receptionists, the press, the friends. He was all alone. The rooms were in disarray; the ashtrays were overflowing; the telephones—here, there, everywhere—were ringing. There was no one to answer. This was defeat. Alone. Deserted.

"Guy," I said, "I have come to say good-bye. In spite of our recent differences, I want to tell you that I enjoyed working with you on the National Committee and I could not leave Chicago without seeing you and telling you so."

"Katherine," he said, "I enjoyed working with you too, but I cannot understand how you, as Secretary, could endorse General Eisenhower."

We smiled, shook hands, and parted. As I turned to leave, the desolate scene of defeat was engraved on my mind.

By now the "shoeless" incident had hit the national press. Could the reporter who asked me why I did it have been from the *Buffalo Courier-Express*? In a featured story he wrote,

> Massachusetts—there she stood, with her shoes off, as she called the roll of states before the speechmaking began.
>
> Her voice was clear and resonant as she sang out the name of state after state. Her manner was cool, poised and assured; serene in the knowledge that the delegates out in front couldn't see her feet, there she stood, with her shoes off—and the people loved it.

The Boston Globe took it up with: "Massachusetts, There she stands—with her shoes off—out of deference to Chairman

Martin—a magnificent gesture, especially for a woman."

One newspaper queried, "Had the situation been reversed, would Joe Martin have done the same for Mrs. Howard?"

Balm to Charlie was the editorial in the *Boston Record*:

Memories Linger On. The Republican Convention has come and gone but the memories linger on, with not the least—to millions of televiewers—their delighted view of a woman official in her stockinged feet as she polled the states on the one ballot which nominated Eisenhower for President . . . The TV camera discovered her, and now Mrs. Howard's pinkies are as famous as Jimmy Durante's nobly-proportioned nose, and Eddie Cantor's pop-eyes.

Before that incident, this Georgia-born woman of stature had resisted all pressure from the 'G.O.P. Old Guard' and, alone, had placed the contests on disputed delegations before the Convention itself for decisions. No smoke-filled rooms for her.

XII

LADY CHIEF OF STAFF

It was good to be home again. I had had a job to do. It had been completed with success, and satisfaction. Now I could relax and enjoy Marblehead and my normal life. But my normal life was interrupted by telephone calls, and a deluge of letters from all over the country. One woman wrote, "I had just taken my shoes off when you did the same." Lawrence Winship, Editor of *The Boston Globe*, sent a photographer and reporter down to Marblehead, and insisted on taking a picture of me with my shoes off. *The Record American* did the same, but they wanted pictures of me stirring up something in my kitchen instead of in the political world. But now all that was behind me. I was no longer Secretary of the Republican National Committee. I sent Jennie and Steve off for a well-earned vacation, and took over the cooking. I thought the family would be pleased and I was surprised when Peggy murmured, "We love having you at home, but don't you think you ought to be *doing* something . . ?"

When Jennie and Steve returned we went to our "Farm" in Goshen for a rest and a change. On Sunday, Charlie went to the nearby town and brought back *The New York Times*. We sat on the porch reading the news. Featured was a story with a picture of party leaders conferring with Ike about campaign plans. There was no woman in the group. I read it several times, getting madder and madder. I fussed and fumed to Charlie. We had lunch. I was still steamed up. I decided to send a protest to Sinclair Weeks, who was at the conference.

Sitting on the porch with Charlie, I composed the telegram and read it for his approval. As we did not have a telephone at our house in the country, I drove down to the village store in Goshen, in my shirt and shorts. There I found a big black telephone, high up on the wall above the deep freeze. Sitting on some boxes, I got out my pocket book, dropped coins in the telephone, and signalled for Western Union. Off went my message to Sinclair Weeks.

After that I felt better.

We returned to Marblehead and toward the end of the week, a *Boston Herald* reporter called me from Denver. He had obtained a copy of my telegram, read it to me, and asked me to verify it. I wondered how it had come into his hands, but I acknowledged that it was a true copy of the message I had sent.

The following Sunday morning Charlie and I were luxuriating in a late morning in bed. Jennie and Steve had gone to Mass. The telephone started ringing. It rang and rang. At first I let it ring, but finally curiosity overcame me. I heard Sinclair Weeks's resonant voice. "Katherine," he said, "you better start packing your bag. You're wanted in Denver."

"Why?" I enquired. He replied, "You have been tentatively chosen as a woman staff member of the Eisenhower Campaign Train. Get in touch with Sherman Adams; he will arrange transportation."

"Sinny, that's exciting! I'll talk it over with Charlie."

By now Jennie and Steve were home, cooking breakfast. We dressed and picked up the newspaper. I was dismayed when I looked at the headline on the front page of *The Boston Herald*, and read:

> Eisenhower Alters His Course On Word Of Our Mrs. Howard. . . .
>
> Our own Katherine Howard, National Committeewoman from Massachusetts, has reminded the General that in the Republican Party the women do a tremendous amount of work in election campaigns.
>
> Either Ike didn't know that or no one bothered to tell him because it is now revealed that Mrs. Howard bluntly informed him a few days ago that

unless this seemingly "indifferent attitude" was reversed, there was a danger that women party leaders would not exert themselves in the next campaign.

The result, women party leaders from all parts of the country have been asked to come to Denver to discuss the role they will play in his forthcoming election battle. . . .

I was really upset. I had just meant for Sinclair to pass the word along, quietly. But a release from Eisenhower Headquarters continued with the account of my telegram to Sinclair Weeks in Denver, and then quoted me as saying—"All I wanted was recognition of the women because they played such an important part in the Eisenhower drive and in the policy committee up to this stage."

Charlie and I had had less than a month together, but now he said, "Darling, this is a once in a lifetime thing. It will only be for two and a half months. You should go." When I telephoned Sherman Adams, from what he said, I inferred this was not to be just a weekend affair. He asked me to come to Eisenhower Headquarters at the Brown Palace Hotel in Denver, and arranged a flight for me the next day.

In the midst of packing, I felt I ought to write a letter to Leverett Saltonstall,

Dear Leverett—

I suppose you saw the article in The Boston Herald yesterday which said I had "rebuked" General Eisenhower. I hope that of course you realize I never did any such thing, or even thought of it. Nothing would be more unlike me.

I offered a suggestion to Sinclair Weeks which Eisenhower Headquarters adopted. They put out a press release saying they were acting on my suggestion and holding a meeting of women tomorrow.

I am flying to Denver today and expect to attend the meeting.

Sincerely yours,

Katherine

Mrs. Charles P. Howard

As he had no secretary in North Haven, Maine, where he was vacationing, Leverett wrote in his own hand on the bottom of my letter to him:

> Katherine, how could I suspect you of "rebuking" anyone? It was good publicity with excellent results!
>
> See you about September 8th. Best to Charlie and yourself—
>
> L.S.

Charlie drove me to the afternoon plane for Chicago—and at the Denver airport it was a pleasant surprise to have a handsome gentleman step forward and say: "I am Bob Burroughs—Sherman Adams asked me to come out to meet you. He is tied up this evening, but wants to see you in the morning." Burroughs was Republican National Committeeman for New Hampshire, and assistant to Sherman Adams.

By my time it was late—a long day behind me—and a challenging one ahead. The Brown Palace was packed. I called Sherman Adams's office to confirm my appointment for the next morning and fell into bed.

Next morning about nine I met with him. After a brief conversation he asked me to become a member of the Staff. Then he strode with me into the room where the women leaders were meeting. There were my good friends Ivy Priest, Assistant Chairman of the Republican National Committee; Bertha Adkins, Executive Director of the Women's Division; Betty Farrington, President of the National Federation of Women's Republican Clubs, and Mary Lord, Co-Chairman of the Citizens for Eisenhower. With little ado he announced that I would be a member of General Eisenhower's Staff to coordinate the women's activities; then he turned on his heel and departed as abruptly as he had come. There was an awkward silence for by implication he put me over their heads. It was up to me. I said that I knew they each had their own important spheres of work and if they would keep me informed I would channel all information to our Candidate. In turn, I promised to keep them informed of developments on the train. I could tell by the expression on their faces and by the way Bertha nodded that harmony was restored.

Before lunch my picture was taken with Eisenhower. I was wearing a French blue shantung silk spectator sports dress, with the I K E pin in gold metal Cabot Lodge had given me at the Convention.

Things were moving fast that day. It was announced that Governor Adams of New Hampshire was directed to open a "policy and strategy" office in Washington, and that General Eisenhower was taking personal control of the Republican campaign strategy. Other members of this directorate were named as Mrs. Katherine Howard, former Senator Fred Seaton, and Ralph Cake.

W. H. Lawrence, writing in *The New York Times* said:

"The announcement means that in a very real sense Adams will be the supreme director of the Eisenhower victory drive, taking orders only from Eisenhower and passing along the nominee's views to the regular Republican organization."

What was surprising on that very busy Tuesday was the decision that *"The General's personal headquarters would be mobile in nature as members of his staff would accompany him throughout the country during his campaign trips."*

And indeed we did!

For my brief stay in Denver I was assigned an office in the Brown Palace Hotel and I went to work. I was in my office quite late when a nice looking young man said, "Mrs. Howard, when you are through will you please let me know, because I sleep in this office." It was Murray Kempton, of The *New York Post.* Being pressed for space, the room was my office for the day, and his bedroom. When I went to my own room at night, I left little notes on my desk in my office as reminders of things to do next day—such as, "Call up Sinclair Weeks," "Get in touch with Bertha Adkins." This went on for a couple of days, when Murray Kempton came to me and said: "Mrs. Howard, I have to tell you that I am a member of the hostile press. I wish you wouldn't leave notes around, because in my professional capacity I have to make use of what comes to hand, and I think I should warn you."

I was surprised. I had assumed that everyone at Eisenhower's Headquarters was for Eisenhower. I hadn't counted on the "hostile press." No more notes.

I had hardly unpacked my bags from Marblehead when Adams announced that on the next day, Wednesday, August

159

20, I would go on the first campaign flight to Boise, Idaho. We made an early morning start, up at 5:30—breakfast—leave for airport 7:00 A.M. On this trip the press was in the same plane with the General, sitting forward in the plane, Eisenhower and the staff sitting in the rear. During the morning I went across the aisle and sat beside Ike and said, "As a new member of your staff, I'd like to have you tell me what you'd like me to do."

He discussed with me his feelings as to the importance of women in the campaign and outlined some of the steps it might be advisable to take in the campaign, such as sending out to the key women his statements as to the importance of the role of women in political life. And this I did.

Finally he said, "Mrs. Howard, my door is always open to a member of the staff, and if you need any help, let me know."

The first stop on this flight was Boise. There Eisenhower spoke from the steps of the Capitol. This speech had been heralded as opening the campaign, and its theme was "the middle way." It expressed Eisenhower's philosophy in broad general terms, but as he spoke to the vast crowds assembled, his words echoed and it was difficult for him to speak with his words coming back and hitting him in the face. It was a good speech, but the reception of the press was disappointing. It didn't seem to catch on. A reception in the Governor's office followed. Many people shook Eisenhower's hand, and finally we sat with a small group in the Executive Chamber, before we returned to the plane by motorcade and soon after we took off, dinner was served. After dinner the lights were dimmed. Our next stop was Kansas City where we were due to arrive at midnight. Everyone was tired.

I sat by myself, and, as a storm gathered, I fell asleep. I didn't awaken until my neck was jerked and I came awake with a bang. We were in Kansas City. It was still raining. It was 1:30 A.M.—a long time since the day began at 5:30 A.M. On our landing in a thunderstorm, we bounced forty feet in the air.

We struggled to our feet. Eisenhower led the way from the plane. The national committeeman and the reception committee were waiting at the airport. We rode to the hotel, found our luggage in our rooms, and prepared to settle down for the night. Across the hall from me in the hotel was Dr.

Snyder, Eisenhower's personal physician, and next door was Homer Gruenther, a member of the Eisenhower staff and brother of General Alfred Gruenther. Dr. Snyder proposed that we all go downstairs for a bite to eat and a drink, so down we went, Dr. Snyder, Homer Gruenther, and I. The snack bar in the hotel was open and we sat on stools at the counter. When asked what I wanted I said, "A nice glass of hot milk would be just fine." Dr. Snyder ordered the same.

On the stool just beyond Homer Gruenther was Ed Darby of *Life* magazine. He was pretty much shaken up by the trip. "Did you see the fire in the rear wing?" he asked. "Well, I just figured that nothing could happen to the Presidential candidate, so I'd be safe, too."

So ended the first day of campaigning.

In Kansas City, the next morning the sessions began at 10:30. They were attended by Congressmen, National Committeemen and Committeewomen, State Vice-Chairmen and Chairmen, and Republican leaders from the Middle Western states. Sherman Adams was there, standing at the rear and observing. Eisenhower went from table to table greeting people. Then he was introduced. He spoke informally and after a few remarks, invited questions. His answers to questions on universal military training, on foreign policy, were to me so satisfying that I came away with the feeling that I'm sure the men must have experienced who served under him in the war—confidence, loyalty, and devotion. On subjects such as agriculture, with which he was not familiar, he said, "I'm not an expert on this." Other times, he said, "My advisors tell me." Later in the campaign he changed to statements in which he said, "I believe," "I recommend," with more authority.

At the conclusion of the morning meeting I invited the national committeewomen and other women state leaders to my room to tell about the activities in their states and of their reactions to Eisenhower's remarks. I got a list of all members present and later sent them notes of appreciation on Dwight D. Eisenhower stationery. I wrote a staff memorandum to Eisenhower reporting the women's favorable response to the meeting and his plan for universal military training and, true to my promise, sent copies to Ivy Priest, Betty Farrington, and Mary Lord.

In the afternoon we took off for the return flight to Den-

161

ver. On the plane Adams came and sat beside me saying that I must be pretty tired after the last two days and the storm. I think he was sounding me out. I said no, I slept through the storm, and I was fine. Jim Hagerty came and talked to Adams. He said the press were disturbed because with Eisenhower leaving the plane first and returning last, they couldn't get any pictures or proper press coverage. This was taken care of, and in all future flights the press traveled in a separate plane which left after ours and arrived before ours so that they could get pictures of Ike's arrival and departure.

On the return flight to Denver, Eisenhower settled down for a game of bridge, which was the only time I saw him play during the whole campaign. For all of us it was work, work, work but it was happy work.

Friday morning I was summoned to a staff meeting with Vandenburg, Seaton, Cake, Bob Burroughs, and Lou Kelly. We discussed the campaign train. Somebody had offered to pay the expense of painting the train red, white, and blue, broad bands running lengthwise. It rather appealed to me, but Kelly said it would be terrible, we didn't want to look like a circus train. The others agreed. Adams dismissed the meeting, but asked Seaton, Cake, and me to remain. He said we would constitute the small inner group. He then asked Seaton for the schedule of the train trip. Cake and I started taking notes as he read the schedule, but Seaton asked us not to, saying he didn't distrust us but it was easy to leave notes around where someone would pick them up.

I gave my notes to him and he tore them into shreds and put them in his shirt pocket. I noticed that Cake kept his. At 12:30 a full staff meeting was held. General Eisenhower thanked all the people who had worked and were working at the Denver Headquarters. He shook hands and said good-bye as he presented each one with a gold pin.

Adams informed us that we were setting up temporary headquarters in New York, to be closer to Washington. The difference in time made communication difficult, and we did not, of course, get the newspaper coverage in Denver that we would in the East.

The next day, Sunday, on the trip to New York, I met Mamie for the first time. She was wearing a black taffeta dress, with a small pattern of deep rose colored flowers, and with the full knife-pleated skirt she liked so much. As she came toward me she was holding the skirt away from her, smiling and saying, "The baby's diaper wasn't waterproof." Young Mrs. Eisenhower and the children had boarded the plane at Chicago, and Mamie had been holding one of them in her lap. She sat down beside me to chat while I was having lunch. I felt immediately her warmth and friendliness. Later on the children were going up and down the aisle of the plane. Ike, who was having a serious talk, suddenly reached out with his big warm smile and grabbed the dress of little Barbara Ann as she ran by. She stopped with a delighted giggle.

The next day we settled in to Eisenhower headquarters on the sixth floor of the Commodore Hotel. Adams's office was next to Eisenhower's, mine was two doors down from Adams', with Cake in between. In this, as in all other instances, the lady member of the Policy Committee was given top consideration.

We returned in time for Ike's speech to the American Legion. New York was gay and sunny, the streets full of Legionnaires. When we entered the hall there was a roar of welcome—and that was the high point. The speech, billed as "nonpolitical," was on a teleprompter which was supposed to unwind as Eisenhower talked, but when it stuck he had to continue without notes. He didn't have his manuscript and the aide who had it was nowhere visible. I gather that the aide heard about this in no uncertain terms, because it didn't happen again.

As I listened to the speech, I didn't get the lift I expected. I had the feeling it was good, but I wasn't excited, and I had expected to be. The press wasn't favorable. The Scripps-Howard papers came out with a front page editorial, "Ike's campaign running like a dry creek." This was the third failure and it was all very discouraging.

The Washington Headquarters was established the next day. Adams, Cake, Seaton, and I flew there to "take up residence." Reservations were made for us at the Hotel Statler, and offices were awaiting us at National Committee Headquarters in the Hotel Washington. After we boarded the plane, Adams requested that the staff members, Seaton, Cake, and Howard join him in a small compartment with just room for four. There Adams took out a proposed speech for Eisenhower to give later to the American Federation of Labor, and read it to us in his musical voice. We discussed it and decided it wasn't good enough, the ideas being old and stereotyped. Adams smiled and agreed. Before leaving New York Bertha Adkins had telephoned to say that she had arranged a press conference for me. I discussed it with Jim Hagerty, press director for Eisenhower, and said that I didn't think I knew enough about campaign issues at this time but he advised me to go ahead and do it. Now flying down on the plane, I told Sherman Adams about it, and he said, "Hagerty, like all the rest of us, has perfect confidence in you. Go ahead and have it."

At National Committee Headquarters, the new publicity woman was so nervous she could hardly breathe. We went down in the elevator together and she was in a state! The National Committe had expected that only the ladies of the press would turn up, but it happened that it was a dull day for news, and a large group was there including Pete Brandt of the *St Louis Post Dispatch*, Bert Andrews of the *New York Herald Tribune,* and others—about thirty in all. How could Hagerty and Adams turn me loose in the nation's capital, with no briefing whatsoever? I had only been a member of Eisenhower's staff for a few days.

The Publicity Director struggled through her introduction; I took my seat at the table and faced the reporters. One of them recorded that I was wearing a "patriotic outfit," a dark blue crepe redingote-style dress, with front panel and cuffs of red and white striped taffeta, and a small red straw beret.

The conference ranged over many subjects—Governor Stevenson's divorce, the role of women in the Eisenhower campaign, and why Eisenhower appealed to women voters. Certainly I had had no briefings on Adlai Stevenson's divorce, I was on my own on that and everything else. A reporter asked if I thought "Governor Stevenson's experience with marriage would have any part in the campaign?" I replied that I thought General Eisenhower's fine family would be an asset to him.

Trying to trip me up, the reporter asked—"Does that mean you think the reverse in Governor Stevenson's case?"

I replied, "I think people would like him better if he had a wife."

Another reporter took it up. "In other words, scandal on either side is bad?"

"Yes, certainly," I replied. "But I don't see that divorce is a scandal. Most of us have had a divorce in our families somewhere along the line."

That seemed to settle that. The *Christian Science Monitor* editorialized that I had dealt with that issue calmly and objectively, and so far as I know, the question was never raised again.

Then I was asked why women should be for Eisenhower. All of a sudden the words came tumbling out—with sincerity and conviction. I said:

> One of the biggest issues in this whole campaign, so far as women are concerned, is the security of the family. That means a lot of things.
>
> It means the Korean War. Is it being handled right? Whose bungling caused it? Will my son have to go to Korea? If he does, will he come back?
>
> It means high taxes. How much pay will father bring home?
>
> It means protecting the family from the inroads of Communism and fellow-travelers in the government.
>
> It means rooting out crime and corruption in government and crime and corruption condoned by government. [Some of Truman's associates had not been scrupulous.]
>
> What can I say to my son and daughter when, after being told how important integrity is, they say "Why should I worry? Look what the White House lets them get away with."

Turning to the subject of women in government I quoted General Eisenhower as saying that he was "very anxious to bring women in on every level of the campaign, and that he had told me to be sure to have the women invited to meet him on the Campaign Train all across the country. I quoted him as saying—"Show me an able woman, and I will see that she gets

165

a job" and also, "I think women have some of the top brains in the country," and I added. "Women see General Eisenhower as the symbol of peace, and of honesty in government."

When it was over, Bert Andrews lingered after the others, and walked upstairs with me. "Oh dear," I said to myself, "Now he is going to tell me what I did wrong." But not at all. He said, "Good for you! You named the six main issues in the campaign—"Crime, corruption, Communism, Korea, high taxes, and the high cost of living." Next day he developed them in a front page article in the *New York Herald Tribune*, giving me credit.

Late in the afternoon, I flew back to New York. My daughter Peggy met me at the plane. She had received her M.A. in literature at Columbia, and had a job as assistant to the fiction editor of *Cosmopolitan Magazine*. She and Dayton Ball were in love and engaged. He was also a Columbia graduate, and was just entering the field of advertising. He asked me, now that the Convention was over, if we could meet in Goshen over the weekend to discuss wedding plans. I agreed.

During the next day I met with Eisenhower and Republican women leaders from the Eastern states; then back to Washington to attend to my mail. (I was provided with a very efficient secretary who, all during the campaign, took care of my mail, answering it, or forwarding it to my office at the Commodore Hotel in New York.) Most of that day was spent in conference with Sherman Adams and members of the National Committee. Actually, Chairman Arthur Summerfield had expected to run the campaign, but now understood that Sherman Adams was Eisenhower's Chief of Staff, and the General's Headquarters was to be a mobile one, with him on train or plane.

All Saturday morning, I dictated to two secretaries, until 11:30, then went across the street to buy my fall wardrobe at Garfinkle's. I asked for a shopper to help me. She confided in me that her husband was a speech writer for Stevenson, then hastily corrected herself and said, "Of course Stevenson writes his own speeches, my husband helps on research." In an hour I bought two dresses, a suit, and a very pretty pale blue feathered hat, a dozen pairs of stockings, and six pairs of gloves,

Republican National Convention—Katherine G. Howard, Secretary of the Convention.

General Eisenhower and Katherine G. Howard as she becomes a member of
Eisenhower's Campaign Policy and Strategy Committee.

Above: First Campaign Flight—Eisenhower confers with Katherine G. Howard and Robert Burroughs. *Below:* Campaign—Katherine G. Howard, Sherman Adams, Jim Hagerty.

Campaign Train—Mrs. Eisenhower and Katherine G. Howard.

then back to my office to sign the letters—a 2:30 plane to New York, where I changed to the flight to Keene, New Hampshire. The plane circled down between the hills, close to a red barn, and onto the small landing strip. There in the twilight were Charlie and Peggy, Dayton and Herbert to meet me.

We drove to Goshen and up the hill to our white farmhouse. Jennie had the fire burning, lamps and candles lighted, a most welcome cocktail, and a delicious dinner. Oh, the joy and peace of the country—the delicious air—and family and love all around.

Sunday was a fine, clear, sunny day. We climbed up on a high hillside behind the house and settled down to talk. Dayton said he and Peggy wanted to get married, and could we set a date? "Either Columbus Day or November —."

Charlie spoke up and said—"I think really the eighth of November might be the best." I agreed. The twelfth of October would have been right in the middle of the campaign. Bless Charlie for speaking up!

Smiling at me, Peggy said: "Well, Mother, if Eisenhower loses, it will be fine for you to have something else to think about, and if he wins, nothing can stop you, you will be so happy." So it was agreed.

Charlie seemed happy in what I was doing. He was interviewed just after I joined Eisenhower's staff for the campaign. "It is," wrote the Reporter, "a complete reversal of procedure in the Howard household during the past 35 years of political life for Middlesex County Treasurer Charles P. Howard. During that period he took time out for two wars and campaigned for nearly half a dozen elective positions. His wife always remained at home to take care of their two children. . . . To General Eisenhower, 'a 'Howard' on his staff is nothing new. During World War II Colonel Charles Howard was on Eisenhower's staff for fifteen months."

Charlie was quoted as saying, "Katherine always helped me. She did everything from licking stamps to speaking at rallies. Now I know how she must have felt every time I went campaigning or joined the Army."

With the swing south, the campaign shifted into high gear—We left the Commodore Hotel at 8:30 September

2—and returned at midnight, September 3, having made a triumphant tour through the Deep South. Huge crowds, sunny skies, vast cheering audiences gave the Eisenhower campaign the lift it so badly needed.

We were met at the airport in Atlanta, rushed at breakneck speed to the center of the city; a ticker tape parade, with tape and confetti gleaming in the bright sunshine; while the crowds cheered. On the platform was the great golf star, popular hero, and good friend of Ike's, Bobby Jones. Governor Talmadge introduced Eisenhower, saying he could have been the Democratic candidate. The General's speech laid it on. He said he had never held to the theory that the Southern vote was a captive vote. There were rebel yells and cheers. I watched the faces, black and white, old and young, interested, responsive, enthusiastic.

On from Atlanta to Jacksonville and another huge crowd in the overpowering heat. We had to fight through the crowd back to the cars and then to the airport. Eisenhower had a hero's welcome.

Miami was our next stop. I had sent wires ahead to the women leaders to meet in my room on our arrival. But when we got there I was told it was too late for the meeting. I went thankfully to my room, stripped off my heat-sodden clothes and ran a bath. I was just stepping out of it when a knock came on my door. "Here we are, Mrs. Howard. We've come to the meeting." "Just a minute," I said, hastily drying myself. I slipped into my brassiere, panties, and dress and welcomed them. We sat around on the beds and talked problems and issues. They were interested in corruption, States rights, FEPC, and Korea. As before I sent a staff report to Eisenhower, the policy group, the women leaders, Ivy, Betty, and Mary Lord.

Rachel and Sherman Adams and I drove together to the rally that night, held out of doors, in the soft Southern air with a huge full moon in the sky. Again Eisenhower was in tune with the occasion and the audience, and received an ovation.

Next morning we left the hotel at seven o'clock. The Florida National Committeewoman was worried about how they could get anyone out to welcome Ike at nine o'clock on a weekday morning in Tampa, our next stop. She didn't need to worry. The streets were full and at the Athletic field where the meeting was held, the stands were filled to overflowing. In his remarks Ike referred to me as his "Lady Chief of Staff."

On to Birmingham. It was the first time a Presidential candidate of either party had visited the city. We drove through crowded streets to the capitol. Standing in a group waiting to enter I heard a voice behind me say, "Come on, Mrs. Howard." "Oh, no," I said, "Governor Adams goes ahead of me." Turning around I saw it was Ike who wanted me to enter with him. I took his arm and he escorted me in. There was a reception in the capitol. I was asked to stand at the head of the line, Adams next, then Eisenhower and Senator Carlson. We four shook hands with the invited guests. On the platform I sat between Mr. Comer who was to introduce Eisenhower and an older lady who leaned across me and said: "Biggest crowd I've ever seen in Birmingham." "Biggest man who's ever been in Birmingham," he replied. The police reported forty thousand in the crowd, listening; twenty-five thousand along the line of the motorcade.

After lunching on the plane, we arrived in Little Rock, Arkansas. We were proceeding into the city when all of a sudden, without schedule, or warning, the motorcade stopped. Eisenhower was told, when he reached the square, that the Armory was on the site of General Douglas MacArthur's birthplace. He ordered the motorcade stopped, strode into the building and paid his respects to the great General.

At Little Rock he gave a prepared speech on civil rights, it was well received, probably because of his immese popularity.

By five o'clock we were back on the plane heading for New York. We had left Miami at 7:00 A.M., on to Tampa, Birmingham, Little Rock, and back to New York at midnight. How did the General stand it? But he had been the one who insisted on the Southern trip, against the politicians' advice. It had paid off handsomely.

PHILADELPHIA

After a grueling expedition like that, it might have been expected that we would have a chance to catch our breath. But not at all. Early the following day we left by train for Philadelphia. The motorcade was a huge one and the town went wild. There were shouts and cheers all the way to Independence Hall. There Eisenhower spoke briefly of the great men who had glorified that building—Washington, Jefferson, John Hancock, Benjamin Franklin. Then on to a meeting of the Republican State Committee. At its conclusion Adams suggested that about six of us go downstairs in the hotel and get some lunch. Sitting beside me he turned and said: "What a fine thing Sinclair suggested your joining the staff." For a man of few words that was saying quite a lot.

The rally that night was unforgettable, every seat was filled and sixty thousand people listening outside to the loudspeakers! This was a major speech on foreign policy and it was received with cheers and enthusiasm. Eisenhower had clicked in Philadelphia as he had in the South. Ike was responding to his audiences and his speech writers were responding to his character. The campaign was off to a good start.

But in the next few days, critical reports came in from all over the country. He had not televised well. He looked old and tired, and his glasses were wrong. He should have dark-rimmed glasses. Eventually he did; he even consented to be made up before a television appearance—hating every bit of it.

CHICAGO

Morning came again very soon. The Warwick Hotel served breakfast in our rooms; bags were picked up at seven and at eight we were on our way to the airport. Mamie did not go with us; she did not like to fly.

When we arrived in Chicago no one met us and there were no cheering crowds on the way to the hotel. This was Taft country. Eisenhower was there to attend the Midwestern Regional Conference similar to the one in Kansas City, with leaders from Indiana, Michigan, and Illinois. The minute we entered the room we could feel the hostility. But Eisenhower handled himself well. As he spoke, faces relaxed, heads nodded in agreement, and there was applause. I had arranged for Eisenhower to meet with the women leaders at this conference. It took a bit of doing, but the women weren't much interested.

174

However, Mrs. Gaines, National President of the Association of Colored Women, had tea with me in my room, and had her picture taken with Eisenhower. It had wide circulation, particularly in the black press.

Eisenhower had a full day in Chicago. That evening, dining with the Cook County leaders and two thousand precinct workers, he disarmed them. "Most of you here," he said, "wanted another person, not me, to be the Republican candidate. You still feel loyal to him, and that loyalty is one of the finest things in life—and you should keep it. The man you are loyal to is one of the great political leaders in America and I expect to work shoulder to shoulder with him in the years ahead." This brought thunderous applause.

Eisenhower had won many hearts in enemy country.

THE PLOUGHING CONTEST

The ploughing contest at Kasson, Minnesota, near Rochester, was our next stop and it would bring together massive gatherings of farmers. Both Eisenhower and Stevenson were asked to speak, Ike in the morning, Stevenson in the afternoon. It was a clear, cool, sparkling day. There was a carnival atmosphere with tents, booths, thousands of people milling around.

We knew this was to be a major speech on farm policy. A great deal of work had gone into it: it was drafted by Congressman Clifford Hope of Kansas, Senior Republican on the House Agriculture Committee, and by Senator Carlson, and Eisenhower himself extensively revised it. Hundreds of thousands of votes were at stake.

Ivy Priest, who had joined our group for a short while, went with me to the Speaker's stand. There before us were one hundred thousand serious, thoughtful men and women, there to listen and make up their minds. They were evidently not there to applaud. They listened solemnly. A plane flew overhead carrying a large Stevenson banner, making it hard to hear. Very poor taste, I thought. The vast audience listened, but they did not clap. When Ike finished there was no ovation—just polite applause. Our staff was nonplussed. How could this happen? What did it mean? We asked people. They

175

came up with the most astonishing answers. They said, "Well, they were crowded in so tight they couldn't applaud." "They were listening so hard they forgot to clap." This didn't seem to make much sense to us—but it was all the satisfaction we got. It was disturbing, and disappointing.

Transportation back to the Snow farm was on a truck. Senator Thye, Governor Anderson, Eisenhower, a few others, and I were on it. Ike came and stood beside me at the front of the truck and waved to the cheering mobs of people who lined the side of the road. The TV camera was just ahead. Suddenly Ike said, "I'd like to see that piece of farm machinery over there." Quick as a flash, he had jumped off the truck before the security men knew what he was doing. He strode over to the machine and examined it with much interest. Then across the road to shake hands with an old lady who wanted to wish him well, and back to the truck.

The Snow farm, where Eisenhower was to have lunch, was a small, tidy, busy place. Several ladies were helping in the kitchen. The table was nicely set for six, with a flower centerpiece. I had supposed lunch would be provided for all the staff and I went upstairs to wash up. When I came down, Eisenhower, Adams, Mr. and Mrs. Snow and speech writer Kevin McCann's daughter were seated at the table saying grace. Ike told me later he had been looking for me to sit with him at luncheon but when I wasn't there, he took in Miss McCann. Ivy and I sat on the porch outside and had a few crumbs from the table.

The General was very much at home with the Snows. His own birthplace in Denison, Texas, was not unlike their house. There, and in Kansas, where he grew up, they spoke the same language as here in Minnesota.

After lunch we attended a large meeting of the Minnesota Republican State Committee. When Eisenhower entered, he strode across the hall rapidly and jumped up the three steps to the platform. His vigor and agility impressed me.

INDIANAPOLIS

I had thought nothing could touch the crowds and excitement of Philadelphia, but Indianapolis streets were crowded—jammed. Ticker tape floated down. The crowd cheered. Ike gave his famous response, arms high in the V sign, alert to the fingertips.

At Indianapolis in the evening there was a mammoth rally. The platform, occupied by Eisenhower, Senator Jenner, and the other local celebrities, was floodlighted. There had been some question as to whether Eisenhower would speak in Indiana. Senator Jenner was opposed to most of Eisenhower's policies. Ike was not pleased with his voting record. However, Jenner was up for reelection and there was doubt as to his being returned to the Senate. To save a Republican seat, Ike was persuaded by political advisors to go to Indianapolis and speak on the platform with Jenner. Just as photograhpers were about to flash their bulbs, and take the pictures for nationwide press and television distribution, Jenner flung his arm around the General, grinned, and waved with the other arm. Eisenhower was furious. His cheeks flushed, and his eyes flashed, but the picture was taken. It was one of the few times I saw Eisenhower really angry. He had a great sense of dignity and propriety. He did not relish this unsolicited personal contact with a man whose policies were repugnant to him.

The following morning we left Indianapolis to spend a few days in New York before beginning the next long campaign trip.

The major event of this period was Eisenhower's meeting with Taft. The Senator had been on vacation in Canada since the Convention. Eisenhower had wired him in mid-July suggesting that they meet. Now it was September, Taft was returning, and the meeting was arranged. When Taft arrived in New York he was met by Eisenhower's good friend and aide, Senator Carlson. Taft gave him a copy of a statement he had worked out to discuss with Ike, and then give to the press. He wanted Eisenhower to have a chance to study it before they met for their breakfast conference. Carlson looked at it and decided not to show it to the General, because he thought it might upset him and he would lose his sleep. Thus, Ike was not aware of what was in the statement until he and Taft met face to face. After breakfast, Taft gave the statement to the press, saying that Eisenhower had agreed to it. All across the country in Citizens for Eisenhower groups, in the press, and among the liberal wing of the Republican Party the cry went up that Eisenhower had "sold out" to Taft. This plagued us until the end of the campaign. In the last days before the election Eisenhower was on a nationwide television show to try to clear up "the surrender at Morningside Heights."

In his book, *Mandate for Change*, Eisenhower says,

> After the bitterness of the preconvention struggle, both of us agreed on the imperative necessity of healing the division within the Party and getting all of its members to pull together for victory.
>
> Accordingly, after we had talked for two hours at breakfast, Senator Taft went out to face reporters and camera men and read a prepared text which I had gone over. Taft said, "I have tried to state here the basic principles in domestic policy which, I think, General Eisenhower and I agree on 100 per cent. Eisenhower admitted that he did not share all my views on foreign policy but emphasized that 'our differences are differences of degree—principally the degree of spending—although there is a fair agreement as to what we want to do now in total spending."

They had buried the hatchet and four days later the Republican National Committee announced that Taft would speak in nineteen states between September 16 and election day. This placed him second only to Eisenhower and Nixon in campaigning for the Party.

XIII

THE CAMPAIGN TRAIN

In mid-September we were off for the long campaign trip which would take us to forty-four states, crossing and crisscrossing the country. At four o'clock Sunday afternoon, September 14, the long black limousines were assembled at the mezzanine ramp entrance of the Commodore Hotel. On the previous day we had been given our space assignments and baggage tags for the "Eisenhower Special."

The rear platform was the first part of the train we saw. So much history was to be made from it, so many speeches, so many cheering crowds gathered around it—even Mamie and Ike responding there to midnight cheers in their bathrobes when the crowd was so insistent they could not be disappointed. This was, of course, the *end* of the train, but it always seemed to me to be the front. From the platform Eisenhower would address audiences—here Mamie would appear beside him, here visiting dignitaries would introduce the candidate to their constituents. Inside one came first to the parlor where Eisenhower conferred with the top members of his staff. Here, too, he would receive the most important people who came to see him on the train. Later, when I accompanied Mamie to all rallies, and Ike was attended by Senator Carlson, or Bernard Shanley, or General Cutler, we were sometimes invited to join Ike and Mamie here for a drink after the rally was over and before bed. The four of us would sit and quietly talk over the events of the day, how the speech had gone, what was ahead. One evening when Bobby Cutler and I were there, Ike said, "On election night, I want you two, and a small group of friends to be with us to hear the results." We were there, but the group was not small! That quiet end to an always hectic day, was something special to be remembered.

This would be the only drink of the day for either the General or Mrs. Eisenhower. There was never a cocktail hour before dinner. Mamie was a very light drinker. She took no more than one drink of Canadian Club whiskey with water. Ike usually had a highball—bourbon on the rocks for me. For the rest of the day, Coca-Cola was Mamie's drink—served in the morning if you went to see her then, or in the afternoon, instead of tea.

The parlor opened into the dining room, which was Mamie's sitting room in the daytime. It was always filled with flowers and fruit. Mamie's secretary, Mary Jane McCaffree, would be busily recording the gifts which were showered on Mamie, and composing thank-you notes. Then there were the bedrooms for the General, for Mrs. Eisenhower, and for her mother, Mrs. Doud, and for Mamie's maid, Rose; then the kitchen. When I took groups of women officials in to meet Mamie, just as we left the dining room where Mamie received them, and the door swung to behind us, they would say, "Isn't she charming!"

Then in the swaying, lurching train, we would emerge onto the platform, passing a security man who stood guarding the entrance to Eisenhower's car. Then into the next car, where the top-ranking members of the staff had their compartments. First there was Tom Stepehen's room; then Senator Fred Seaton's room; next mine; then Rachel and Sherman Adams; and one occupied sometimes by Senator Carlson, sometimes by Senator Knowland; then General Cutler's compartment; and another one used for various visiting dignitaries. Many people rode the train—we were the permanent group with our own permanent compartments.

Following forward, one came to the V.I.P. lounge. Here Eisenhower would greet all the people who were invited to board the train. There would be the Governors and Senators of each state, the Party leaders, both men and women, and members of the Finance Committee and influential people. The more important leaders rode the train all day—lesser groups rode from one stop to the next. The car was arranged like a sitting room, with chairs along the walls. It was soon found to be too exhausting for Mamie to walk from her car, through ours, and back to meet people in the lounge car, so she, her secretary, and I worked out a system whereby I would meet the women, talk with them, introduce them to Eisenhower, and then take them into Mamie's dining-sitting room for a chat with her.

Mamie's training as an army wife stood her in good stead. She always got the name of the person introduced to her, picked up whatever information I might add to the introduction, and brought it into the conversation; chatted gaily and personally with each woman present. Once I took a group of about twelve in, and said of one whom I introduced, "She is a Gold Star Mother." Before we left, Mamie singled her out and drew her aside for a few minutes of quiet personal talk. The Eisenhower's only child, John, was in active combat in Korea at the time. After about ten minutes I would give the signal, and we would say good-bye and file out, each woman glowing from the warmth of Mamie's personality.

We would then go to my room, or to the V.I.P. lounge for a talk about issues, policies, and what was of particular concern to this region. This I would relay to the Policy and Strategy Committee and to the three top women leaders, Ivy Priest, Betty Farrington, and Mary Lord.

In one of the midwestern states the whole group of women officials was upset because they said Eisenhower was not a church member! How could he lead a moral crusade when he did not belong to a church? They reported that in their state the women wouldn't vote for him because of this. Quickly checking, I could tell them that Eisenhower's family and he had belonged to a Protestant sect called "The River Brethren." Then when he went to West Point he attended chapel there, and from then on, attended services at whatever army post he was stationed. He was a deeply religious man. It was good that the report was brought to me. I could resolve their doubts at once, and send them away happy.

When National Committeewomen were on the train, I would entertain them for lunch or dinner. One fortunate thing was that, from being Secretary of the National Committee, I had warm and friendly relations with the Party officials in each state, and I also knew personally many of the Senators and Congressmen who boarded the train.

Back of the lounge, going toward the engines, was the press car. One had to go through it to reach the dining car. It always fascinated me. There was the clack-clack of typewriters and teletype and mimeograph machines. One wondered what word was being sent out to the world from this nerve center. Each major reporter had his own typewriter and station, and they might be busily typing, as I walked through.

In the dining car you sat wherever there was an empty seat. It might be with Roscoe Drummond or Bert Andrews of the press—or Adams—or a secretary, or a visitor on the train. All the staff, press, everyone except the Eisenhowers had their meals there, so you had an infinite variety of table companions. I can remember at one touchy time in the campaign, as I entered the car Stewart Alsop motioned to me to come to sit at his table. I did so with pleasure—but I could see Fred Seaton looking agitated and worrying for fear I would say something indiscreet to the press.

The train extended back—or forward—toward the two engines which pulled the eighteen cars. It was a long trip for Anne Wheaton, Mamie's press secretary, from way back there to the Eisenhowers' car. She frequently used my room as an office when it was available.

When we rolled out of New York on that September afternoon, the original staff group which had gone to Boise, and on the Southern trip, was vastly augmented. Adams had consulted with me about additions and in particular about Bobby Cutler, since we both came from Boston. Of course, I had no objection to General Cutler. Joining us now for "the duration" of all train trips were Mamie and her mother, affectionately called by almost everyone "Miss Min." She was a great favoite of General Eisenhower's, and he frequently sought her advice. Quite often, when he would be speaking from the rear platform, she would be in her darkened room inside, watching the crowd. Afterwards she would say, "That point didn't go over so well. You'd better either refine that or try something else." Or she would say, "They liked that. That was a good point, it hit them." There was a wonderful rapport between them. Mrs. Doud was tall and slim, and had a fine sense of humor and a twinkle in her eye.

Her great companion was Dr. Howard Snyder (General

Snyder), who was Ike's personal physician. But he was much more than that. He soon took on the aches and pains of all the staff and press, for from time to time almost everyone had a cold or a stomach upset. He had an attache case filled with pills of many colors, and they seemed to be efficacious. When, several weeks later, I was sick for two days, he said, "Oh, Katherine, I shouldn't have let you get so tired. I should have given you one of my big brown pills sooner!"

Gabriel Hauge, Robert Cutler, Stanley High, and Kevin McCann were the chief speech writers—every candidate has to have speeches written for him, but Eisenhower could never take a speech written for him and deliver it verbatim. He had to make the text his own before he could or would deliver it, and his ideas had to be incorporated in the first draft. Frequently, he made changes up to the last minute, which his invaluable secretary, Ann Whitman, would type out just in time for release to the press. Also with us was Mary Jane McCaffree, Mrs. Eisenhower's secretary.

Others joining us were Eisenhower's longtime friend and associate, General Persons, and Homer Gruenther, brother of General Alfred Gruenther, and also a close friend of Ike and Mamie. They both had golden personalities and did much to add to the generally happy atmosphere of the train. But Ike and Mamie really set the tone.

When Eisenhower introduced Mamie at the conclusion of his rear-platform remarks, he would say, "And now folks, here's my Mamie!"

She told me that if he were miffed with her, he would say, "And now here is Mrs. Eisenhower," but when everything was fine, he would say, "And here's my Mamie." I never heard him say anything but "Folks, here's my Mamie."

In times of stress, when everybody was agitated, Gabriel Hauge was a tower of strength. He would come striding through the cars to Eisenhower's "parlor" from his compartment further back in the train, unruffled, objective, carrying on calmly, no matter what.

Fred Seaton's job was to schedule the campaign stops. He was always being importuned to add one more, the threat being that if you don't stop for us, we can't deliver the vote. He was usually adamant, for every day and evening was filled to the limit. He would answer, "The program won't expand."

In regard to his difficult job he said in an interview, "Ike has the background to appreciate the need for organization. When we hand him the day's chart he accepts it as the best that could be done, and goes to work.

"But," said Seaton, "this week when the General saw the schedule for the third day in a row calling for thirteen hours of steady speechmaking, greeting, and auto touring he said, 'You're slipping Fred, you almost left me enough free time to shave'."

Mamie, too, was importuned to add to her full schedule. She was unyielding. She said, "Katherine, if I push myself too far I will be sick. If I am sick I am no help to Ike." By resting and conserving her strength she was radiant when she appeared on the platform or in the motorcades, and full of warmth and personality when she met the hundreds of women who rode the train and met and talked with her.

Fred Seaton was deputy to Governor Sherman Adams. Sherman was definitely top man in every way. He had Eisenhower's complete confidence and he assumed strong and commanding leadership. A short, wiry man who had started life as a lumberjack, he was terse, laconic, self-contained. And yet, he could surprise you with a twinkle in his blue eyes, and a warm personal smile, an arm flung around you—when he addressed you as "Honey." He and Rachel loved each other dearly. His name for her was "Plum"—but that was his own term of endearment. We called her Rachel. Sherm's nickname was "The Rock," and Rachel called herself "The Pebble."

In the early days, when just a few of us were traveling with the General, and Sherm was new to the job, he would prepare each day a one-page summary, go forward to sit with Eisenhower and brief him on what was coming up, and on the political developments. At this time he said that although everything was correct and satisfactory he didn't seem to get through to Eisenhower on a personal basis. But later, a strong and close friendship developed. Eisenhower believed in the staff system to which he was accustomed in the Army. Adams was his Chief of Staff—and as time went on, and he proved his competence, he was given more and more duties and responsibilities. We all recognized his authority, both on the train, and later in the White House.

As I have said, my compartment was between Seaton's

and the Adams—"the buffer state." Each of us used our bedrooms for offices in the day—Adams sometimes had conferences with visiting political dignitaries in his room—a drawing room in the center of the car—at night. Rachel hung an orchid on the wall nearest my compartment with a sign, saying "Remember, Katherine Howard sleeps here." Mamie kept Rachel and me constantly supplied with orchids—so many were given to her and she could not possibly use them all.

Rachel was a rare woman. She, too, had Yankee charm. She had dignity and sweetness and tremendous reserve strength. But such a sense of fun and lack of stuffiness! She did not wish to be treated as the governor's wife. She was just along to be with Sherm, fit in anywhere, do whatever job needed to be done.

Quite often, Rachel did not go in the official motorcade to evening rallies. She preferred, sometimes, to go along with the press on the press bus, and sit with them to get pictures of the rally. This didn't always work out so well. Once, she got left behind, and had to get a sheriff's car to speed her to the next train stop. Another time, I was frantic. It was in New York State. The Eisenhowers were staying in Albany at the Executive Mansion. Sherm and Tom Stephens were in conference with Governor Dewey. I returned to an empty car. No Rachel. Where could she be? As the evening grew later and later, I becme more and more perturbed. What to do? After a long time, when I was considering desperate measures, Rachel appeared, calm and unruffled. The crowd had been so enormous that she could not find her way through it to get to either the motorcade or the press bus. She was stranded, but eventually had found someone to drive her back to the siding where the train was parked for the night.

In her hand she had a cake of very nice toilet soap, which the New York ladies had given to her. A bath was one of the most sought-after luxuries of the campaign—as recorded in the poem we sang frequently both during the campaign and after, to the tune of "I'm Looking Over a Four Leaf Clover." It said:

> How Ike's Train keeps rolling
> With so many men controlling
> Will always be a mystery.

Seaton makes the schedules
So does Summerfield!
Adams settles most scraps
But Cutler never yields
There's no use complaining
Kelly's still explaining
The jolts and bumps we have each day
With music played by Homer
Snyder's patients in a coma
We've all seen the U.SA.
We Really Mean It
We've all seen the U.S.A.

As Ike's train keeps moving
Its passengers are proving
A bath is needed every day
Sometimes it's three days
Other times it's four;
Mum's the word they're saying
When it's a week or more.
There's no use complaining
It needs no explaining
We're doing it for dear friend Ike
'Twould take atomic power
To scrape off the soot each night.
Without a Shower!
We've all seen the U.S.A.

As time went on other verses we added in which most of us figured. The song was always sung when "The Friendly Sons and Daughters of President Franklin D. Pierce" met on rare occasions when we had a night on the train without an evening whistle stop or rally. It was organized by Fred Seaton. I never knew why he chose the name. Perhaps because it was so improbable—Franklin Pierce having been a very unhappy Democratic President in the 1850's. We would meet again in Washington at the time of the Inaugural in 1953, and at the nominating Convention in San Francisco in 1956.

As I scanned the list of staff and press for the September 14–26 train trip, I was impressed with the star-spangled group of press correspondents aboard the train. There were Steward

Alsop and Bert Andrews, *New York Herald Tribune;* Jack Bell of the Associated Press; Frank Bourgholtzen, N.B.C.; Raymond (Pete) Brandt, *St. Louis Post Dispatch*; John Mason Brown, *Saturday Review*; Frank Cancellare, U. P. Photos; Marquis Childs, "Washington Calling"; George Dixon, King Features; Roscoe Drummond, *Christian Science Monitor*; Doris Fleeson, Bell Syndicate; Edward Folliard, *Washington Post*; Martin Hayden, *Detroit News*; Fletcher Knebel, Cowles Publications; Max Lerner, *New York Evening Post*; Charles Lucey, Scripps Howard; Ralph McGill, *Atlanta Constitution*; Crosby Noyes, *Washington Star*; Beverly Smith, *Saturday Evening Post*; Esther Waggoner Tufty, Michigan Papers; John O'Donnell, *New York Daily News*; James Reston, *New York Times*; James Shepley, *Time* Magazine; Duke Shoop, *Kansas City Star*; Don Wilson, *Life*. In all there were sixty-five including five from London papers, and a representative of the British Broadcasting Company. It was customary for a group of reporters to accompany Eisenhower for two weeks, and then, perhaps, at a Chicago stop, the group who had been with Stevenson would come to us, and the group from our train would go to Stevenson. I noticed that there was never a word said about anything connected with Stevenson or his activities when they joined us. There was complete confidentiality. On the train I was on easy terms with most of them. All told, as we started on our first full-scale swing, there were 163 people aboard the train.

September 15 was our kick-off and it was a grueling day. I was up and dressed, had had breakfast, and hoped that my room was made up when I greeted the first group of women who, at 7:40 A.M., boarded the train at Monroesville, Indiana. Mamie was dressed and ready to greet them too. The General's first speech that day was not from the rear platform, but in the Fort Wayne Station at 8:00 A.M. Off-the-train speeches always involved more effort and were more "formal" occasions. Between that stop and the next one at Warsaw, an hour later, I took the next group of women in to meet Mamie. At 9:00 A.M. at Warsaw, there was a rear-platform speech and a presentation of a corsage to Mrs. Eisenhower. She had begun her full participation in Ike's campaign.

On that crowded day, Eisenhower made five rear-platform speeches and eight off-train speeches. He had smiled and waved, and met people from 8:00 A.M. until 10:00 P.M., when we returned to the train. I wrote, in my diary, "Beautiful sunny day, then evening and dark—motorcade reached our train one hour late. No dinner. Had started the day at 7 A.M.—a killing day, but successful. After we boarded the train, about 10 P.M., Mary Lord and I had dinner in the dining car with Bert Andrews of the *Herald-Tribune*, to bed about midnight." I fell gratefully into my berth for the overnight trip to St. Paul.

It was on this trip that the very successful rear-platform speech routine was put into action. Like everything else in the campaign, no detail was overlooked. Everything was scheduled to the minute.

Although the schedule was exact—and the timing was perfect—each rear-platform appearance seemed spontaneous and different. This was because Eisenhower sensed the feeling of the people waiting there to hear him. The faces were different, the voters might be different—in Indiana, Virginia, Montana—but always there was curiosity, admiration, and affection. The train would slow down, and Homer Gruenther would start the music: "The Sunshine of Your Smile." There was an air of expectation in the train. What would this group be like? How would they respond? In each state Senator Carlson would escort the Governor and Senator, and ranking party officials to the rear platform. When the train wheels stopped turning Eisenhower would step onto the platform. No matter how tired or worried he might have been, his spirits would rise when he saw the upturned faces, eager to see him and listen to him. There would be families together, perhaps with a child on the father's shoulder, legs dangling down. There would be children, young, middle-aged and older people, joining together in shouting "We Like Ike." "We Like Ike and Mamie." Eisenhower would be introduced by the ranking official—Governor or Senator—and then he would make a five-or seven-minute speech. They were never read. He would know *where* he was, and had been briefed on what the local problems or points of pride were; he would refer to them, and then share his philosophy with his listeners, his spirits and his eloquence rising, as he could see and feel the response. After the introduction, the local candidates would withdraw to the parlor, so that Eisenhower was alone on the platform. As he concluded, he would say, "And now folks, here's my Mamie." A radiant Mamie would step onto the platform. There would be a tremendous roar of approval. The music would start again, and Ike and Mamie would wave. The people would wave back until the train pulled out of sight. There was an emotional quality, a personal give-and-take to these platform speeches which could never be duplicated in a vast hall or on a television screen. For these stops, the press would emerge from their quarters, listen, take pictures, get the crowd's reaction, then scramble aboard again.

Mamie was a tremendous help. As time went on, "The Sunshine of Your Smile" (Ike's) was alternated with Fred Waring's, "Mamie, What a Wonderful Word Is Mamie."

With all these short rear-platform speeches in the small towns, the press was becoming increasingly restive. Ike was using the inflation topic, illustrating his remarks with two pieces of board, one long—"You got *so* much before Truman became President; now you only get *so* much," Showing a much shorter piece of board. The same with eggs. Before Truman, a dollar would buy *so* many eggs; under his Democratic administration—only *so* many eggs. It was simple and understandable to the audiences gathered around the rear platform, but there was nothing for the press to write about. They longed for Stevenson's polished phrases—something to make headlines—and they soon had it.

Now we were leaving the smaller towns and cities for St. Paul. We arrived under cloudless skies, "the lucky Eisenhower weather." In the whole campaign we only felt rain once; that was a drizzle in Iowa, where they had been praying for rain. As most meetings were out of doors, the sunshine made all the difference.

St. Paul's Union Station was crowded when Eisenhower's special train pulled in from Northfield and thousands lined the curbs along the parade route through the St. Paul Loop. Confetti streamed down, gaily lit by the dazzling sun. In some places after the parade passed, it was three inches deep on the street. The General spoke from the Capitol steps to one of the largest and most enthusaistic crowds that city had ever seen. As always with him, their enthusiasm buoyed him up. He said, "This kind of meeting is to me an inspiration. From you I gather strength and determination to carry on the job I have laid out for myself." The press noted that for the first time he said, "*When* we win the election on November 4."

St. Paul and Minneapolis gave the biggest ovation to date. Bronzed and smiling, feeling more confident than at any time, arms high over his head in his victory sign, he waved good-bye and boarded a plane for New York, where he was to make his American Federation of Labor speech the next day. A few Aides went with him. For the rest of us it was a welcome night in a hotel—a bath—and no grinding railroad wheels going around beneath our beds.

Next morning, early, we were off again. Now we were in Iowa, where Ike had joined us. Twelve stops and speeches, including Iowa City, where six thousand people stood in a drizzle to hear him. They loved it when he said, "In Kansas we always thought of Iowans as rich, and if we ever lost five cents through a crack in the floor, all six boys would have been out looking for it."

What with the whistle stops and three slow-downs for waving, an off-the-train speech in Des Moines, people to be met and photographed with Ike, it was quite a day; 180 visitors came aboard. At the rally in Omaha that evening, he was enthusiastically applauded when he said, "The Federal Government has gotten into your house and you'd better watch it." "Farmers," he declared, "like all other citizens have had enough of what it humorously called the 'Fair Deal'. What we all want now and what we are going to get is an honest deal."

The next day, Friday, the Nixon affair broke.

THE NIXON ISSUE

"Nixon Issue Hits Ike Train Like Bombshell," reported Drew Pearson.

Aboard the Eisenhower Campaign Train: Ike Eisenhower had settled down to whistle-stopping with the verve and gusto of Harry Truman when the $16,000 Nixon bombshell hit him.

After a hesitant start during the first part of the trip, the General had really learned how to harangue the crowds and seemed to like the hustings.

Then suddenly came word that the candidate for Vice President had received $16,000 a year for expenses from a "millionaire's club" in California while serving in the Senate.

Ike looked pretty grim the next morning when he spoke at little mid-west towns along the way. Back in the rest of the train Eisenhower's advisors discussed the pros and cons of the gift.

Talking with Sherm Adams about it that day, I looked out the window at a whistle stop and saw Fred Seaton walking across a field with no apparent objective in sight. I said, "Where is Fred going?" Sherm replied, "He's going to telephone Nixon." Their schedules and the pressure of events made it extremely difficult.

At lunchtime as I went through the press car, Bert Andrews tackled me and asked me to come out on the platform between cars where we could talk "Would I make a statement?" Of course, I wouldn't make a statement. He was incensed and wanted me to condemn Nixon. Naturally I wouldn't. But the press now had something to write about. The air was electric in the press car and press lounge.

Meanwhile, Eisenhower had continued with rear-platform appearances in five different cities before going on to Kansas City, Missouri. Sitting with Sherman Adams at the Muehlbach Hotel, I realized that he was becoming more and more impatient and upset as no reply arrived.

"Why don't we hear from Nixon?" he exclaimed.

But before the evening speech, contact had been made and Eisenhower prefaced his already prepared remarks by a reassuring statement in which he quoted Senator Nixon as saying:

Because of continued misrepresentation concerning disbursement of a fund which was collected and expended for legitimate, political purposes, I have asked the trustee of this fund, Dana Smith of Pasadena, California, to make a full report to the public of this matter. . . . The facts will show that not one red cent was spent by me for my personal use. The facts will make it crystal clear that such a legitimate political fund originated in an earnest and unselfish desire on the part of the contributors to support my fight against communism and corruption in government."

Eisenhower added, "Knowing Dick Nixon as I do, I believe that when the facts are known to all of us, they will show that Dick Nixon would not compromise with what is right. Both he and I believe in a single standard of morality in public life."

But by now, the nation was in a furor. The papers were carrying articles about how the Vice-Presidential vacancy would be filled if Nixon should withdraw. Most agreed that in this case the Republican National Committee would fill the vacancy.

After the speech, our motorcade left for the Union Station and we spent the night on the train, parked on a siding. We left at 7:20 the next morning for St. Louis, where the National Federation of Women's Republican Clubs was meeting.

When we arrived, the station was jam-packed with people. The security guards had difficulty in clearing a path to the waiting motorcade. As his Lady Chief of Staff, I sat beside Ike in his car along with Ivy Priest and, as we drove through the St. Louis streets, between responding to cheers, he said to me, "Katherine, it's the hardest thing in the world in a campaign to get time to think, to make decisions. You're always having to see somebody, or say something. You don't have time to reflect."

Considering that a day could begin at 7:40 with guests boarding the train and continue with platform speeches, motorcades, speech after speech, and delegation after delegation to be greeted on the train, and ending the day at ten, eleven, or midnight, this was necessarily so.

And each event, to that particular town or group, was of enormous importance and to each person on the train the moment of meeting Eisenhower and Mamie was an event of a lifetime.

In St. Louis, at the Women's meeting, he had the longest ovation and the most colorful one of the western trip. Each member of the audience had been given a small American flag to wave as he came on the stage. Eisenhower gave his famous arms-over-head greeting, and, as the applause, cheer-

192

ing, and whistling continued, he brought his arms down to his side and stood grinning by the speaker's stand. The flagwaving and cheering continued.... After four minutes Ike pointed to his wristwatch to indicate he was losing radio time. Shortly thereafter, the crowd sat down and subsided. The longest applause for him came when he said, "I have commanded your sons in war. They and I hate war and all its evil works."

But the Nixon issue was not resolved. Next day the *St. Louise Post Dispatch* in a front-page story said, "Eisenhower Insists Nixon Explain Gifts Completely." Sub-headline: "If Report is Satisfactory, Senator Can Stay on Ticket. If Not, He Will Be Dropped."

It is known that Eisenhower feels, from the facts now available to him, that Nixon did no wrong in accepting the money. But the G.O.P. Presidential Nominee was expected to begin a searching inquiry into the matter, starting with a telephone call which was to have been made last night. Later, Eisenhower probably will meet Nixon face to face.

That Sunday, September 21, we laid over in St. Louis, and telephone contact was made by Nixon with the Eisenhower staff and with the Republican National Committee. Newspapers, radio, television, all concentrated on the Nixon affair. In the main, the theme was "Dump Nixon."

On Monday we were off again. We were coming into Taft territory and needing Republican votes from this region. Now all of those who boarded the train, who introduced Eisenhower from the rear platform or at off-platform speeches or large rallies, were those who had confidently expected that their man, Taft, would be the candidate. They were the leaders who had fought for years in the National Committee, or at the conventions of 1948 and 1952 to make him the Presidential nominee. The Eisenhower Program for Tuesday, September 23, Middletown, Ohio, to Cleveland, says:

At all train speeches the following will be on the rear platform:
Senator Robert A. Taft

Senator John W. Bricker
Charles P. Taft
Mrs. Katherine Kennedy Brown,
Republican National Committee

Katherine Kennedy Brown was a power in the Republican National Committee, a Vice-Chairman, and the head of the Women for Taft in the pre-Convention Campaign. We arrived in Cleveland at 6:15 with guests on the train including David Ingalls, Taft's cousin and pre-Convention campaign manager, Congresswoman Frances Bolton, Congressman Bender, and many others. All in all, one hundred people boarded the train, were introduced and greeted by Ike and Mamie.

Meanwhile, Nixon had decided to go on nationwide television to place his case before the American people. Eisenhower and Mamie, Adams and Arthur Summerfield and a few others decided to view it in a small room upstairs in Cleveland's Public Hall.

As National Committeewoman from Massachusetts, I was expected to appear with Katherine Kennedy Brown, Ohio Republican National Committeewoman at the large rally downstairs. With other political personalities we sat in the front row of the platform and watched Nixon on a large television screen.

When the broadcast was over, Representative George Bender leaped to his feet and asked if they wanted to keep Nixon on the ticket. The audience roared its approval and the band played "California Here I Come" amidst tremendous cheers. As far as that audience went, Nixon was "in."

Upstairs in the small room, when the broadcast was finished, Ike turned to Arthur Summerfield, Chairman of the Republican National Committee, who had allocated National Committee funds for the broadcast and said, "Well, Arthur, you certainly got your $75,000 worth!" But Eisenhower was not as enthusiastic as the audience in the hall. He still had the decision to make. Before coming down, he dictated a telegram to Nixon.

A grim-faced Eisenhower strode to the platform. He began by saying that he had intended to speak on inflation tonight (much research and careful writing had gone into this speech; it was to be a major policy statement), but wisely he

194

put it aside and talked about what was uppermost in everyone's mind—Would Nixon stay on the ticket?

He said that the Chairman of the Republican National Committee would want his judgment and that he, Ike, must be prepared to give it.

> I am going to say to the Chairman that my decision, or at least my conclusion, is based upon this: Do I myself believe that this man is the kind of man that America would like for its Vice-President?
>
> It is obvious that I have to have something more than one single presentation, necessarily limited to thirty minutes, the time allowed Senator Nixon. But so far as I can see—and I am sure that there is complete agreement here at this point—he made that presentation as full, as frank, as naked as he possibly could under the means and in the time allotted to him. I am going to ask Senator Nixon to come to see me.
>
> In this case, therefore, except for asking for such divine guidance as I may be granted, I shall make up my mind and that will be done as soon as I have had a chance again to meet Senator Nixon face to face and talk with him. And I want to tell you that I have been deeply impressed by his sincerity, by his frankness and by his courage. . . .

And so the Nixon issue still was not settled. Nixon was heartsick and baffled. He stated that he had no intention of resigning. At audiences when he appeared, his reception was enthusiastic.

In his speech over the air he paid a fine tribute to General Eisenhower. "Remember, folks, Eisenhower is a great man, believe me. He is a great man and a vote for Eisenhower is a vote for what is good for America."

So back to the train. As usual, I washed out a pair of white doeskin gloves in my washbowl so they would be fresh and dry to wear the next evening at a rally. And so to bed. . . .

The train pulled out of the Cleveland station at 3:00 A.M. We were mercifully asleep, knowing that we must be up and ready to greet people at Chillicothe at 7:45. The train was winding through West Virginia. At luncheon I was struck by the beauty of winding river, steep hillside, as the train curved on its way.

We arrived at Wheeling that evening for what was to be a momentous event. So far, all had proceeded according to schedule, but from here on, the events were dramatically different. Nixon was breaking his campaign schedule and flying to Wheeling for a rendezvous with the General in West Virginia. It was a cold, raw evening in late September and darkness arrived early. General and Mrs. Eisenhower drove to the airport to be on hand to greet Nixon. I went with the staff and the press. Standing in the dark and the cold, people kept saying, "This is a very historic occasion." Like so many other historic occasions, it was uncomfortable to those participating. The cold was penetrating. The wait was long.

Finally Nixon's plane swooped down from the sky. In a flash Eisenhower was out of his car and, as the steps of Nixon's plane were lowered, Eisenhower was up them and inside the Nixon plane.

After a few minutes' wait, they came down together, and it was evident that everything was all right. The General and Nixon drove the twenty miles from the airport to the rally together.

But then Eisenhower had another terrible worry—Mamie was not at the rally. I was in her motorcade, which somehow or other had become separated from the General's car. We drove for miles and miles along dark, curving roads, with no sign of towns or even road signs. We reached the rally one-half hour late and saw how disturbed Eisenhower was—this must never happen again!

Eisenhower spoke to the vast crowd—out of doors in the chilly evening air of a September night—and said: *"Nixon is completely vindicated."* He introduced Nixon, who spoke with emotion and—at the finish—with tears of relief and joy in his eyes. After days and nights of doubts and fears—the team of Ike and Dick was together again.

The Nixon "Checkers" speech was behind us. The terrible cloud that hung over the train through those long days and nights of meeting schedules, and people, making speeches, waving in motorcades, with a difficult decision to be made hanging over you—nagging at the back of the brain for attention all the time—the terrible cloud was dissipated by the decision and reconciliation at Wheeling, West Virginia. Now the team of Ike and Dick were working together again—each continuing their own grueling schedules.

Exhausted by the tension and high emotions of the events which led up to the reconciliation in Wheeling, we fell into our beds, with no appointments until 9:30 the next morning when we pulled into Cumberland, Maryland. There was an off-train speech, with introduction of Eisenhower by Governor McKeldin, who had made the nominating speech at the Convention in Chicago. Then on to Baltimore, another motorcade to the Lord Baltimore Hotel. A tremendous meeting in the Fifth Regiment Armory, Governor McKeldin again introducing the General. For our appearance in Baltimore there was a fifteen-page schedule outlining in detail times, places, people who would be participating—nothing overlooked.

Then back to the train heading for North Carolina. When I awoke in the morning, I looked out to see the familiar red clay soil and pine trees of my former home state.

The train backed into Charlotte, so that we would be headed in the right direction for Winston-Salem. Somehow word had gotten out that there would be a service stop for ice and water at Salisbury, and at 5:30 A.M. a crowd gathered around the Eisenhowers' car. The cries of "We want Ike. We want Ike and Mamie" were so insistent that the Eisenhowers slipped on bathrobes and dressing gowns and appeared on the rear platform to smile and wave—and to be photographed by just one sleepy photographer who had struggled out to see what was going on. There was consternation among the other photographers at this scoop of an unscheduled appearance. Jim Hagerty pleaded with the Eisenhowers to give them a break, and a few hours later, Ike and Mamie slipped on their bathrobes over their regular clothing. Mamie tied a pink ribbon around her hair with bow on top, and they smilingly obliged the other members of the press.

As we came into Charlotte, the September sun was brilliant. Even at 8:30 in the morning, the streets were lined with people, and the stadium was packed. All rallies in the South, where segregation then existed, were held out of doors, so all could come. And come they did. It was a happy, successful meeting.

197

As the train pulled out heading for Winston-Salem, General Eisenhower asked me to join him in his parlor to tell him what to say in his speech. Remarks had been prepared for him, but he preferred to have me tell him about the city in which I had grown up.

I told him about the Moravians in Salem and the leaders in tobacco and in textiles in Winston. I told him about Salem Academy and College where I had spent eight years before going on to Smith. I had been pressed by those heading up the drive for the restoration of the eighteenth-century buildings in Salem to ask the General to mention "Old Salem" in his remarks.

Eisenhower listened to me intently and asked some questions. He took no notes. But when he spoke, he covered all the points I had made. Not only that, he also paid me a very high compliment when he said,

> One reason I am particularly delighted to be in Winston-Salem is because of the location here of what I believe to be the oldest school and college for women in our country. Originally founded as Salem Female Academy, it has become both Academy and College.
>
> Now it happens that my principal advisor for women's affairs in this campaign is a graduate of that school. If she is a sample of what that school has been turning out since 1772, you have got one of the prize institutions in the United States here in your city.
>
> I need Mrs. Howard very badly because, as I see it, women have a special place in this campaign, not merely because of their numbers, although, of course, that is important. There are two million more of them in this country than men. So they are not to be slighted merely from this very practical angle. But their value is far greater than that.
>
> My associates and I are engaged in a crusade that is firmly based on *ideals*, on purposes that we think reflect the highest of moral standards. In such a crusade the concern of women for that kind of value is important to us. Women never forget that

the moral tone of the *home* is the basis of our civilization. As a consequence, they carry that kind of crusading spirit even into a campaign. I should say they instinctively carry it into a campaign; and we need exactly that at this moment.

General Eisenhower's compliment was completely unexpected. I blushed with pleasure. My father, who had worked so hard to bring me up, would have been pleased and proud. In addition, Ike *did* speak of Old Salem too.

There were three more rear-platform speeches that day in Roanoke, Lynchburg, and Petersburg, Virginia. Then on to Richmond for an outdoor meeting. A platform had been erected over the Capitol steps. As we emerged from the old and historic building onto the platform, the surrounding beauty made you catch your breath. There was a full moon in the sky bringing out the beauty of the Capitol and the dark glossy green of the surrounding boxwood and magnolias. Overhead, the Ike dirigible floated, pinpointed by floodlights. The air was soft—so were the voices, and the crowd was enormous. Ike's instinct about campaigning in the South had been correct. He knew and liked the Southern people. They liked and trusted him. You felt the charm and beauty of this Capitol of the Confederacy, and you were happy at the vast outpouring of people.

But at the end of the speech there was consternation. As too many people mounted the platform, it cracked and splintered under us. Ike stumbled, but was caught in his fall by Senator Knowland. Ike laughed it off. Mamie had just left the platform. Dismay turned to relief when it was found that Ike and Mamie were both all right. No one was injured and we returned to the train, going by the modest brick home of General Robert E. Lee. So back to New York by nine o'clock the next morning, September 27.

It had been a long and eventful trip. There had been the telegrams and letters pouring into the train recording the resentment of the Citizens for Eisenhower-Nixon over Ike's having to appear with Jenner, and there had been the worry over the farm speech at the ploughing contest in Kasson and the Nixon crisis.

We had visited twelve states, all but three of which Truman had carried in 1948. Ike had delivered seventy speeches, eight of them major ones. But in spite of worries and crises, one remembered the cheering crowds in Baltimore and St. Paul, the earnest faces gathered around the rear platforms in the farm states: Kansas City, Louisville, Winston-Salem, Richmond—what a variety of climates and people and problems, and always, even in the dawn, "We like Ike. We like Mamie. We want Ike and Mamie."

When I was in Winston-Salem I had felt in glorious health, but by the time I arrived in New York on Saturday, some virulent flue bug had hit me. It was no wonder. Confined to the train most of the time, everyone caught everyone else's bugs. This one laid me flat. I went home to Reading. Charlie, attended by Jennie and Steve, had left Marblehead to spend the fall there. The grapes and the apples were ripe; it was a good time to be there. Charlie met me at the airport and I went home to bed, with a temperature of 103°. On Tuesday, when Eisenhower and the staff flew to Columbia, South Carolina, I was unable to go. My southern cousins in Columbia wrote to me about the hero's welcome and how, from the capitol steps, Governor Byrnes introduced Ike, saying, "In this hour of peril I would rather have a professional soldier than a professional politician as President of the United States. . . . If we want to avoid a third World War, bring an end to the war in Korea and bring an end to corruption in Washington, we can best do it by electing as President of the United States General Eisenhower."

Governor Byrnes thus bolted the party which had made him Secretary of State and Associate Justice of the Supreme Court.

Next day the train rolled without me. I asked Rachel Adams to greet the women boarding the train, keep the guest book, and introduce the ladies to Mamie until I returned. Now Eisenhower was campaigning in Michigan, Illinois, and coming into Wisconsin. The problem of what to do about Senator Joseph McCarthy had to be faced. When the Senator had won a sweeping victory in the Wisconsin primary in September, Senator Taft had declared he was "delighted." In New York at the same time when questioned by newsmen as to whether he would support McCarthy for reelection in November, Eisenhower replied, "No comment." Democratic

Senator Sparkman commented on McCarthy's victory by saying, "This must make this one of General Eisenhower's darkest days. I wonder about his sad plight in the wake of his endorsement this week of Bill Jenner, who stood on the Senate floor and declared that General Marshall, Ike's benefactor, was a living lie. . . . Now General Eisenhower must come out with the same endorsement for Senator McCarthy, who also stood on the Senate floor to declare General Marshall a traitor, or words to that effect."

Certainly there were prolonged discussions in the staff about the Milwaukee speech. Early in the campaign Eisenhower had told the staff to make no plans for his appearance in Wisconsin, but in spite of that, it was included. In the daily demands on Eisenhower, with his meeting the strenuous schedule assigned him, he was not aware that Wisconsin was included until it was too late to make the change. When Ike found out that he was expected to appear with McCarthy, he was angry. His first impulse was to include in his speech a paragraph praising General Marshall, and it was inserted. His political advisors strongly objected: they said it would be a pointed affront to McCarthy. Governor Kohler asserted that it would defeat the whole state ticket. Eisenhower was almost alone in his determination and with genuine distress he agreed to delete his remarks. The press were aware of the deletion, and because of it Eisenhower was flayed by the press and by friends he admired and liked.

I returned to the campaign train in Milwaukee while the staff was listening to this speech and as I was still feeling weak and washed out, I hoped to take it easy the next day. But about 6:30 A.M. Bobby Cutler was rapping on my door saying, "Wake up, Katherine, Ike wants you to be Mamie at the next stop." It was Duluth, Michigan, an off-the-train speech in the cold, raw early morning. I stood beside the General while he spoke, and was given a huge bouquet of long-stemmed red roses for Mamie. The ribbon with which it was tied would be pressed out by Mamie's maid, Rose, rolled up, and kept for future use.

The only Sunday we spent on the train was the fifth of October. At breakfast, I was sitting with a man from the advertising agency of Batten, Barton, Durstine and Osborn. I said, "It would be nice if there could be a church service on the train." "Impossible," he said, "you couldn't have a religious atmosphere and people would think it was phoney."

But Sherman Adams and Bobby Cutler, both devout Episcopalians who always attended church with Rachel Adams, on every Sunday of the Campaign, had other ideas. After breakfast when I returned to our staff car, I learned that Governor Adams had arranged to have a minister board the train at Livingston, Montana. In the lounge car the Eisenhowers and members of the staff gathered. The Episcopal rector donned his vestments and conducted Morning Prayer. Everyone was reverent. Just a quiet Sunday morning service on the train in the beautiful Montana country, a refreshment to the spirit.

At the next stop, Whiteface, the minister left us. Looking out the windows as he departed, we saw western riders on handsome mounts there to greet the General. As the train pulled out, they galloped along beside us until the train gained speed and left them behind us.

I had never seen this part of the world. As I walked back through the train to lunch, I paused on a platform between cars where Sherman Adams was standing, drinking in the beauty of the scenery of the Continental Divide and taking deep breaths of the invigorating air. He was standing quietly and alone. I realized the strength he drew from the solitude and the mountain views.

At dusk we were in Missoula. This scene is indelibly impressed in my memory. The people crowded around the rear platform. I watched their faces as Eisenhower spoke. They stood as far as one could see, some women with babies in their arms, men with children on their shoulders. They were listening, looking, finding what they had been seeking. There was joy in their faces—that Ike was all and more than they had hoped—that Ike was really leading a crusade for the things that every American has a right to expect in its President. As the train pulled out and away, they were silhouetted against the sunset with hands held high, waving, waving till we were out of sight.

The following day we were in Portland, Oregon, where Mrs. Dorothy McCulloch Lee was Mayor. In the motorcade through the city, she and General Eisenhower rode together, and her presence prompted him to make a downright statement about women in public life:

> I want to speak for just a second about my honest belief, my deep convinction, that we should have more women in public life. It is not only that we have two million more of them than we do of men. I have a deeper reason, arising out of my conviction that our civilization, our form of government, has its roots firmly based in moral and spiritual values—indeed in a deeply felt religious faith; and I have the further belief that women as the homemakers of our nation are more concerned with the preservation and the strengthening of those values in our consciences all the time than do the men. . . .
>
> I feel that today we probably have the greatest group of Republican governors that we have ever had at any one time in all the history of the United States, and we have more than half of them. And I think that their caliber might even be enhanced if we could include an additional one or two of the women next time.

When Eisenhower made a remark like that, it wasn't just hot air. He meant it.

Olive Cornet, the Republican National Committeewoman, boarded the train at Portland for the overnight journey to Sacramento, California. She had learned that the train was to stop for water at Klamath Falls, her home town, at midnight, and immediately she started agitating for the Eisenhowers to make another platform appearance in their bathrobes. It was a lot to ask of a candidate working eighteen hours a day and reluctantly Ike and Mamie agreed to make a brief appearance, wave, and return to their quarters. But when Olive escorted them to the rear platform, the crowd was so large, the cheers so enthusaistic, the response so overwhelming that Ike and Mamie lingered on. People sang and cheered and as time passed, I became worried and went back for help. Everyone was in bed and asleep—Adams, Seaton, Stephens. Homer Gruenther was several cars back. Finally I found Senator

Knowland in my car and still up. "Bill," I said, "you've got to come and rescue Ike and Mamie and close this act so they can get some sleep." He passed the word to the engineer and at last got the train rolling with everyone waving good-bye.

Next morning Sacramento was hot, with brilliant sunshine and waving palm trees. Then to Oakland, Senator Knowland's city, and finally to San Francisco.

There at the St. Francis Hotel, a mistake had been made and Mamie was furious! Ike's suite was on one floor, and hers on the one below. She made her feelings known vehemently until she was moved to the same floor as the General.

In San Francisco, Eisenhower received a tumultuous welcome; one hundred thousand people turned out to cheer him. His speech, delivered to sixteen thousand people jammed into the Cow Palace, was one of the key addresses in Eisenhower's campaign. The General was tense; his son John was in active combat in Korea where the biggest Communist attack in more than a year had just been launched. The headline next day read: "Ike says, 'Reds seize Seoul Road Key; Truce Talk Trap'." Dispatches from Seoul indicated that thousands of Chinese were engaged in the drive, menacing positions guarding the Korean capital. Eisenhower quoted the Korean Ambassador as saying, "Give us your guns. Spare your sons." Eisenhower said the South Koreans should be manning most of the battle lines against the Communists and that American soldiers should be pulled out. He concluded with a four-point plan for peace, saying:

In this enterprise which I describe we are not trying to remake the world in the image of America. We are not trying to force any man to our way if it is not his. We are not trying to buy peace or bring peace with the sword.

But we are a people who are strong in faith and purpose and moral courage. And we have an appointment to keep with history. . . .

And that appointment is the most important that history has ever made, for it can bring peace on earth.

In San Francisco I suddenly felt that all my clothes were awfully tired. The things I had bought in Washington in August had had a lot of wear. I had also brought along some suits and dresses I already had. Except for my spanking white gloves every night, and the white orchid Mamie invariably gave me, I felt everything I had had seen its best days. I remarked on this to a young and capable Republican leader in San Francisco. Her response was immediate, "We'll be in Los Angeles tomorrow. I'll call Bullocks-Wilshire and I. Magnin and have them send some clothes to the hotel for you to choose from." The next day when I arrived, several dresses and hats were in my room. I bought a new daytime outfit, and a black taffeta two-piece suit and white hat, which was perfect night after night, on different platforms in different cities. With the white hat, white gloves, white orchid, I was ready for everything from that very evening to the final night of the campaign in Boston. At that time hats were always worn in the evening in public places.

We flew from San Francisco to Los Angeles. The drive to the city from the airport was twenty long miles. The sun was hot. All along the way there were cheering crowds. From his open car, hot sun beating down, Ike had to wave to the cheering crowds. He made it very clear that he was never going to do that again. He said it was worse than ten speeches. Then, when we reached the city, there was a motorcade to end all motorcades. Confetti streamed down; people roared and cheered. It was exhausting.

But by the time for his speech at night, he was revived. This time he spoke on civil rights.

He said he wanted to make equality of opportunity a living fact for every American, regardless of race, color, or creed. He said he would start by eliminating segregation in Washington, the nation's capital, and in every civil and military establishment of the Federal Government, which indeed he did.

After his address we returned to the V.I.P. Lounge on the train to entertain some of the Hollywood stars who had been on the program at the auditorium before Ike spoke and others who were personal friends. George Murphy took Ike and Mamie around to chat with Irene Dunne, a staunch supporter; Ethel Merman, John Wayne, June Allyson, Anne Baxter, Edgar Bergen, and others, but somehow the party lacked gaiety and spontaneity. Ike was still angry and upset over the interminable motorcade in the hot sun to which he had been subjected, and weary from the effects of it.

And the next day would be another day of people to be greeted, motorcades to be endured and speeches to be made.

Visiting reporters were always interested in where the power lay. Was the lady member of the staff just window dressing? Was she just a hostess?

Ruth Montgomery, syndicated columnist, came aboard the train and questioned me sharply as she visited me in my bedroom office. She was trying to find out if I were just "along for the ride" or if I really rated.

"Eisenhower," she wrote, "has given Mrs. Howard only one instruction: 'My door is always open to every member of my staff. Let me know what you need to insure that women are a big part of my campaign, because this is a moral crusade and women guard the morals of our country.'

"As the campaign train crosses each state, groups of women politicians get aboard and Mrs. Howard interviews them to glean their suggestions and reactions. She is Ike's sounding board with the women."

Robert Allen, in his syndicated column for September 23, 1952, put it in more military terms:

> *Ike's Staff:* In keeping with sound staff doctrine Eisenhower's campaign organization consists of three groups, or echelons, each separate, distinct, but all interrelated and working as a team with the usual amount of minor personal and other hitches.
>
> These three key groups are
>
> (1) The personal, advisory staff which is comparable to the G (top) sections of a general staff. This group of advisers is the heart of Eisenhower's campaign set-up; he leans on it most heavily in determining policies and plans.
>
> (2) A research unit headed by Gabriel Hauge which is comparable to the Special Staff sections of a general staff.
>
> (3) The Republican National Committee which is functioning in a manner comparable to that of the supply, finance and maintenance elements of an army. In Eisenhower's campaign the National

Committee is not a command organization. National Chairman Arthur Summerfield is not the campaign manager. He operates under the direction and constant scrutiny of the personal advisory group.

This all important unit consists basically of five men, all personally hand-picked by Eisenhower .... They are Governor Sherman Adams of New Hampshire, who acts in the role of a Chief-of-Staff; Senator Frank Carlson, Kansas; Senator Fred Seaton, Nebraska; Oregon National Committeeman Ralph Cake; and Mrs. Katherine Howard, Massachusetts National Committeewoman and former Secretary of the Republican National Committee.

The day after Los Angeles, we were off by air to cover three states, Arizona, New Mexico, and Utah. After such a long time on the train, it was a pleasant change to board a plane. Walter Swan, the member of the staff in charge of air transportation, was a Vice President of United Air Lines and we always had the best—the best plane and the most superlative food and service. The luncheon or dinner tray would arrive with a small gold-bordered menu card carrying the heading, "The Eisenhower Special Plane," and the date. A typical dinner would be shrimp cocktail, filet mignon, baked potato, green salad, a lemon meringue tart, and coffee. When we had lobster, paper bibs were provided. Nothing was overlooked for the comfort and pleasure of the General and his staff. Eisenhower was always the last to enter the plane and the first to leave. His seat was always the first one to the right in the rear half of the plane. The seat beside him was kept vacant so that he could confer with various staff members during the flight. Sometimes place cards were on the other seats in the rear section, if not, the upper echelon sat in the rear seats across from, or behind, Ike. The front section was for others on the trip. Ike's personal secretary, Ann Whitman was always along and available to take down a new draft of a speech, as he made revisions, sometimes up to the very last minute. Ann worked interminable hours, with complete devotion and dedication.

Another person always part of the entourage was the masseur, who gave the General and Sherman Adams a vigorous workout the very last thing at night—to release tension and help relaxation.

Another plus about air travel was that we spent the night in a hotel room, which meant a good hot bath, and a comfortable, unshaking bed to sleep in. When we arrived, our bags would be in our rooms, keys on the bureau, there would be flowers, and sometimes complimentary liquid refreshment. Our rooms were assigned more or less in accordance with train arrangements. When traveling by air, mine was usually next to Sherm and Rachel Adams. Mamie did not go on the flights, but when we had a night off the train, mine was near Mamie's.

On this trip, our first stop was Tucson.

In the almost blinding sunshine and overpowering heat, we saw another part of America of different tradition and history. But there was still the same appeal of the man, Eisenhower, and still the same respect for his character as well as his accomplishments. As Lew Douglas, former Ambassador to the Court of St. James, said in introducing him, *"There is no substitute for integrity!"* This was another case of a prominent Democrat endorsing Ike. In his remarks Eisenhower called for the election of Barry Goldwater, candidate for the United States Senate. At that moment, no one could have imagined that he would become the Republican Party nominee for President twelve years later.

Then on to Salt Lake City for a major speech in the Mormon Tabernacle. Everyone was a little nervous lest someone should not act with suitable propriety in this place of worship. We were all cautioned against smoking there, particularly the newspaper men. This was the home city of Ivy Baker Priest, Assistant Chairman of the Republican National Committee. She and I sat on the platform behind Eisenhower, and listened with rapt attention to the Mormon Choir whose glorious singing opened the ceremonies. We were impressed by the privilege of being received there. As I listened, my eyes roamed over the Tabernacle, with its predominantly brown color and heavy, dignified architecture. Eisenhower's speech was in keeping with the occasion. He spoke on "a better way" than the right or the left—*The Middle Way*. It was a reaffirmation of his basic political philosophy.

XIV

IKE'S BIRTHDAY

"*Rest*"—the word struck us with amazement as we were handed the schedule for the next trip. It read, "Denver Saturday and Sunday—Rest!" It was the only time in the whole campaign when that word appeared. For most of us it was a busy day nevertheless, but Ike did get some golf in. As Mamie avoided flying whenever possible, she and Mrs. Doud left on the Campaign Train for New Orleans, where we would fly on Monday to join them. Later Mamie chided me a little for not being with her, but no one had asked me to go.

En route to Denver, acting on a suggestion from General Persons, Sherman Adams called a staff meeting in the sky. General Persons, who had served on Eisenhower's staff at Supreme Headquarters in Europe and who was a close personal friend of Ike, told Sherm that it was a tradition at SHAPE for Ike's top staff to celebrate his birthday with a small staff party, and he thought Ike would appreciate the same sort of observance from his close personal political staff in this campaign.

As the General's plane flew between scheduled stops, Sherm summoned us. He, Jerry Persons, Walter Swan, Lew Kelley, Stanley High, and I gathered in the open space near the entrance to the plane, Sherm, Jerry and Walter and Lew Kelley seated in a circle on the floor. They insisted that I occupy a seat. "Katherine," announced Adams, "as the only lady member of the staff, will be chairman of the celebration." Then and there we made plans—*where* the party would be, *who* would be invited, *what* we would give him, and the *Cake*.

On the fourteenth day of October, Ike's birthday, we would be in Texas, where Eisenhower was born and where he first met Mamie. Thus it would be a very appropriate place for the party. A prime consideration was the press, a hundred of whom traveled with us by plane and train. It was decided that this would be a private party, not to be spoiled by picture taking and the crush of reporters trying to get stories or pictures. However, the press were part of our campaign set-up, and we decided to invite representatives for the first part of the party and then, after the presentation of their gifts, they would leave and it would be an Eisenhower staff party with no publicity.

We agreed to have our celebration in San Antonio and to give him a large sterling silver Paul Revere bowl. Stanley High would write the inscription. As for the cake, Walter Swann would arrange to have it baked at the Shamrock Hotel in Houston and flown to San Antonio.

On this weekend in Denver, Stanley High wrote the inscription for the bowl: "To General Eisenhower from those who have worked with him in his campaign and loved it. October 14, 1952."

It seemed only fitting that a Paul Revere bowl should come from Massachusetts, so I telephoned Shreve, Crump and Low in Boston. They agreed to give first priority to having the bowl engraved with the inscription, and Walter Swann arranged to have it picked up and flown to San Antonio. Making these plans, I started thinking about a poem, and in no time at all, there it was! I printed it myself on attractive paper, with a few sketches, and my birthday gift was ready.

But for me on that Sunday, there was also the matter of my *New York Herald-Tribune* Forum speech. At the conclusion of the Republican National Convention in Chicago, Mrs. Ogden Reid of the *New York Herald-Tribune* asked me if I would be the woman speaker for the Republican Party at the Forum to be held in New York in October. This was a great honor and I readily agreed. Mrs. Helen Hill Waller, who was Director of the Forum, wrote in September that I was appearing at the evening session where Eisenhower and Stevenson would speak, as well as Mrs. Dorothy Vredenburg, Secretary of the Democratic National Committee. Mrs. Waller suggested that Mrs. Vredenburg and I talk about campaign strategy and the role of television and asked for a first draft by October 10. So over the weekends and on the train I had been working on the speech, and my first draft reached her on time. Her telegram in reply was delivered to me at the Brown Palace Hotel in Denver, where we were "resting": "I have your script and request for comments. Believe it needs some word pictures like 'Bikes for Ike' (teenagers on bicycles promoting the campaign) or information about coffee parties to illustrate general points you make so well and, above all, to leave audience remembering definite examples of your ideas."

So that Sunday in Denver I stayed in my room, rewriting the speech, and, when it was finished, asked Gabriel Hauge, Ike's top speech man, to read it. He wrote, "Katherine, I think this has a splendid, intimate flavor. It's swell. Now, good luck on delivery. —Gabe."

In addition to my speech and plans for our private party for Ike's birthday and for the nationwide birthday celebrations which I had been asked to coordinate, I telephoned Bertha Adkins about the one hundred thousand birthday parties sponsored by the National Committee and to Betty Farrington about the four thousand Women's Republican Clubs which were also having parties. Then, having mailed my revised speech, I packed my bags for an early morning start. So ended my day of rest.

Monday was a day of travel such as you would not believe possible. Our instructions said that a buffet breakfast would be served from 5:00 to 5:45 A.M. in the Brown Palace Hotel dining room. This mean that at 5:00 A.M. you were up, dressed, bags packed and in the lobby ready to go. And you were all set for the day, which would end between eleven and twelve o'clock at night in New Orleans.

From Denver we flew north to Casper, Wyoming. There, on the platform at the airport, we could see our breath in the cold, crisp morning air. As the General spoke over a radio hook-up to twenty-five stations, his breath congealed. It was *cold*. Then on to Cheyenne, where the Governor was attended by his mounted guards dressed in Civil War uniforms and fringed deerskin jackets.

At half past one, Eisenhower spoke to another large

gathering in 80° weather at Oklahoma City. There, before his speech a woman member of the local committee presented him with a broom to symbolize that he would sweep the Capitol clean. Then off to the airport for the long flight to New Orleans. Mamie and Mrs. Doud had already arrived, and Ike joined them on the train after which we set forth in a motorcade. It was frightening. People swarmed into the streets to such an extent that they were pressed against the Eisenhower car and our cars which followed. In the soft Louisiana air, the picturesque city with the torch lights, the swarming crowds of friendly people gave Ike a heartwarming welcome but a little alarming all the same as they crowded so close.

The General spoke in Beauregard Square. At the conclusion we returned by motorcade to the Union Station, where we rejoined our train. There, on the rear platform, Eisenhower was given a giant birthday card, signed by a thousand people, and a huge cake. In his book, *Mandate for Change*, Ike says, "On October 13 as we were leaving New Orleans, friends brought a huge cake to the train. The anniversary of my birth was celebrated the following day. The cake was the largest example of the confectioner's art that I have ever seen, almost large enough to eat and have it too, but the entire company of campaigners feasted on it (one of them, I believe, accidentally sat on part of it) and the cake disappeared." Now at last this day was done . . . a speech in Casper, Wyoming, at 8:00 A.M., and ending with a major speech in New Orleans. How did Ike do it!

Next day was really Ike's birthday, and there was no let-up. At Houston he spoke, having left the train for campaigning by air, going on to Waco in the morning, Lubbock in the afternoon, and finally back to San Antonio. Meanwhile the staff, Mamie, and I proceeded by train. As soon as I arrived in San Antonio, I started checking about the birthday party. Had the cake arrived? "Not yet, but it will be here." Had the present arrived from Boston? "Oh yes!" Lew Kelley, staff member in charge of rail transportation, had had a parlor car brought in and set up, just across the tracks from the Campaign Train. The seats had been removed and just one small table left for General and Mrs. Eisenhower and Mrs. Doud, with plenty of room for guests.

But by the time of our party that evening, Eisenhower must have wished that he had nothing more to do than to have a quiet evening with Mamie and "Miss Min" and go to bed. Wherever he had flown from Houston to Lubbock and Waco and back to San Antonio, all through the day he was greeted with "Happy Birthday, Ike" and cakes and presents. When I called for the General and Mamie to escort them to the party, General Snyder, the General's genial personal physician, looked at me more sternly than I had ever seen him and said, "Katherine, the General has to rest for another half hour. Actually, it would be better if he didn't go at all."

My face fell as I thought of the special private car brought in, of the silver bowl which did arrive in time, of all the loving care which had gone into planning the party.

Half an hour later, to my great relief, General and Mrs. Eisenhower and Mrs. Doud appeared. We went across the short space which separated the two cars, and as we stepped through the doorway, there were shouts of "Happy Birthday, Ike, Happy Birthday." All our pent-up love and devotion went into those words, and Ike himself seemed refreshed.

As cocktails were passed, representatives of the press were invited in. For a week or so, at one period, Ike's rear platform talks had been concerned with inflation. Remembering these remarks about eggs and lumber, the reporters had brought Ike two beautifully wrapped presents which, when opened by General Eisenhower, proved to be a china egg and a length of lumber. There were shouts of surprise and laughter. Ike was delighted! We all roared approval. Then the press withdrew and our party went on. Ike cut the cake; we sang "Happy Birthday." I presented the Paul Revere Bowl and read my poem:

Listen my friends, with all your power,
And hear of the ride of Eisenhower.
Through September, October of '52
To win the election for all of you.

The feet are running—the people cheer
For Ike and Mamie at last are here!
Ike talked to crowds in the village street;
He talked at Tucson in the western heat.

Miami by moonlight, Missoula by dark
And wherever he went he struck a spark
In the hearts of men to arise and fight
For a better America and all that's right.

It was past midnight at Klamath Falls,
But the people are cheering—Ike hears their calls
Mamie and he on the platform appear,
Olive Cornet is there, and Katherine near.
Bill Knowland at last sends the crowd away
Before they keep Ike 'til the break of day

So through night and day rode Mamie and Ike.
The country has never seen the like
Of their smile and their charm and their message of hope
Which roused the millions and sent them to vote.

And we say with the poet who wrote in the past
"Through all our history to the last"
There was never a leader like Eisenhower,
Who came to us at the very hour
When the world and the nation most needed his power.

We'll remember forever the year '52
Happy Birthday, dear Ike
Happy Birthday to You."

Ike and Mamie beamed. The General was genuinely
happy. He responded with his warm and heartfelt thanks for
his sixty-second birthday party. We were a close-knit, affectionate group, bound together by love and admiration for Ike
and Mamie, and devotion to Mamie's mother, Mrs. Doud.

But the evening was not yet over. Ike's major speech was
at the historic Alamo. He was in a mellow mood as he was
presented to a cheering crowd by Democratic Governor Alan
Shivers, who called on modern Texans to stage a revolt for
independence in Presidential elections.

Next day Eisenhower and Adams and the majority of the
staff and all the press departed by plane to attend the Al
Smith Memorial Dinner in New York. En route Ike cam-

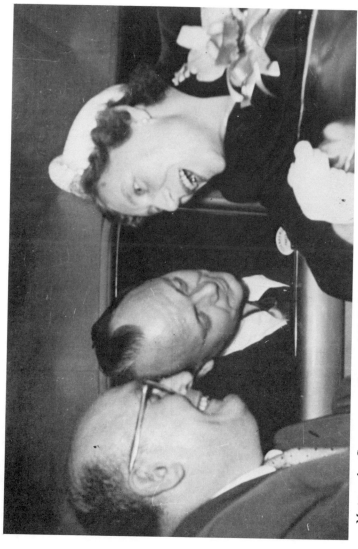

Motorcade—Congressman Leonard Hall, Senator Seaton, Katherine G. Howard. This photo was used as a placecard at the farewell lunch to Katherine G. Howard at the White House.

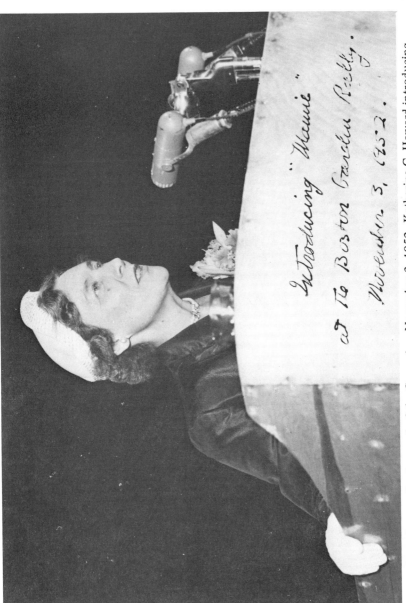

Introducing "Mamie"
at the Boston Garden Rally.
November 3, 1952.

Rally at Boston Garden, end of the Campaign, November 3, 1952—Katherine G. Howard introducing Mrs. Eisenhower.

Howard family in President Eisenhower's office at the White House as Katherine G. Howard is sworn in as Assistant Administrator, FCDA.

Katherine G. Howard takes oath of office in President's office as she is sworn in as Deputy Administrator of Federal Civil Defense.

paigned in Tennessee, West Virginia, and Pennsylvania, arriving in New York for the dinner on Thursday, October 16.

Sherm had said to me, "We'd like to have you come to the dinner as part of Eisenhower's Policy Committee. Mamie would like you to stay on the train with her. You decide."

It would have been interesting to go to the dinner and I would have liked it, but I was glad Mamie wanted me to stay with her, and so I did.

After the hustle and bustle of the campaign, with the train full to overflowing with staff, press, photographers—very important people getting off and getting on—it was lonesome on the train.

There were Mamie and Mrs. Doud and Mary Jane McCaffree, Anne Wheaton, Mamie's Press Secretary; Senator Carlson, and Homer Gruenther. But the empty train rattled and banged and one time stopped suddenly, jarring Mamie. But it was a unique experience. It was probably the first time any Presidential candidate's wife was on a Campaign Train alone. No plans or schedules were made for Mamie. She just simply and naturally did what was the courteous and gracious thing to do. When a crowd gathered around the Eisenhower Special in Texas, Mamie went onto the rear platform and said, "Didn't you know the General isn't here?" "Oh, yes," came the reply. "We came to see you!"

In Indianapolis in the railroad yards, there was Mamie, the trouper, on the rear platform chatting with the railroad crew, and police officers, and handing out Ike buttons. At Cleveland she was greeted by a reception committee and made a rear-platform appearance, and a charming A.P. wire service picture went out across the nation.

One of the most interesting events of this trip was a visit Mamie and I made to Eisenhower's birthplace in Denison, Texas. A large number of citizens turned out to greet her. Wearing a bright colored two-piece suit with pleated skirt, a small blue pillbox hat and black gloves, she responded to their friendly greeting with outspread arms, like Ike.

The small frame house was attractive inside and out, but Mamie shuddered at the idea of having had to make butter with a churn. "Imagine living like that," she said.

Saturday morning our train pulled into the station in New York. For three days and nights we had "campaigned" from

Houston, Texas, across the countryside, back to New York, where we were to spend the weekend.

Charlie came down to New York to be with us. It was wonderful to have him there, joining me on the campaign train and sharing this experience.

Mamie came back to our room and sat with him for a visit, and they had a great time chatting about Barbara Eisenhower's father, Colonel Thompson, who was in Vienna at the same time Charlie was in 1945–46. Mamie enjoyed Charlie's humor. They had a good time together.

Now we were off by train for New England. In Providence our own Senator Henry Cabot Lodge and Congressman Christian Herter got on. Charlie was having a fine time, at home in the political world to which he had introduced me. Minority Leader Joseph W. Martin, Jr., also a long-time friend, boarded the train at Attleboro. His geographical area had been for Taft. The editor of the *New Bedford Standard-Times* had recently declared for Cabot Lodge's opponent, young Congressman John Kennedy, in his race for the Senate against Lodge. The editor, Basil Brewer, had been a pro-Taft delegate to the Republican National Convention which nominated Ike; now in revenge he was backing a Democrat.

Truman had just been campaigning for Stevenson through this area. The press were watching to see how Ike crowds would compare with Truman crowds, and how much disaffection with the Republican candidate would be revealed. We motorcaded all through New Bedford, Fall River and Taunton. In the biting cold, people waited for an hour, building bonfires in the streets to gather round to stomp their feet, warm their hands, and declare there were lots more folks here than turned out for Truman.

Then back to the train and on to Worcester. We were running late. Would any appreciable number turn out in the dark and cold? We needn't have worried. They waited—a tremendous crowd—twice as many as Truman had drawn.

We spent that night on the train, Charlie and I sharing our cozy compartment.

Next morning we were in Sherman Adams's country, where it had all begun in March, when Eisenhower consented to have his name placed on the ballot in New Hampshire as a Republican candidate for President and went on to win the first primary contest in the country.

It was a proud day for Governor Adams, now Ike's right-hand man, to introduce the General to his New Hampshire friends and constituents. There was a light dusting of snow in the early morning, which seemed altogether suitable. But there was nothing frosty about Ike's reception.

At noon we reached Boston, By that time it was a warm sunny day, clear blue sky, and still some foliage on the trees. There was a motorcade from the North Station to Boston Common. I stood on the platform with Eisenhower as he spoke to that vast throng—sixty-thousand people—completely filling the Common from Charles Street, where the speakers' platform was, all the way up to the statue on top of the hill.

It is interesting to note that in this whole campaign all across the country there was no instance of protest or heckling. The crowds were enormous. They were interested, curious, friendly, and sometimes carried away by a sort of emotional intoxication.

Late in the afternoon, Mamie and I joined the General, Sherman Adams and Charlie, to fly back to New York. For this was the night of the *Herald-Tribune* Forum. Ike was to speak and Adlai Stevenson and Dorothy Vredenburg and I. This was the speech I had been working on for such a long time. I thought to myself, "I will stand there, and I will wow them. Invitations to speak will come pouring in from all over the country. This will be a big plus for the campaign." I had a suitable dress to wear, a long black lace dress. Everything seemed OK. We marched onto the platform from the wings—the two presidential candidates, the secretaries of the two National Committees. Behind us on the platform were city and state officials, and a few leading members of the two campaign staffs. Out front, the hall was filled with prominent men and women from all over the country. Down in front, just below the platform, were representative high school and college students; up in the front row of the balcony were Charlie and my volunteer secretary, Sylvia Breed.

My speech started off all right. Gabe Hauge had liked it and OK'd it. But when I got to "Bikes for Ike" which Mrs. Waller had asked me to include, I could feel I was losing the young people just below me. I shifted into high gear and finished the speech. There was polite applause, but no thunderous acclaim. I had not swept anybody off his or her feet.

Dorothy Vredenburg, Secretary of the Democratic National Committee, spoke next. She also wore a black lace dress, but crisper and smarter than mine. Her speech was better too, I had to admit. Whether she wrote it or the Democratic Speakers Bureau, I do not know, but it was a polished and skillful speech, well presented.

I have recorded many victories and triumphs. To be honest, I would have to put this down as a failure. Charlie and Sylvia met me in the wings as I left the platform. We just didn't say very much.

But in a campaign like this there is no time for repining. Next morning we were off again by plane for Hartford, Connecticut. It was a crisp sunny day, deep blue sky, sparkling sunshine, brilliant fall foliage. Handsome Governor John Lodge stood silhouetted against the sky as he introduced Eisenhower to the enormous gathering.

Francesca Braggiotti Lodge, the Governor's attractive wife, came aboard the train. She was wearing a red, white and blue "I Like Ike" costume, complete with tricorne hat, "I Like Ike" stockings and Ike jewelry. It was effective, but to me it did not seem appropriate garb for the Governor's Lady.

Then on to Springfield, Pittsfield, and Albany for a night speech in Troy, New York. Next day, October 23, there were appearances in seven cities in upper New York State and then on to Ohio. The climax of this trip was in Detroit with the speech in which Ike announced, "I shall go to Korea."

When the campaign train took off for Ohio from Buffalo, I took the night train back to New York to attend to things in my own sphere of the campaign. Now was the moment when letters over my signature were to go out to campaign workers and to women who had met the Eisenhowers on the train, all across the country. It was planned to mail the letters in the last days of the campaign to get the maximum benefit. All through the months I had been collecting quotations from Eisenhower's speeches in regard to the importance of the women's vote. I had composed a letter which was mailed on this day, October 24, 1952, with Ike's quotations enclosed, on Office of Dwight D. Eisenhower stationery. The letter said:

Dear Co-Worker:
Since the first of September, as I have travelled with General Eisenhower on the Look-Ahead-

Neighbor Campaign Train or the Eisenhower Special Plane, I have heard him pay tribute over and over again to the important part women are playing, not only in the home and the community, but in public life as well. I am enclosing four significant statements along these lines.

General Eisenhower believes that his crusade, with its stress on moral and spiritual values, has a particular appeal to women.

You and I know that women have the decisive vote in this election. In these closing days of the campaign let us be sure that every woman we know goes to the polls on November fourth. More than this, let each of us try to influence as many people as we can to do likewise. By so doing, we shall elect General Ike overwhelmingly, and finally have a leader of whose honesty and integrity we can be proud.

With best wishes to you.

Sincerely yours,

Katherine G. Howard,
Mrs. Charles P. Howard
Eisenhower Campaign
Strategy Committee

Sixteen-thousand of these letters went out to the women members of the regular Party Organization, The Presidents of the Clubs of the National Federation of Women's Republican Clubs, to the citizens for Eisenhower and the Young Republican Organizations.

In addition, each of the almost six hundred women who were guests on the Train received a personal letter from me, enclosing a note of gratitude signed by Ike.

I had written my letters previously. Bertha Adkins, Mary Lord, and Betty Farrington had supplied me with the lists of their organizations. The Citizens for Eisenhower had cooperated in the printing. Now the letters were in the mail to stimulate the devoted women workers. As there were two million more women than men, it could make all the difference.

Also, on this day in New York I was getting ready for my

speech in Philadelphia the next day. I didn't intend to have a repetition of the *Herald-Tribune* disappointment. This was an important all-Pennsylvania event, the Annual Candidates Luncheon of the Philadelphia Congress of Councils, at the Bellevue-Stratford Hotel. I was the guest speaker. It always seemed silly to me to bring in a guest speaker when the candidates want time and attention for their pleas. Congressman Hugh Scott was there and Senator Martin and I was the out-of-state person, fresh from the Eisenhower Train so I was meant to be the drawing card. I took as my title, "The Look-Ahead-Neighbor Train."

After the usual tribute to the candidates present and to the occasion, I spoke in direct personal terms of experiences on the train, of Ike and Mamie and their appeal. I outlined the six issues of the Campaign; I spoke of Korea; then finally:

> Who can bring peace? No one can bring peace better than Ike Eisenhower. He is known and respected throughout the free world. No one can bring peace better than the man whose organizing genius reduced ancient national antagonisms and conflicting ideologies into the common denominator of NATO. Ike knows the capacity of the U.S., of our allies and of the Communists. He has the confidence not only of the rank and file in this country and abroad, but is an intimate and confidante of the leaders of the Western World. If there is any man who is deeply interested in peace, it is the man who lived with and had to carry the burden of war. Ike has suffered with it as a soldier and as a father. . . .
>
> When we can have the best, will we choose anything less? In the mining towns, in the farm villages and big cities, the answer is the same—"We Want Ike," "We Want Ike," "We Want Ike and Mamie!" Let each one of us here dedicate the remaining days and hours of the campaign to translating that great cry "We *Want* Ike and Mamie" to "We H̄ave Ike and Mamie!"

Thank goodness, this speech was a success.

XV

THE LAST WEEK–IKE'S TRIUMPH

Now we were down to the last week. The decision was made for Eisenhower to visit states with crucial blocs of votes—Pennsylvania, Illinois, New York, and Massachusetts, the home state of Cabot Lodge, Ike's pre-Convention Manager, now a candidate for reelection to the Senate.

First to Pennsylvania. We boarded the train Sunday evening for an overnight trip to Philadelphia. Early in the campaign we had been there. On his way back to the Al Smith Dinner by air, Ike had visited six Pennsylvania cities. Now we made a return trip to Philadelphia, then on to Lancaster, Harrisburg, Altoona and Johnstown. Mamie thought that their daughter-in-law, Barbara Eisenhower, should have the experience of the Campaign Train and arranged to have Barbara go in her place on this trip. She said she was putting Barbara in my care. It was a short trip and an interesting one which Barbara thoroughly enjoyed. She made rear-platform appearances with the General and entered into the life of the train. It was a full and taxing day, but a sunny and bright one. In a motorcade at noon I was riding with the General in a great downfall of confetti. As we approached the Capitol, Ike tried, with his hands, to smooth out his hair, which was full of confetti. I reached into my pocketbook and offered him my comb, which he accepted gratefully. As he combed out the confetti, he turned to me and said, "By golly, Katherine, that's the first time I have had a comb in my hair for years!"

After speeches in Altoona and Johnstown, back to the train and on to Pittsburgh. There the General and the small group with him had free time from 6:30 to 8:20. Barbara went to her hotel room across the hall from mine, and changed into a pretty red dress for the evening. I had time to bathe and change. Then on the General's invitation, Barbara and I joined him and Fred Seaton for dinner in his suite.

Off again at 8:20 for the mammoth meeting in the Hunt Armory, with speeches by Governor Fine, Senator Duff, and a half-hour speech by Ike with live television coverage. At half past ten we returned to the train for an overnight trip back to New York.

Next morning, Tuesday, October 28, we went from the train in Pennsylvania Station for a motorcade tour through Queens County and Nassau County, then back to home base.

Now the days were ticking off. As Wednesday dawned, it was less than a week to go. No one seemed tired. In spite of enthusiastic crowds everywhere we went, we kept wondering—could General Eisenhower possibly win? After all these years of Democratic rule, could the Republican Party gain the Presidency? Or would it be another 1948 all over again—when Dewey couldn't lose but he did. I steeled myself against such an outcome. Fortunately the full days and evenings didn't leave much time for contemplation. Every hour, every minute, there was something to be done.

Wednesday, Governor Dewey and Senator Irving Ives joined General Eisenhower for campaigning through Westchester County; then to the Bronx. It was a day of scrambling in and out of the motor cars. At one stop I saw Murray Kempton of the *New York Post*, who in Denver had used my office as his bedroom at night while I had more comfortable quarters elsewhere. I greeted him happily. "So glad you're back!" I exclaimed. "Mrs. Howard," he said severely and ungraciously, "I am *not* glad to be back." He was an ardent supporter of Adlai Stevenson.

That night Eisenhower participated in a nationwide television show, beamed at liberal Republicans and Independents and Democrats. This broadcast was in part a result of the messages I had gotten on the train from Mary Lord of the Citizens for Eisenhower that many Republicans and Independents had become disenchanted with Eisenhower since his breakfast meeting with Taft and since the appearances Ike had made with Jenner and Senator Joseph McCarthy.

Thursday was a day of campaigning in Manhattan, but I spent this day in my office at the Commodore Hotel. There were innumerable letters to be dictated, reports to make, telephone calls to make, and to answer. The grand climax of the day was the huge rally at Madison Square Garden.

There was a notable stage show with many stars, but Mamie and I always missed these, for her appearance was scheduled after the stage show and before the General spoke, and I always came on with her. On this evening Fred Waring came to visit Mamie below stairs. When we did come to the platform, what a sea of faces and what contagious enthusiasm from that vast audience. Of course, we were going to win! But were we? Remember Dewey!

Next morning, early, we were off to Chicago! As I dressed in my room at the Hotel Commodore, it seemed to have been a short night. Now, in October, I had two basic wardrobes, one navy blue and one black. To simplify things, I had bought shoes exactly the same, one pair blue, one pair black. Of course, the inevitable happened. When we arrived in Chicago in full daylight, Tom Stephens discovered that the left shoe was blue, and the right shoe was black!

Fortunately it didn't show in the tremendous ticker tape parade, nor on the platform that night when Eisenhower made his first major speech in Chicago. We had been there to meet with party leaders early in the campaign; this was his first "big" appearance. Here in the citadel of the *Chicago Tribune* he declared that *"Isolation in America is dead as a political issue."* He also reviewed the issues of the campaign, stressing corruption.

Next morning I had breakfast with Eisenhower and the other Campaign Strategy Committee members, Adams and Seaton, in Eisenhower's suite. Only a small number of the staff had gone to Chicago. Back to New York with a myriad of things to do. Charlie joined me there for this final weekend.

On Sunday, General Eisenhower participated in a television-radio recording session in which Ivy Priest, Assistant Chairman Republican National Committee, Mrs. Caroline Simon, a member of the New York State Commission Against Discrimination, and I asked him questions. This had been "cooking" for a long time. It was one of the things I discussed with the General when I was first appointed to his staff. About a month before, on one of our long flights, Gabe Hauge had asked me to write a script for it. The final version was a composite, as usual, of my script and others. I never saw it nor heard it because the recording was released on Monday at 12:30 and 4:45 P.M., and that Monday I was in Boston with every minute filled.

LAST DAY OF CAMPAIGN: NOVEMBER 3, 1952: BOSTON

The campaign train rolled into Boston's South Station at 10:15 in the morning. Eisenhower invited me to join him and Mamie on the rear platform as we pulled into the station. Ike and Mamie were greeted by Cabot Lodge, Leverett Saltonstall, and Sinclair Weeks, and others from Republican circles in Massachusetts. As I followed them down the steps, it warmed my heart to accompany them as they were greeted by the "great" of our party in Massachusetts.

We went from the station to the waiting cars and participated in a motorcade through Boston. It was a warm, sunny day. In the first car, Senator Henry Cabot Lodge rode with General Eisenhower and Mamie.

In the next car were Congressmen Christian Herter, the Republican candidate for Governor, and his wife, Mary MacArthur Herter, called "Mac." In his previous campaigns, she had not participated. To my surprise and pleasure she was sitting beside Chris, up high on the tonneau. Wearing a gray tweed suit, she was smiling and waving, having overcome her natural shyness and reticence, to help her husband win.

I rode with Leverett Saltonstall. As he was not up for reelection, he came quite far back in the motorcade. In the intervening cars, between Herter and Saltonstall, were many of the celebrities from the Campaign Train, important in their own right but unknown to the Boston public. So they waved and cheered for Eisenhower, Mamie, and Cabot Lodge—the same for Congressman and Mrs. Herter. Then came people they did not know. By the time Leverett Saltonstall and I came along, they were ready to wave and cheer again for someone they did know. On this particular motorcade through South Boston, Dorchester, and Roxbury, I was im-

228

pressed with the spontaneous enthusiasm for Leverett. As our car came along, there would be a ripple of happy recognition, "Hi, Lev!"—"There's Salty!"—"Hello, Gov!" rang out.

Knowing that Mamie and others would be in Boston and free at lunchtime, I had invited Mamie and Pat Nixon to my house at 124 Beacon Street for lunch. Others invited were Jane Weeks, wife of Sinclair Weeks, Mary Lord, Co-Chairman of the Citizens for Eisenhower, and Mary Jane McCaffree, at that time Mrs. Eisenhower's secretary, and later to be her White House social secretary. And, of course, Anne Wheaton, Mamie's press secretary and a long-time friend of mine. Also, Mrs. Swan, and Mrs. Kelley, whose husbands had been responsible for air and railroad transportation of the Look-Ahead-Neighbor Train, and the Eisenhower Plane, Rachel Adams, Gladys Seaton, Fred's wife; and Bess Gruenther, wife of Homer of the campaign staff and a close friend of Mamie.

At the end of the motorcade I went to Eisenhower Headquarters at the Copley Plaza Hotel to escort Mamie to my house. Tom Stephens was sitting in the living room of the suite just outside Mamie's room.

He looked up at me and said, "Better look out; Mamie is angry and upset. During the motorcade when she accompanied Ike for a short speech, she was accidentally hit on the head. I don't know whether she will come to your party or not."

I knocked and went through the door to Mamie's room. She was standing in front of the mirror of the bureau, looking unhappy, cross, and angry.

"Katherine," she said, "I've been hurt; someone knocked me on the head this morning. I don't know whether I can come or not."

"Mamie," I said, "of course I want you to come but there is no necessity if you would rather not. My house is only a short distance—lunch will be completely informal—with just your own good friends and Jane Weeks. You might enjoy getting away from the campaign atmosphere."

She considered for a minute and then said, "All right, I'll come." We drove the short distance to 124 Beacon Street.

When she came to my house and upstairs to the drawing room, in a completely social atmosphere with no pressure and only good friends, she relaxed and was happy.

For luncheon Jennie made her special fish chowder. It was served from the Staffordshire soup tureen into the Staffordshire soup plates which had come to me from my great-grandmother. Of course, we had "common" crackers with the chowder, then tossed green salad, and for dessert, a homemade deep dish apple pie, served with cream and cheese and coffee. It was a real New England meal.

When I returned with Mamie to the Sheraton Plaza, she was smiling and said, "Katherine, you did me a lot of good. I was hurt and angry and now I am happy again."

After luncheon there was only time to freshen up before the reception for Mamie and Pat in the ballroom of the Copley Plaza. It was an "invitation only" affair, given by the Women's Republican Club of Massachusetts, of which I was a former President.

Mamie was wearing an olive green tissue taffeta dress with V-neckline and full skirt of unpressed pleats, and carried a cluster of deep pink orchids. She wore a small pillbox hat. I wore my black taffeta outfit with the pale blue feather hat.

Mamie was radiant. After I introduced her, there was thunderous applause and she said, "Thank you, one and all, for giving me the chance to meet you."

She and Mrs. Nixon stood together on the platform, and the guests came up four steps and met first Mamie and then, Pat Nixon. Each person seemed almost transfixed by Mamie's personality, and almost in a daze as they moved on to meet Mrs. Nixon. Pat was pretty and slender and blond, wearing a royal blue wool dress with black velvet collar and cuffs. There was something a little touching about her fragile young figure as she stood on the platform beside Mrs. Eisenhower. Perhaps it was this that prompted one of the women to say, "I hope you're not too tired." But Pat Nixon smiled sweetly as she said, "Oh, no, but *you* must be tired waiting all this time in that long line."

As each guest wanted to linger to talk with Mrs. Eisenhower, I tried to move them along faster, but Mamie asked me not to.

After about an hour of hand-shaking, Mamie took a break for a few minutes, sitting down and having a glass of water. A photographer snapped her picture. Mamie protested vigorously, and the plate was destroyed. She never permitted a picture with a glass in her hand. There were too many people ready to misinterpret the contents of the glass. But Coca-Cola was much more Mamie's drink than anything else.

After the brief rest, Mamie resumed her place in the line again and shook the hands of all the women who were still waiting there, chatting gaily with each one. I said, "Mamie, you can shake hands with three thousand people and make each one of them feel that you care." "But, Katherine," she said, "I do!"

After the reception, we went upstairs to her room. The General was going to have dinner in his suite with some men. She asked if I wouldn't stay and have supper. I said that I'd like to. Then she reconsidered and said, "No, you ought to go home and have dinner with Charlie. I think I'll have dinner by myself tonight." It was a generous thought.

After dinner, as usual, I accompanied Mrs. Eisenhower to the Boston Garden for the final rally of the campaign. It was jammed to capacity and many of the Eisenhowers' friends from the entertainment world came to participate in the final hours of the campaign. Rosalind Russell and Irene Dunne, who had been at the party on the train in Los Angeles, were there; Buddy Rogers was present as well as Irving Berlin, George Murphy, Robert Montgomery and Fred Waring and his band.

The Boston Garden, holding fourteen thousand, was filled to capacity at an early hour. There were loudspeakers for the overflow crowd outside. On the platform were the Governors and Senators and Congressmen from all the New England States, and our own state ticket and Charlie.

As usual, Mamie had given me a white orchid to wear, and she was wearing one. We came on the platform together as Fred Waring's band played "Mamie, What a Wonderful Word Is Mamie." Then I was introduced, went up to the podium, spotlight on, and introduced Mamie to that vast and welcoming audience. She came forward, arms outstretched, to wave and bow and accept red roses—then back to her seat.

General Eisenhower had done an unusual thing. He had taken the afternoon off to rest and work on his speech. It was not a partisan speech; it was a statement of his philosophy. He said he had seen the forces of evil in the Nazi world and the fight against the forces of evil was a constant and unremitting

231

one. He spoke of the Communist issue, of corruption, of equal opportunity, and of the pledges he had made in the campaign.

He said, "I believe in the ability, the decency, and the initiative of Americans. They are to be helped by Washington, not smothered by Washington. They are to be listened to by Washington, not disregarded by Washington. They, and not an entrenched handful in Washington, make up this great nation. Next Tuesday, we citizens go to the polls. I have an abiding faith in this country and the spirit of its people."

When the triumphant rally was over, General Robert Cutler and I drove with the Eisenhowers to the WBZ studio for the final broadcast of the campaign. General Cutler sat in the front seat with the driver, and I sat sandwiched in between the Eisenhowers on the rear seat.

The General leaned across me and said to Mamie, "That was my best speech of the campaign. In that speech I said the things in my heart which I have wanted to express."

General and Mrs. Eisenhower, Senator and Mrs. Nixon, as the Republican candidates, were to make their final plea to the nation from this station at 11:00 P.M., urging all citizens to vote and thanking supporters across the country.

A photographer, Hank Griffin, wanted a picture of Ike and Mamie under a clock with the hands at the stroke of midnight when the TV broadcast was over and the campaign finished. Ike consented. So Griffin got a cardboard clock stuck up on the wall, with Eisenhower sitting under it. Just as he took the picture, the clock banged down on Eisenhower's head. It cut a gash and blood flowed. Eisenhower didn't swear; he didn't say anything for a minute. The studio people and Hank Griffin were so upset that Eisenhower ended by reassuring them and laughing if off, saying, "Gee, I'm glad it wasn't a real clock!" as he wiped the blood away with a handkerchief.

The campaign was over. That night I went home to Charlie, to sleep in my own bed, and to vote with him at the polls next day. My job was done. I'd been on loan, and I'd come home. As I went to sleep, I remembered the General's face as he had said to me that morning, "Katherine, you've been a good sport and a wonderful help."

Next morning I went to Reading with Charlie to vote. He

232

was one of the leading citizens of Reading, and it meant a lot to have him come to the polls with his wife at his side to vote. That was the way Charlie wanted it.

That done, we packed our bags to go to New York to hear the returns with the Eisenhowers at the Hotel Commodore. Ike had told Bobby Cutler and me that he wanted us to be with him when the returns came in. We were there. So were countless others. My special badge for the evening admitted Charlie and me to certain "restricted" areas.

Friends and supporters came from all over the country. Parties were given by many people in their suites; radios and television sets in many places bringing in good news from state after state. People milled around, visited around, but the enormous tally board in the Commodore ballroom was the focal point.

From 8:00 P.M. on, there was a rising tide of enthusiasm in the Commodore ballroom. At 10:00 o'clock General Eisenhower, accompanied by Mamie and Mrs. Doud, appeared there, having just arrived from their home on Morningside Heights at Columbia University. They were greeted with shouts and cheers and cowbells ringing wildly. Ike seemed relaxed and easy.

"Folks," he said, "I was particularly anxious to get to see you this evening before the returns came in. . . . It has been a long campaign and, at times, a hard one. But I want to express to each of you now my warmest thanks for your support throughout the campaign." Then the Eisenhowers went to their third floor suite, and Ike went to bed and to sleep.

However, all over the three floors of the hotel, completely occupied by Eisenhower friends and workers, enthusiasm was mounting. At 10:30 Arthur Summerfield predicted victory, saying, "Ike is running ahead in Virginia, Colorado and Illinois. The news is good from Montana and Nebraska. It seems certain Ike will carry North and South Dakota. I predict victory!" Pandemonium reigned.

However, there were many there who remembered the Dewey campaign, and they kept back their full-fledged enthusiasm. All the time, the professionals were keeping their eyes on the key states. Pennsylvania was still doubtful. How would New York State go?

In between the announcing of returns, and the appearance in the Eisenhower column of additional states, Fred Waring and his band were playing "God Bless America," "The Battle Hymn of the Republic" and their familiar tunes. Parties were held in various suites and people visited about, but always the magnet was the tally board in the ballroom.

At midnight the outcome was still in doubt. Early victories had been recorded in Oklahoma and Virginia, states which had not voted Republican since 1928. Soon after midnight the Democrats lost Connecticut and Maryland, and the Republicans held New Jersey and Ohio. Enthusiasm was mounting, but still Pennsylvania and New York, with large blocs of votes, were hanging in the balance. Now more and more people were crowding into the ballroom. Cheers and yells were heard as Michigan went into the Republican column, and then the Chairman of the Democratic State Committee of New York conceded that the Republicans had carried that state. As we watched the mounting total, we were almost overcome. We hadn't let ourselves believe that this could happen. Now—*now* Eisenhower swept ahead in Pennsylvania. Yes, Ike *was* winning! Massachusetts and Rhode Island broke their Democratic voting record. He carried Texas, whose Mineral Wells delegate fight had all but prevented Ike's being nominated; and Ike even carried Illinois, Adlai Stevenson's home state. Now joy was the overwhelming emotion. Ike *had* won! *He had won!*

At 1:45 Stevenson conceded his defeat in a telegram to Eisenhower in which he said, "The people have made their choice, and I congratulate you. That you may be the servant and guardian of peace, and make the vale of trouble a door of hope is my earnest prayer." Someone asked Stevenson how he felt about it. He replied by quoting Lincoln: "Too old to cry, but it hurt too much to laugh."

Radiantly Ike and Mamie entered the ballroom to joyous and tumultuous shouts at 2:00 A.M. Arthur Summerfield, as Chairman of the Republican National Committee entered with them. Standing quietly and unostentatiously off to the right were Sherman and Rachel Adams, Charlie and I with them. Summerfield as titular head of the Republican Party took the spotlight with the winning candidate. Adams, the Chief of Staff and Ike's right-hand man in the campaign, was content with the victory. There was such an ovation that it was several minutes before Eisenhower could even make himself heard.

Rested and jubilant, he began his remarks by reading Stevenson's telegram and shared with those present his reply: "I thank you for your courteous and generous message. Recognizing the intensity of the difficulties which lie ahead, it is clearly necessary that men and women of goodwill of both parties forget the political strife through which we have passed and devote themselves to the single purpose of a better future. That I believe they will do. . . ." Then he addressed himself to us: "This is a day of dedication rather than of triumph. I am indeed humble, as I am proud of the decision the American people have made. I recognize clearly the weight of responsibility you have placed upon me . . . a more personal word of appreciation, of the courtesy, the warmth of the greetings that Mamie and I have experienced everywhere, has been something that is unforgettable. . . . It's been great to meet you, to work with you for a common cause."

The band played, we shouted and cheered and embraced each other. It was almost unbelievable. The campaign was over. Eisenhower was victorious.

In the succeeding days as the returns were analyzed, it was apparent that the campaign strategy had paid off. Ike had been advised not to waste his time in the South—he campaigned vigorously there. He carried Texas, Virginia, Florida, Oklahoma, Maryland. What about Indiana and Wisconsin where, at some cost to his personal feelings he appeared with Senator Jenner and Senator Joseph McCarthy? Yes, both states were carried, and the Senate was Republican by *one* vote. The House of Representatives was Republican once more, 220 Republicans to 211 Democrats. Joseph W. Martin, Jr., of Massachusetts, would be Speaker.

Ike had made a special point of including a woman in his high command. He had insisted that women were to ride on the Campaign Train along with the men leaders in each state. He had made speeches appealing for the women's vote; they went to the polls in overwhelming numbers to sweep him to victory. The women's vote was a decisive factor.

It was a glorious victory; the largest outpouring of voters in history gave Eisenhower 415 electoral votes, 149 more than the 266 required for election. Ike had won by a margin of six million votes. Adlai Stevenson had only carried eight states. It was an unending satisfaction to have been part of it.

Along with Ike's victory thirty states elected Republican governors. There was additional rejoicing for Charlie and me in the fact that Chris Herter, who enjoyed his work in Congress but had been induced by Sinclair Weeks and others to come home and run against the incumbent Democratic Governor, Paul Dever, had won. It was an uphill battle, but Herter was victorious too and now Massachusetts also had a Republican governor.

The *Boston Herald* editorial summed it up: "Eisenhower's huge vote was much more than a personal victory; it was a popular demand for change. It was a small revolution against deterioration of the government in Washington—against cronyism and corruption, against indifference, against communism at home and abroad, against a government so sure of itself that it had lost touch with the people."

Ike and Mamie personified what America was looking for. They had won. The campaign, with all its rigors and pleasures, was over. What would the next chapter be?

XVI

TO BE OR NOT TO BE— CIVIL DEFENSE

For the time being I lived with the exhilaration of the victory. It would have been hard to return quietly to domesticity after my long identification with the campaign and the stimulus of traveling within the sound of Ike's voice and the cheers which greeted him in the motorcades and in the halls. Fortunately for me, I had an exciting family situation which demanded all my energies.

My daughter Peggy was getting married to Dayton Ball, a Columbia graduate embarked upon a career in advertising. This left no chance for me to pause and sort things out.

Peggy had been right when she had said, "Mother, if Ike wins, you will be so happy nothing can stop you!" We returned from New York on Wednesday, after being up until the small hours of that day at the victory celebration. Peggy's wedding was Saturday. No time to unwind. Just keep on walking on air! All arrangements had been made well in advance. My brother's family, John and Elizabeth Graham and their three daughters, would stay in our house in Reading. Dayton's mother and father would be our house guests in Boston. Dayton, his ushers, and other out-of-town guests were put up elsewhere.

Jennie was in her element getting 124 Beacon Street shined up for the reception to be held there after the wedding ceremony in St. Michael's Church, Marblehead. Peggy and I

237

had bought her trousseau and wedding dress in New York. With part of her inheritance from her grandmother, she had bought an attractive cooperative apartment at 163 East Eighty-first Street. The invitations had been engraved, addressed and mailed. Traynors did the flowers; Fosters did the catering; everything was fine and right for the marriage of my first-born child and only daughter. It was a smallish wedding with family from near and far, and close friends. And it was such a happy day! Peggy was a lovely bride, and Dayton, handsome and attractive. After the reception we had a supper party for family and out-of-town guests. Then the bride and groom departed for a honeymoon in Quebec.

Next day, when all the guests had left, Charlie said, "I am going to take you away for a short vacation."

My heart sank. I had traveled and traveled and traveled—fifty-one thousand miles by train and plane, through forty-five states! Now I was home, I wanted to stay home. But Charlie had his heart set on taking me away from people, from press, from telephone calls or callers. He wanted me all to himself, just the two of us, away somewhere, where we could not be reached or bothered. So we departed for Martha's Vineyard, to an inn still open where we could be quiet and enjoy the Indian summer. We left Tuesday afternoon.

On Wednesday morning the headline all across the front pages of the Boston papers proclaimed in large print:

"SLAYING OF READING COUPLE LINKED TO CRAZED BURGLAR"

"Mr. and Mrs. Stanley Porter of High Street, Reading, shot to death." Further down in the story we read that the burglar had broken into our house in Reading before going across the railroad tracks to murder the comfortable elderly couple.

When we telephoned Jennie and Steve, we found that they and all of Reading were paralyzed with fear. We knew we had to return. Next morning as we packed up our bags to go back to Boston, we realized it was going to be more press, more interviews, more problems. That morning's headline, still across the top of the page, proclaimed: "Mass Round-up Ordered. Still No Clues to Reading Murder."

It was later revealed that on Saturday afternoon, having

read about Peggy's wedding in Marblehead and reception in Boston and suspecting that the Reading house would be empty, the slayer broke through the back door. He was attempting to open the safe in the pantry off the kitchen when the furnaceman, with his own key, came in the front door and went down the cellar stairs, just the other side of the pantry door, to stoke the coal furnace. The burglar hastily gathered up some silver and jewelry, went out the back door, down through our orchard and across the railroad tracks to the Porter home, where, as a child, he had been a ward of the family. There he broke open a bulkhead and got into the cellar. He found a dusty bottle of bourbon in the playroom, had several drinks, then went upstairs to Mrs. Porter's bedroom. When he opened her door, she screamed. He shot her. Mr. Porter came stumbling from his bedroom to see what was the matter, and he was shot dead. The murderer escaped, and the Porters' bodies were not found until Monday morning. On Sunday morning, the slayer taught his Sunday School class as usual. It was not until Tuesday evening and Wednesday morning that the story hit the press in screaming headlines on the front page.

So back we came to reassure Jennie and Steve, be interviewed with the District Attorney and try to help in the investigation.

In about ten days, the murderer was caught and confessed; he admitted that our silver and jewelry were buried in a bandana handkerchief at the foot of a telephone pole near the Highland School in Reading. Accompanied by a police officer, we found the pole, dug up the loot, and our valuables were restored. The murderer, a young man, was tried and given a life sentence.

Meanwhile, Truman had asked Eisenhower to appoint aides to confer with his aides so as to have an orderly transition of government. He had sent a top secret document to Eisenhower by a special aide in a special plane. On Sunday, Senator Henry Cabot Lodge, who lost his Senate seat in winning the victory for Ike, flew down to confer with Eisenhower, who had appointed him Primary Liaison Representative.

On the following Tuesday, Eisenhower, accompanied by Lodge, went to Washington to confer with Truman. I was in

New York on that day to help settle Peggy's apartment and welcome the Balls home the next day. Late in the afternoon I dropped into Eisenhower headquarters at the Commodore to pay a visit to Sherman Adams. He said he was going to the airport to welcome Ike on his return to New York, and would I come along. As we drove to the airport, I spoke of the picture in the paper of Eisenhower and Lodge entering the White House gates on the way to call on President Truman. "Let him have his hour of glory," was Adams's comment.

The Eisenhower we met was more sober than I had ever seen him. I assumed later that Truman told him of the hydrogen bomb and the heavy burden of responsibility it entailed.

At Eisenhower's headquarters at the Commodore, Adams was secure in his position as Ike's chief of staff. He would soon go to Washington to see about office space in the White house and the Executive Offices of the President. Herbert Brownell was screening applicants for positions and the scramble was on. Thomas Stephens and Jim Hagerty were continuing in their positions. Gabe Hauge was there helping. Most of the others, like me, had gone home to take up life there again.

Now Charlie did take me away—this time to Bermuda and there I began to confront the decision which I had thrust to one side.

At the triumphant conclusion of the campaign I was riding high. I had emerged from the long and arduous months of Eisenhower's appeal to the voters by train and plane, with the respect and affection of Eisenhower, and Sherman Adams, and with a close and affectionate relationship with Mamie. No woman had ever had a comparable position in any campaign. There was speculation in the press that I might be the first woman member of the White House Staff. I could not resolve in my own mind what role I wanted.

It was all rather heady and I was tormented by indecision. Also I felt guilty. Charlie was the politician when I had married him and set out to help him. Now I wanted to give whatever prominence or kudos I had back to him. Charlie's misfortune was that his best years, when he could have served with distinction in Washington in a high federal position, were dominated by President Franklin Roosevelt and the New Deal.

Charlie was a Republican. When he went off to war, he was fifty-four years old, almost fifty-eight when he returned. Now he was 64, successful in his job but capable of doing a bigger one.

We sat in the library and talked. I wanted to know if he would be interested in a position in Washington, now that the Republicans had won after the long, lean years. He said "Yes!"

My other concern was that women—not necessarily myself—should be well represented in high government positions in the Eisenhower Administration. To this end I made an appointment to see Eisenhower on the first day he returned from his vacation in Georgia to his temporary offices at the Commodore Hotel in New York. I asked Ivy Priest, Bertha Adkins, and Mary Lord to meet with me and go to see Eisenhower with me.

Had I felt as I did later, that I wanted to be part of Eisenhower's administration, this would have been the time to say so—the field was mine.

But I had Charlie and "the girls" on my mind.

Eisenhower was in his former office; Sherman Adams, Chief of Staff, was in his; Jim Hagerty, Press Secretary, was there. They were all glad to see me and ready to welcome me aboard. Eisenhower suggested I might be interested in the Civil Service Commission.

I was asked to confer with Herbert Brownell, who was making recommendations on appointments. He came quickly to the point. What position was I interested in, in the new administration? This was my opportunity to ask for a position commensurate with my campaign responsibilities, but I said that I didn't want a position for myself; I would prefer that my competent husband, who had extensive governmental and political experience, be appointed; and that I wanted to be sure that women were represented in responsible positions. I was not sure I wanted anything for myself. Politically, my whole approach was unrealistic. But I was acting in character. I really hadn't been working for any reward but victory for the Republican Party—and we had that!

One of the three associates who had been invited to join me in my appointment with Eisenhower, Mary Lord was in Europe and could not come, but sent word that she wanted to be appointed to the United Nations. Ivy wanted any job that would pay enough so that her family could move from Utah to Washington. Bertha, who had been running the Women's Division, wanted to be Assistant Chairman of the Republican National Committee. But in her own true and generous way, she said, "Katie, why don't *you* be Assistant Chairman?" I said I didn't want it, but her generosity was characteristic.

The Commodore Headquarters was alive with people that day, most of them wanting an important job in the new administration. Eisenhower had just made his first appointments: John Foster Dulles, Secretary of State; Charles Wilson, President of General Motors, Secretary of Defense; Douglas MacKay of Oregon, Secretary of the Interior.

Of our appointment with General Eisenhower, John Harris of *The Boston Globe* wrote:

Women to Get High Positions in Government, Ike Says—General Eisenhower couldn't find his specs, so a bit nervously, he reached out and borrowed the glasses of Bay State's National Committeewoman, Mrs. Katherine G. Howard, and read and approved the only sanctioned words of quotes that came back from his office during the frantic day of commotion of his first day back from campaign vacation.

He had dictated them, but he wanted to see how they read.

At the invitation of General Eisenhower, Mrs. Ivy Baker Priest, Mrs. Katherine Howard, Miss Bertha Adkins discussed with General Eisenhower the appointment of outstanding women of ability to executive posts in his administration.

Mrs. Howard described it this way:

"Ike looked marvelous. He was wearing a gray business suit. He looked fine—ruddy. We went into his office. When we got there, he said,

'Let's go into the living room.'

"So we went in and he pulled up some chairs.

"He said that in the campaign he had said he wanted to have both men and women in his government and he meant it; it was not just campaign stuff. He was in wonderful form and humor."

From the way Mrs. Howard described the interview you could tell that there must have been a lot more. . . .

Just a natural question. Are you interested in a Cabinet post? Mrs. Howard smiled in her most charming way and replied,

"I have not been asked."

From Mrs. Howard came a true note of sincerity and willingness to fit into anything the President may elect.

What Harris seemed unaware of was my own indecision.

The question would not let me alone. Before long I learned from Sherman Adams that Oveta Culp Hobby was to be appointed to a very high position, probably the Cabinet. Eisenhower had known her as the capable head of the WACs in World War II. She had proven ability. He knew she would do a good job. But I realized at once how Republican women would react when the first woman appointed was a Democrat! Eisenhower had gone to Korea. I telephoned Jerry Persons and Sherm Adams to say this just would not do. Eisenhower must appoint at least one Repbulican woman when he appointed Oveta.

As a result, Ivy Priest was appointed to the job which had become traditional for a woman, Treasurer of The United States, a marvelous title but not too much responsibility. The Treasurer does not make policy, but she does have her name on the green money, and Ivy became an instant success.

Meantime I had gone home feeling the issue was settled, returning to working with the Ladies Visiting Committee of the Massachusetts General Hospital, and to other volunteer civic work, from which I had taken a leave of absence, and carrying on Republican activities in and around Boston. But soon a bid did come from the incoming head of the Foreign Operations Administration, Harold Stassen. He was calling from Washington to ask me to be Assistant Secretary of the Foreign Operations Administration. I asked him about the duties. They were extensive. It was a policymaking position. William Rand, former President of Monsanto Chemical Company and a friend of Charlie's, was to be Deputy Director. I asked for time to discuss it with Charlie and to make a decision. Stassen was going off the next day to Europe and would not return until just before the Inauguration. We made a date for me to have breakfast with him then and to give him my answer.

No word came from Brownell about Charlie. The whole atmosphere had changed. Eisenhower laid down the principle that he owed nothing to anybody. He would appoint no one on that basis. He wanted his administration made up of capable people of proven ability, regardless of politics.

I discussed the Foreign Operations job with Charlie. But I was still torn by indecision: whether to give it all up and settle down at home, or to continue my identification with the Eisenhower administration.

Late one afternoon Charlie walked down Beacon Hill from his office, came in the front door and closed it with a bang, as he always did. He came up the stairs to the library where we sat at the end of the day and, giving me a kiss, he announced, "I'll be darned if I am going to Washington! *I live in Boston.* You can go on down and do a job if you like, but I'm going to stay here!"

So that was that!

The launching of Eleanor Roosevelt's book, *Ladies of Courage*, which has a chapter about me in which I was described as "The National Committeewoman of the Year," took me to Washington, and, while there, Bertha Adkins pleaded with me to take an active position. I told her I could not decide. I thought I would probably stay at home in Boston. She said, "You could come down for a while anyway." But I couldn't do anything halfheartedly. In the past I had known what I wanted. Now I felt torn in two. I loved my home, my husband, my life, but there was no challenge such as I had been experiencing.

The time drew near for the Inauguration. I decided that I'd had a wonderful experience, that the job offered by Eisenhower and Adams through Stassen would demand too much and strain a happy marriage. It would send me traveling a lot. The duties would drain my energies and I'd have nothing left for Charlie. So Stassen and I had breakfast. He had confidently expected that I would say yes. But my answer was no.

244

Charlie and I then attended the Inauguration. For Charlie and me it was glorious, the climax of so many years of hope and endeavor. All of our friends from the campaign and from previous year's mutual associations were there. We were swept up into not only the official functions but many other inner circle parties. I had a long talk with Mamie in her suite, and she called Charlie to come over and see Colonel Thompson, Barbara Eisenhower's father. The car assigned to us had an official Eisenhower plate, our box for the parade was very close to the Vice-Presidential one, where the little Nixon girls were too, and just opposite the Presidential stand.

The day after the Inauguration and Ball, there was a meeting of the Republican National Committee, and in the afternoon, the Women of the National Committee and other prominent women in Washington were invited to the White House to have tea with Mamie. It was rainy and cold. A friend drove me over. As I approached Mamie, receiving in the Blue Room, her face lighted up; she took both my hands in hers; and said, "Katherine, why don't you stay after the tea and come upstairs for a little visit with me."

After the tea we went in the elevator to the second floor and Mamie took me with her to look over their private quarters in their new home. It was almost as new to Mamie as to me. They had only moved in the previous day, which had been filled with the Swearing-In, the Inaugural Parade, and the Inaugural Ball. We went to the Lincoln bedroom. Mamie examined the window curtains and said they needed cleaning. In the study there were new boxes of Crane's stationery. She opened one. It said "The White House." I noticed it was just the sort of Crane's stationery I had at home. In another bedroom, the dresses from the Inaugural Ball and the Inauguration were hanging, not yet put away. Mrs. Truman's bedroom was a surprise. It was a small corner room. There was a fireplace, catty-cornered; an ordinary and unattractive bureau, single bed and chair. That was all.

For herself, Mamie took the large room next to it. She had it painted a delicate shade of pink with a king-sized bed and beautiful furnishings, many pictures and photographs including autographed ones from Queen Elizabeth and Prince Philip. It was a charming room.

As we went from room to room, a message came up that the Cabinet was going to be sworn in, in the East Room, and would Mrs. Eisenhower like to attend? "Come on, Katherine," she said, "Let's go." The chairs were set up lengthwise in the East Room, facing the wall where the portraits of George Washington and Martha Washington hang.

Standing between the portraits were the President and Chief Justice Vinson ready to administer the oaths of office. As soon as Mamie and I entered, the ceremony began. So many of my friends, Sinclair Weeks, Oveta Culp Hobby, Sherman Adams, and many others were there.

After the swearing-in, shaking hands, congratulations, Mamie said, "Come on upstairs and we'll have an old-fashioned."

The President and Chief Justice had disappeared, but when we went to the second floor, they were sitting at one end of the very large corridor, which is used as a family living room. There were sofas and chairs, a coffee table, lots and lots of flowers all about. Mamie and I went over and joined them. They were talking seriously, and Mamie and I listened quietly.

The President was troubled about the Rosenbergs. They had been convicted as spies, but the decision as to whether or not they were to be executed had not been made by the previous administration. Now it was up to Eisenhower. He said to the Chief Justice, "I wish you could give me some guidance about the Rosenberg case."

The Chief Justice replied, "Well, I can't do that, but I just want to give you one piece of advice, that I'd like to give to every President. That is, surround yourself with some people who won't be overimpressed with the power of the Presidency, and who will have the gumption to say no to you.

"For instance," continued Vinson, "yesterday I called you Ike. Today I address you as Mr. President."

The President looked rueful for a moment, rubbed the back of his head, then, with that delightful grin said, "Well, I'll still call you Fred!"

I said, "I'm sure what the Chief Justice has said is true, and there's one person in your Cabinet who will always give you a straight answer, and that is Sinclair Weeks."

Turning to another subject Ike said, "I'm not going to have politics mixed up in my Administration. Any person who is a member of the National Committee, and accepts an appointment, will have to get off the Committee." (This meant that Weeks, now Secretary of Commerce; Frank du Pont of Delaware, now Commissioner of the Bureau of Roads; Charlie Thomas, now Secretary of the Navy, would have to resign from the Republican National Committee and Republican National Finance Committee.)

Then I began to wonder—should I make the move to go, or should the Chief Justice, or would Mamie give the signal?

So I said quietly, in an aside, to Mamie, "I think perhaps I'd better go." She whispered, "Wait till the Chief Justice goes, and then go after that." And just then he rose to say good-bye.

After he left, the telephone rang. Mamie answered and said to Ike, "It's John and Barbara. They have met some friends and want to know if it is all right to have dinner with them and not come home to supper here."

The President said, "Well of course, if they want to, fine."

Such a family touch. Their first night in the White House—dinner at home—but the children want to join friends, and it is all right.

Then Mamie said, "Ike, why don't you get a car for Katherine?"

When the car was announced, I kissed Mamie good-bye, the President came down with me in the private elevator, and escorted me to the front door, just as he would have done in his own home.

As we walked across the marble floor to the door, he said earnestly, "Katherine, I want you in my administration. I shall tell Sherm Adams I want him to find something interesting for you, and I want you to come down and talk with him."

I thanked him. We shook hands, and I drove off in the long, black, sleek White House car.

That night Charlie and I took the Federal Express back to Boston. Before I came to my decision and said no to Stassen, I had prayed long and hard to make the right decision and then to accept it. Now, another chapter was closed. It seemed cold and dark and lonesome in that station. There was a little twinge of regret in my heart.

Back in Boston Jennie was running the house. Peggy was in New York; Herbert at Harvard; Charlie gone all day. I missed the team I had worked with. I missed not being called on for the full use of my energy. And no word came from the White House. The adjustment was hard. I tossed at night and couldn't sleep. My sparkle was gone. I was pale and uninterested. Finally Charlie said, "You'd better go on down to Washington and do a job. The President wants you."

Adams was Chief of Staff. Much as he liked and respected me, he saw no place for a woman on the White House Staff. There was a great hue and cry from the women's organizations to have a woman on the White House Staff—and to have me. I would have liked that. But Adams said he wasn't going to have an Arab for the Arabs, a woman for the women, and a Negro for the Negroes on the White House Staff, but he wanted me to continue to be part of the team. Would I be interested in the Women's Bureau of the Labor Department?

I didn't know too much about labor and social welfare laws. It didn't appeal. How about the Children's Bureau? The same there. We went over many possibilities, and finally hit on Civil Defense.

CIVIL DEFENSE

Sinclair Weeks had his doubts that Civil Defense was good enough, but Eisenhower believed in it. He had seen it in operation in England during the war and so had my husband. The job was nationwide in scope; it needed help and I could help it. It reached into every home, or should reach into every home. I could help take it there. So it was decided. Governor Val Peterson, of Nebraska, was Administrator. Now Eisenhower was making me Assistant Administrator. Both appointments were interpreted as a demonstration of the President's belief in the importance of the Agency and its mission. He further demonstrated this by asking the Administrator, Val Peterson, to sit with the Cabinet, and Peterson was a full-fledged member of the National Security Council. Eisenhower made a strong statement about the importance of Civil Defense in his State of the Union message, and in his historic speech at the United Nations on December 8, 1953.

Where to live? Charlie and I decided on the Westchester, an apartment hotel where Sinclair Weeks and Jane were, where Homer Gruenther and Bess lived, where Bertha Adkins was just across the street. We took an apartment just like the Weeks, and the duPonts. Each apartment had an entrance foyer and to the left of it a dining area, and just beyond that, the kitchen. A wrought iron railing separated this area from the large living room, three steps down from the foyer and dining area. There was a fine view from the windows out over the park which surrounded the Westchester. Beyond the living room was a large bedroom and an attractive bath. It was just fine in every way, but it was the only place I ever lived which did not become "home." Home was still Boston. My office where I spent my working hours got the homemaking touches. Every weekend I returned to Boston and Charlie came to Washington from time to time for White House dinners or receptions, a dinner at the British Embassy or at the Saltonstalls' or just to be with me.

Having arrived and taken up residence, I called Val Peterson and said, "I'm here, Val. Shall I come in at nine o'clock tomorrow morning?" "Come anytime you like," he said. "The office opens at 8:30. I am usually here at 8:15." So next morning I walked up the steps and reported to his office at 8:30. It seemed very early to me.

When I went to the Westchester dining room for breakfast the first morning, I found that it would not open till eight. No one could have breakfast in the dining room at eight, have a fifteen minute drive, and get to work at 8:30. Frank duPont solved the problem. He bought electric percolators for all our group—the Weeks, du Ponts, Honewells, Mills, Howards—and we all got up at six-thirty or seven, cooked our own breakfasts, and got to work on time.

Everyone was feeling very conscientious and hardworking. A Democratic friend in Washington said to me, "Why don't you Republicans relax and enjoy yourselves?"

Within a few days, my swearing-in ceremony was arranged. It would be in the President's office in the White House, and Mamie would attend. This was considered newsworthy. Charlie came down from Boston, Peggy from New York, and Herbert from Harvard University. I was told I could invite friends, and it was an impressive list of White

House Staff, Cabinet members and wives, Senators, Congressmen and wives, and National Committee members and top-ranking staff. After I was sworn in, and the President and I were having pictures taken, he said, "Katherine, if I had known you had all these friends, I never would have worried about the election!"

During the picture taking, too, I was telling him about our breakfast difficulties at the Westchester, and he said, "Lots of times I get up so early there is no one around and I cook my own breakfast."

But the remark that went out all over the country in the astounding nationwide publicity was his remark when he shook hands with me and handed me my commission. "Now, Katherine," he said, "you're a full-fledged bureaucrat!" The picture of the President and me with that quotation under it was featured all across the country. Clare Boothe Luce wrote me, "Dear Katherine, Congratulations. The President couldn't have given the job to an abler or sweeter woman. If you're a full-fledged bureaucrat, bureaucrats are going to be a good deal more popular throughout the country than they have been up to now. Affectionately, Clare"

After the swearing-in ceremony was over and I emerged from the door of that wing of the White House, I found a microphone set up, and with no previous notice, I was asked to make a statement. The words rolled out, "I agree with the President that an adequate Civil Defense is a sheer necessity to the defense of our country. There's a tremendous job to be done in the Civil Defense field. I shall devote my best efforts to bringing the necessity for an adequate Civil Defense to every family in the nation." Val Peterson looked at me and said, "Katherine, what office are you running for?"

So there I was, and what were my duties to be? Val went off to an atomic test in Nevada and told me to sit in his office the first week and read "Project East River," the basic paper on Civil Defense Assumptions and plans for implementing the defense; and to read all the laws and regulations governing Civil Defense.

When Val came back from "Operation Doorstep," the atomic test in Nevada, he went about setting me up with an office and a secretary, as I had been using his office and secretary while he was away. His assistant said, "You've got to get a secretary for Mrs. Howard who can take pressure, for she's a high-pressure woman." They got Jeannette Thuman and later Henrietta Parker in addition. After providing me with a secretary, the Administrator walked me down the corridor to a large, attractive office and said, "How would you like this office?" I said, "It's very nice, but it's Colonel Chambers' office. I couldn't think of taking his office." But Val had decided it was to be mine, and Colonel Chambers accepted it graciously as one of the political facts of life. He had been Acting Deputy of Civil Defense under Truman, after his predecessor Jerry Wadsworth left to go to the United Nations. Chambers was a very convinced and active Democrat. He had a feeling: "These people come and go. She'll be here for a while, and after she has gone, I'll be Deputy again, or something just as good."

My office was a joy. It was a great big room. My desk had its back to the windows, and the United States flag and Civil Defense flag in standards behind it. There was a large conference table with enough chairs for a staff meeting, and a large brown leather sofa with coffee table and two arm chairs. The walls were a soft green color and there was wall-to-wall carpeting, my own private bathroom, and a large adjoining office for the two secretaries, I soon had and kept busy. There my life centered. I kept fresh flowers; the coffee pot was always perking; and usually I came out from behind my desk and sat in an armchair to meet and talk with people.

The next week, Peterson called a staff meeting of all the Assistant Administrators, General Counsel, and Heads of Departments. A matter of policy was being discussed. After about half an hour's discussion, I made a suggestion—Val looked at me—said, "That's it" and he adjourned the meeting. My political training on high policy levels had paid off. Then he asked Paul Wagner, his personal assistant; Mr. Aitken, his executive assistant; and me to meet with him in his office. From then on, we were the policy group, meeting in Val's office at 8:30 every Monday morning, and at other times when necessary.

From the beginning Val and I got along famously. Although we had not known each other personally, we had been on the same side in the fight to nominate Eisenhower when Peterson was Governor of Nebraska and I was Secretary of the National Committee. While I was in the final stages of making the decisions on the Texas Delegates before the 1952 Convention, he was at the Republican Governors' Conference which drew up and signed the manifesto in favor of the Fair Play Langlie Amendment, so important in the Eisenhower victory.

In the Federal Civil Defense Administration he consulted with me, gave me wide responsibilities, and we were friends. I never had to "pound on the door." He opened doors for me. Some of the assignments he gave me almost took my breath away—they were so unusual for a woman—but I went ahead and did them.

Val is a man about six feet tall, of robust build, quick and agile in mind and body. He spoke easily and forcefully and had an agreeable personality. The only thing we differed on was that he and his personal assistant, Paul Wagner, were always watching their weight, while I was always being sure to eat a good breakfast and lunch as well as dinner so as to have plenty of energy for what I was doing. I was burning up calories at a fast rate. One day when Peterson, Paul Wagner and I were having lunch together, they ordered cantaloupe for dessert and I ordered honeydew melon. Paul said, "You ought to eat cantaloupe; it has twenty-five less calories." I kept on eating honeydew; I needed those calories!

Because of the atomic tests then in progress, Civil Defense was one of the three most sensitive security agencies, the others being the Atomic Energy Commission and the Central Intelligence Agency.

As for my duties, as Assistant Administrator for Educational Services, they were many; all of the manifold publications on as many varied subjects as Chemical Warfare, Fire Prevention, Biological Warfare, Home Shelters, Home Protection, were issued from our office, and had to be studied, reviewed, and finally approved. We had two staff colleges for disaster training, one on the East Coast, one on the West Coast; men and women volunteers attended. Women's participation and all radio and television were part of my responsibility. We were the only agency specifically designated by law to disseminate information. Our task at this time was to alert the American public that a danger did exist, that we were no longer protected by the great Atlantic Ocean, that bombs *could* be flown from Moscow and dropped on American cities, and that, with proper preparation and precautions, we could survive an atomic attack. One of our tasks was to prepare the booklet, "The Home Protection Exercises." I learned that in the bureaucracy it took a long time for all the agencies and departments to review the text and "sign off" in agreement. After many months they were printed and promulgated with endorsements on the inside of the title page by President Eisenhower, Val Peterson, and myself.

We had a dedicated staff. There was John deChant, whose idol was Franklin Roosevelt. He was a man of great integrity, a devout Catholic, who had been a Vice-President of Hill and Knowlton, advertising agency, and had left it to become Public Relations Director of Civil Defense, at a lower salary. John would come strolling into my office, or the Administrator's, cigarette in a holder like Franklin Roosevelt's, tilted at the same angle, and he would tell us frankly where we were good and where we hadn't done so well. He was a Democrat but loyal to the new administration; he believed in civil defense and wanted us to do a good job. In addition to Jack deChant, Public Affairs, there were Hal Goodwin and Jack Greene on the scientific and medical side, and one of our liaison men with AEC; and Pete Hotchkiss of Public Affairs "who broods in his office and comes out with the *Atlantic Monthly* slant on what we should or should not be doing a year from now."

It soon struck me that the majority of the staff did not like to make decisions. They would do the staff work, present you with alternatives. It was up to us, the political appointees, to make the decisions and take the consequences. I always liked making decisions; this, I thought, was the best part of the job.

I had been sworn in as Assistant Administrator on Friday, March 13, a lucky day for me. But In June, Val Peterson, Sherman Adams, and President Eisenhower had decided to promote me to Deputy Administrator.

My new position required Senate confirmation. The President appoints. The Senate confirms. This was the time in Washington when Charles Wilson, President Eisenhower's nominee for Secretary of Defense, was given such a hard time by the Senate Armed Services Committee and made the classic remark, "What's good for General Motors is good for the country." He and other presidential appointees were being mercilessly grilled by the various Senate Committees.

My loyal staff of Educational Services were worried for me. They briefed me on what to say and what not to say. When the appointed day came, they went with me to Capitol Hill. As we waited outside the Armed Services Committee Room, they paced the floor, looked worried and chewed their finger nails. All I could think of was a mother about to give birth to a baby, and the agonized father pacing the floor. After quite a wait, Harold Stassen came through the door looking as if he had been on the rack. Then almost immediately, I was summoned, and went into the august room alone. I was seated at the end of the table, nearest the door through which I had entered. At the other end of the table was the smiling face of the Senator from Massachusetts, Leverett Saltonstall, Chairman of the Armed Services Committee, with the other members ranged up and down the sides of the table. Leverett introduced me. I knew many of them anyway. I made a brief statement, then Leverett asked for questions. Senator Case, Republican from New Jersey, said something favorable. Senator Margaret Chase Smith, my long-time friend, said in her flat, down-right way, "All I can say is, they are lucky to get her and the President should have appointed her Deputy in the beginning." So it went, all the Republicans saying pleasant things, asking easy questions. Finally Leverett turned to Senator Stennis of Mississippi, the ranking Democrat on the Committee, and enquired if he would like to question me. Senator Stennis replied, "As long as she was born below the Mason-Dixon line, she's all right with me!" With this, I was allowed to withdraw. Later that day the news went out and Leverett sent me the ticker tape "Senate unanimously confirms Mrs. Katherine G. Howard of Boston as Deputy Administrator of Civil Defense."

Several days later the swearing-in was in the President's Office at the White House. As he handed me my commission as Deputy Administrator, Ike said, "Katherine, this is getting to be a habit."

Again my family came to Washington for the ceremony and after it, Charlie and I gave a luncheon at the Sulgrave Club for the family, close friends, and senior staff members of FCDA.

I was the first woman deputy of any federal department or agency. My deputy's car was equipped so that in an atomic attack or civil defense emergency, if our Headquarters were destroyed, my car could become Headquarters with communications to the White House, other agencies, our regional offices, and our secret command post.

In many of his speeches Eisenhower referred to "The Age of Peril" in which we live. The cold war was on, and the importance of civil defense was underlined by the fact that the Administrator was a member of the National Security Council, and by invitation of the President sat with the Cabinet. When Val was away, I was Acting Administrator and as such, attended meetings of the National Security Council. If a disaster occurred in his absence, I was expected to take charge.

I had learned and was learning so much—important things and trivial things. I found that the *size of your desk* in bureaucratic Washington was important. To me, a desk was a desk, but when I was promoted to Deputy Administrator, my secretary insisted that I should have a larger one, commensurate with my exalted position. She had her way. So I had a deputy-size desk, described in the Federal Supply Schedule as "desk, executive, 40 x 66, wood, walnut, chambered corners, double pedestal, Class A"—but it was all I could do to reach across its vast expanse to place signed letters in the outgoing letterbox. However, I couldn't let my secretary down.

Then there was the matter of the buttons on the telephone. In my volunteer job for the past ten years I had had an office and a secretary but calls went through the switchboard. When I was confronted with a telephone with six buttons—HOLD—375—376—COM—BUZZ—each with its own light—it took concentration to master such intricacies. Our telephone extensions were 375 and 376. HOLD was the button to push when I wanted to hold a call on one line in order to pick up another. COM was the intercommunication line to my secretaries, and BUZZ, for ringing my outer office. I would press 376 before BUZZ and again we were cut off. I must say, Jeannette and Henrietta were tactful and patient! Matters of policy, yes—decisions, yes—learning a whole new field, yes—but, oh, those buttons!

And a *whole new language* had to be learned. Around the conference table every sentence had alphabetical abbreviations with their own peculiar pronunciations. "P.S.B." they blithely said. I had no pride as everyone knew I was new. "What is that?" I would say. "Oh, Psychological Strategy Board." Then there was B.D.S.A., Business and Defense Services Administration, and O.E.E.C. (pronounced O-Double E-C)—Organization for European Economic Cooperation, and many, many more.

A year later I had learned most of them and didn't realize how much of a bureaucrat I had become until one morning when I was talking to General Wilton B. (Jerry) Persons, Deputy Assistant to the President in the White House about the improvised hospitals for which the Federal Civil Defense Administration was seeking appropriations.

"Jerry," I said, "in addition to all their other vitures, these hospitals are purchased through 'As-ma-pah'." "What!" said Jerry, "what in the world is that?" "Armed Services Medical Procurement Agency," I explained. Jerry laughed and said, "Well, don't let the President hear you talk that way—if there's anything he hates, it's alphabetical abbreviations!"

All of our telephone calls were monitored. No extemporaneous speeches could be made, so I was assigned a speech writer. We would confer in my office. I would tell him what I wanted to say. He would check out the scientific background, use my written notes and quotations, submit a draft to me for revision, put it in final form, and then distribute it to the press and to our regional offices. In the beginning, at Civil Defense, I learned a great deal from the speeches I made, for from the beginning I had a heavy load of speech making.

Charles Ellsworth, my speech writer, sent a letter which I cherish, soon after I became Deputy. He wrote:

> Although I have not asked them all, I think you have long since been elected to the Club. Certainly you passed with flying colors the first quick inspection of the professionals, the men who know the hallmarks of ability and how to recognize them in others. . . . Your speeches, for one thing, have had a profound effect on the people *inside* Civil Defense as well as on the outside, and that's a good thing.
>
> The fact that you allow yourself to say simple, understandable things to plain people seems to be reassuring—it takes you out of the stuffed-shirt

class. I think they like the fact that you are translating a terribly complex subject into terms that can be understood by the average householder here and now, instead of addressing the faceless millions for posterity. . . .

You have many friends in Civil Defense, and thus far, no enemies.

You look very good indeed to the boys and girls and they're for you. My suggestion as a consultant is that you keep right on doing what you're doing without any further reference to the White House. . . . Aside from that, I don't think anyone could ask for a more letter-perfect boss.

Jack deChant raised the question of my going home every weekend. Wouldn't it look better and show more interest if I stayed in Washington? "Jack," I said, "I am a married woman. I have a husband and a home in Boston. If I neglect that fact, I am open to criticism. I can do the job here, but I can't and don't want to neglect my job there."

I worked it out so that I had the maximum time at home. Along with young Chris Herter, General Counsel at Foreign Operations Administration; John Cabot of the State Department, later Ambassador to Sweden; and sometimes Leverett Saltonstall in the summer, I would take the 5:30 plane to Boston Friday afternoons, and be home early Friday evening. All day Saturday with Charlie, and all day Sunday, even Sunday night supper. Then, without any fuss or bother to anyone, a taxi would come about 9:30, I'd kiss Charlie good-bye, and proceed to South Station, and the Federal Express back to Washington. One could board the train at ten, it pulled out at eleven, and I was asleep by then. As a regular customer, I arranged to have the porter wake me early, bring coffee and toast and orange juice to my berth, so that when the train reached Washington, I could go without delay to that 8:30 policy meeting in the Administrator's office. One morning when the train was late, I arrived to find that they had just decided on the names of the National Civil Defense Advisory Council with only one woman member instead of two as previously. It didn't take long to fix that!

The pleasure Charlie and I had in being together was

heightened by our separation. Love was fresher and stronger and more spontaneous and rewarding. There was so much to talk about and to share—a whole new batch of anecdotes on Charlie's part—stories of Washington on mine. I was happy and fulfilled, and it radiated outward.

One weekend when we were at our house in Reading, the telephone rang and I answered a long distance call. "Katherine," a woman's voice said, "I want your advice because there is a possibility that I may be asked to be a candidate for Congress. If I am the candidate, I may not be elected, but before I consent to become a candidate, I wanted to talk with you and find out if you think it is possible to have a position in Washington and maintain a happy home."

I said, "For almost a year and a half, I've worked it out happily and successfully, and I'm sure you can if your husband is willing, and you can stand the loneliness. Of course it will be a strain on your marriage to be separated five days a week; the weekends together must be sufficiently rewarding to carry you through. You have got to be careful not to lose your head in the new prestige. The balance between your home and your career must be carefully adjusted. It can be done. Good luck!"

When I went home for weekends, I traveled at my own expense, but when I went on speaking trips, or to Atomic Tests in Nevada, it was at government expense. It was useful for me to have a salary even though Charlie complained that it put us in a higher income tax bracket.

I always imagined that when Cabinet Secretaries, Administrators and Deputies traveled, they were provided luxurious accommodations on trains or ships, and impressive suites at hotels.

My awakening was rude when I discovered that the government allowed minimum first-class accommodations on the train, that is, a lower berth, and the magnificent sum of *nine* dollars a day to cover hotel room, meals, tips, and any other tranportation except a taxi when you arrived and departed. This was in 1953.

My husband had rather spoiled me and I liked to travel comfortably so the difference between what the Government allowed and the "style to which I was accustomed" came out of my own pocket.

When I was promoted to Deputy, my duties and responsibilities were even more interesting. In the absence of the Administrator, I was Acting Administrator. At other times I was second in command; Val assigned to me the responsibility for Congressional liaison, for NATO affairs, and the Office of Women's Participation reported directly to me.

Again Colonel Chambers figured. In the Democratic Administration, Congressional liaison had been his responsibility. Now we had a Republican President, a Republican Congress, and a Republican Administrator for FCDA. It didn't make sense for a Democrat to represent us on the Hill. Peterson asked Chambers to take me up to the Capitol, introduce me around and show me what went on about Congressional liaison. When we returned from a morning with the Congressmen and Senators, he said to Val, "I think Mrs. Howard is a natural," and to me he said, "I can see that Val is going to turn this over to you and that you are going to do all right."

He was a Marine Colonel, and a man of purpose and high standards. I think he took it all very well. So Congressional liaison became my responsibility. This meant that I must keep in touch with legislation affecting Civil Defense, and must try to get the maximum amount of Congressional support for increased appropriations for our Agency. Bowie Johnson from the legal department was assigned to me as "leg man" on the Hill. He knew all the Clerks of the Committees, kept in touch with what was going on, went with me when I called on members of the Armed Services Committee and Appropriations Committee.

Margaret Chase Smith was again helpful. She said, "Katherine, when you go to see a Congressman or a Senator, have a piece of paper with you with some facts on it, and when you say good-bye, leave this with them. Then they will have something to look at which will summarize briefly the points you have been making."

From being National Committeewoman, and from the campaign, I knew most of the Congressmen and Senators. It was a natural sphere of work for me. Joe Martin of Massachusetts was Speaker of the House, and at that time, Charlie's friend, Congressman John McCormack, of Massachusetts, was Minority Leader.

I liked to go to the Hill. I knew a lot about the workings

of the Congress. I knew a lot about the Senators and Congressmen with whom I was working. I knew their backgrounds, what they were interested in, and I believed in what I was asking for, so that I could speak with conviction. I had studied so hard, learned to much, and I believed so truly.

But this I noticed after a bit. When I was National Committeewoman and I wanted to get in touch with a Congressman or a Senator, he would invite me to lunch in the House or Senate dining room, and put himself out to be pleasant. Now when I came up, hat in hand, from a government agency asking for money, they felt they were doing me a kindness when they gave me ten or fifteen minutes to explain what we needed for Civil Defense.

Bowie Johnson was my liege man—loyal, devoted, competent. But his boss, the General Counsel, did not like having him working directly under me. I was surprised at the General Counsel's hostility. I had counted on him as a friend, as I had known him favorably as the young, attractive Chairman of the Republican State Committee of one of the New England states. But in our organization, he was no friend. Nor was the newly created Executive Assistant Administrator. Whether they resented me as a woman, or resented my White House and National Committee ties, or resented the considerable responsibilities Val entrusted me with, I do not know. It might have been all three, but they were not friendly.

It was, of course, a help to me that we had a Republican Congress to work with. Senator Homer Ferguson, of Michigan, was Chairman of the Senate Appropriations Committee, and once as Acting Administrator I had to go before his Committee to make a prepared statement for Civil Defense and then to answer questions. Members of our staff were there to back me up. The Senate Appropriations Committee Room features a long mahogany table with a vast brown leather throne at one end for the Chairman. Other senators—all members of the Committee—were seated facing one another across the table, Republicans on one side and Democrats on the other. Each senator's place was marked with a silver plate bearing his name. At the far end of the room a huge marble mantel supported an even bigger gold-framed mirror, and a magnificent crystal chandelier seemed to dwarf them both in the attempt to light the murals on the walls.

It was an impressive setting, and I was aware of the great responsibility I carried, in being the spokesman for FCDA. At the end of an hour I came away, gratified by their attention to what I had said.

Another day was more eventful. I was up at seven on a warm summer's day. I put on my light blue linen two-piece suit and after breakfast, left for appointments on Capitol Hill in the morning and a meeting at the White House in the afternoon. I had kept the lunch hour free in order to go to the Westchester to pack my bags and take them back with me to my office, for on Friday afternoons I went straight from the office at five to the airport to fly home. Most of the morning was spent on the Hill talking to various congressmen. Then I went to the anteroom of the Senate Appropriations Committee for a chance to speak with Senator Ferguson.

Time dragged by, although it was enlightened by Senator Joseph McCarthy coming out to engage in conversation with May Craig of the Gannett Press. I wondered what sharp and penetrating question she would put to him. Finally Senator Saltonstall came by and found I was waiting to speak to the Chairman; he went in, asked Ferguson to come out briefly and in five minutes our business was concluded.

By now it was half-past twelve, and word of the House action in regard to FCDA appropriations was passed to me. It had not been favorable, and I was so disturbed, I decided to go back to the office before going home to luch.

CHESTERTON DISASTER

As I walked into my office, the telephone was ringing. It was the White House. There was a disaster in Chesterton, Maryland. The President directed me to proceed there and take charge; Val Peterson was out of the country and so I had a job to do.

The first move was to try to get the necesssary staff to my office, but they were out for lunch; then to hear the reports from FCDA regional and state directors. Next, a request to the Defense Department for transportation. They called back to say that a plane would be ready at Bolling Field if I could get there fast. Lunch came up from the cafeteria, which I ate while I was briefed on the situation, and arrangements were made. With Civil Defense's top staff at lunch, I couldn't help wondering if this is the way it would be if a national emergency arose. Fortunately, one expert was on hand who really knew the answers.

Soon I was tearing through the heart of Washington with a motorcycle escort to Bolling Field. There Colonel Beers, FCDA liaison to the Department of Defense, met me and we were off in an Army F-37 with a pilot and copilot, two men from Civil Defense and myself.

We had been told to fly carefully, for a nitroglycerin plant in our path might blow up. About twenty miles away from Chesterton, the acrid smoke filled our nostrils, even in the enclosed plane. We flew over the town and could clearly see the large devastated area.

At the Chesterton plant they had been assembling fireworks and Army training shells. Fireworks on an assembly line suddenly blew up. Sky rockets shot up and roman candles flared, aerial bombs burst, then the plant exploded with a thunderous roar, heard thirty miles away. Firemen who had led the workers to safety had to dodge flying debris and blasts of flame. Eleven workers were killed. Chesterton was partially evacuated by Army crews, wary of treacherous explosives.

As soon as our plane landed, we proceeded in a car to the disaster area—but the car needed gas! The road was blocked off, but our official sticker let us through. I hurried to emergency headquarters to take charge. There I received reports of what had happened, the extent of the disaster and what steps were being taken. All employees of the firm had had civil defense disaster training at our Staff College. Names of survivors were being checked—Civil Defense, Salvation Army, and Red Cross and National Guard were all working together. Fifty wounded who were on the lawn were moved to the hospital. I visited the hospital and talked with the injured, moving from bed to bed. There was still danger that two more plants might blow up, but the disaster was averted.

All that long afternoon I coped with the disaster, visited the wounded, issued directions to be carried out by our Regional and State Directors who would take over, and at last I returned to the Army plane which flew me back to the National Airport in Washington. In that short flight I caught my breath and reviewed what I had done. My plane for Boston was leaving in a few minutes. I had just time to walk from one plane to another. With no coat or luggage, just my pocketbook in my hand, I flew back home to Boston.

VICKSBURG TORNADO

About six months later I was at home for the weekend in Reading with Charlie. On Sunday morning in the midst of a "line" storm, with heavy winds and rain, Hal Aitken, the Executive Assistant Administrator, telephoned from Washington to say that President Eisenhower wished me to go immediately to Vicksburg, which had been devastated by a tornado. My boss, Val Peterson, was in Puerto Rico attending a Civil Defense meeting. I said to Charlie, "I wouldn't go anywhere in a storm like this, except for an emergency or my daughter's wedding," but off I went to Washington to be briefed by the staff before I flew south, suitably clad in a tweed coat and ground-gripper shoes. I curled up in the seat, shut my eyes and comforted myself with the Biblical saying, "Underneath are the everlasting arms."

In Washington it was still raining hard, as we drove up to the FCDA Headquarters. In less than an hour we reviewed the provisions under which the President had declared Vicksburg a major disaster area; went over the FCDA-Red Cross agreement and after a bite of supper, I took off for Memphis in more wind and rain. When I arrived, it was midnight. There a National Guard plane had been requisitioned for me and before I went aboard (it seemed a macabre note), I had to sign a statement saying that in case of my death, the military would not be held responsible. Having signed my death warrant, I sat down in a metal bucket seat, in a cold plane, and proceeded, alone.

At Jackson, Mississippi, the State Civil Defense Director met me, drove me to the hotel, and asked me to meet him for breakfast at 7:30. It was now 4:00 A.M. It seemed only minutes later, when the telephone rang and a cheery Southern voice said, "Good mawning, honey, it's seven o'clock," and I knew I was below the Mason-Dixon Line. Turning on the radio, I heard, "World News Roundup" and the announcement, "Mrs.

Opposite: Administrator of FCDA Val Peterson and Deputy Administrator Katherine G. Howard, at FCDA Staff College. Demonstration of Rescue Training.

Below: Destruction caused by Vicksburg tornado.

Delegates to NATO Civil Defense meeting, Palais Chaillot in Paris.

Katherine G. Howard speaking at NATO Civil Defense meeting, Palais Chaillot, Paris.

Katherine Howard, Acting Administrator of Federal Civil Defense, arrived early today from Washington on telephoned instructions from President Eisenhower in Bermuda."

After a good breakfast of ham and hominy grits, we went to call on the Governor. I gave him a message of sympathy from the President and then the State Civil Defense Director and I flew to Vicksburg.

There the situation was tragic. The tornado had struck Saturday afternoon, and the movie theatre was filled with children. The building had collapsed, killing the majority of them.

At mounds of debris, volunteers were digging desperately to free those who might be still living, and to recover the many bodies of the dead. We walked miles through rubble and broken glass. We saw streets completely filled with tumbled buildings and demolished cars, and swaying overhead, incongruously, the glittering Christmas garlands, torn and tattered. The city was plunged into mourning.

I went to visit Mercy Hospital where the wounded were being cared for. The Director, a nun, told me of their experiences in the night. For hours they had to do the best they could in darkness. "Oh, the *blessedness* of the light, when it came," she said. "There were not enough doctors. Anaesthetists were sewing up cuts and wounds. Everyone did the impossible."

Walking through the wards visiting the victims, I stopped to talk with one who had an early edition of the afternoon paper in his hand. He said feebly, "See that name there? That fellow was beside me eleven hours while we were trapped in the rubble waiting to be rescued. He just didn't make it."

As I drove with Mayor Pat Kelly through the streets which had been cleared, I heard over and over on the radio the message of sympathy I had brought from the President, his congratulations on the courage they were showing, and the assurance that federal help would be forthcoming. It seemed strange to listen to my own voice.

At the end of the day, a National Guard plane flew me to Monroe, Louisiana, a totally different world from the one of death and disaster I had just left.

Months earlier I had agreed to speak at "The Woman of the Year" banquet in Monroe, Louisiana, on that very night.

In all my rush I had stowed an evening dress in my suitcase. My speech was there too although it needed some additions in view of my activities of the past twenty-four hours.

Civil defense was not all disasters. I settled happily into the routine. So many doors in Washington were open to me: Ike's and Mamie's at the White House, the Deputy President, Sherman Adams's in the White House offices. He was undisputed as the number two power in the government. I liked and admired him; we had become good friends on the Campaign Train and Plane. Of medium height, he had a strong and wiry frame. One felt that his body was all muscle and with not an ounce of extra flesh. From time to time I went to see Sherm on civil defense or political matters. His door was always open to me, no matter how busy he was.

Sherman had the large office on the first floor of the White House, in the opposite corner from the President. Often I would sit in the chair facing Sherm. He was a smallish man in a huge chair behind a huge desk. My presence did not deter him from talking on the telephone in the most frank and open way. He must have had perfect confidence in my discretion. Sometimes a telephone caller, who wanted to "pass the time of day" in polite preliminaries, would be greeted with an abrupt "State your business." As Adams talked, I would look through the long windows on each side of his desk out onto the White House lawn. In the foreground there were beds and beds of pansies all in bloom. Or I would look at the pictures on his walls; some were by Rachel, an accomplished artist. In addition, there was a valuable collection of Currier and Ives prints of the Presidents of the United States.

Sometimes while we were talking, Tom Stevens, the President's appointment secretary, and also a Campaign Train Alumnus, would come in from an inner passage, connecting Adams' office with the President's, to discuss some matter of importance.

Adams had the complete trust of the President all the time I was in Washington. He worked tirelessly, and he wielded enormous power, and wielded it wisely and well. The nice thing, too, was that the secretaries I had known on the Campaign Train were now the secretaries to the President, to Adams and to Tom Stephens, Ike's appointment secretary; to

Jim Hagerty, the White House Press Officer, and to Mamie. If I had a cold or slight indisposition, I went to see Dr. Snyder or Dr. Tkach at the White House and was treated there. But in all the period in which I served on a full-time basis in Washington, I never missed a day for sickness.

Then, too, Leonard Hall and Bertha Adkins headed up the National Committee, and although I had resigned as a member of the Committee when I was appointed, all the staff and members were friends. Bertha gave great leadership and was instrumental in having many women appointed to high government positions. She was a real and true friend. The women in Government met regularly for lunch and were a friendly group.

My brother and his wife lived in Georgetown. John, a Democrat, had served as Assistant Secretary of the Treasury under Truman, and his wife had the distinction of being a Washington "cavedweller," her Breckenridge family having been prominent in Washington for several generations.

Then, too, there was our own group at The Westchester, all under the same roof, all part of the Administration. We would often meet informally for a cocktail, if we weren't going somewhere else, and go down to dinner together in the Westchester dining room. Life was full and stimulating, and I thrived on it.

WASHINGTON PROTOCOL

I was fortunate that the Saltonstalls and Wigglesworths were friends from home who extended the welcoming hand. In their typical warm, friendly and hospitable way, Alice and Leverett Saltonstall said they would like to give a party for me to introduce me to Washington. One could not be launched under better auspices! They suggested either a tea or a dinner party. Since Charlie was such a long-time friend of Leverett's and could share a dinner party with me, I chose that.

It was a warm spring evening. Cocktails were served in the lovely walled garden behind the Saltonstalls' Tracey Place house. They had assembled a delightful group of people, old friends like Secretary of Commerce Sinclair Weeks and Jane, General and Mrs. Persons from the White House, and others whom it would be helpful for me to know in my new civil defense position, such as Secretary of Defense Wilson and Chairman of the Senate Appropriations Committee, Senator Ferguson and others.

In my happy memories of that evening two amusing incidents stand out. One was the worried look of some of the men who were being, or had been questioned, by various Senate committees prior to confirmation. During cocktails, they clustered together at one end of the garden while Admiral White and I were having a delightful time at the other end. Every once in a while I would hear out of one ear their indignant tones and the name of Margaret Chase Smith, who had been particularly probing in her questions to them regarding stock holdings and conflict of interest.

The other was my amusement at myself as I almost took the wrong seat at the table. Since the party was given for me, I started toward the seat on Leverett's right, where I thought the guest of honor always sat. Dear Jerry Persons, my dinner partner, took my elbow and guided me to my seat beside him, further down the table. Among our mutual suppressed laughter he explained that in Washington the ranking guest always sits at the host's right, regardless of who is being honored. In this case Mrs. Wilson was the ranking guest, being the wife of the Secretary of Defense. Mrs. Weeks came next, being the wife of the Secretary of Commerce—Defense outranks Commerce because that department was created before the Department of Commerce. Fortunately this is all spelled out in Washington's Bible of Social Usage, *The Green Book*. The ranking guest must also be the first to leave a party and woe to her if she lingers too long, for high government officials work long, hard hours, 8:00 or 8:30 A.M. to 6:00 or 7:00 P.M. Then out to a dinner party at eight, night after night, and preferably home before eleven.

I was having such a good time that I was disappointed when Mrs. Wilson broke up the party soon after the gentlemen rejoined us. But it was a happy and memorable evening. After that, I learned to look at the seating chart, if there was one!

Different protocol customs kept popping up. One afternoon I was asked to "pour" at a reception. As I took my place behind the tea urn, I saw Alice Saltonstall ensconced behind the coffee urn at the other end of the table. Mrs. Burton, wife of the Supreme Court Justice, came up to me and exclaimed, "My dear, you are presiding at the wrong place!"

"What do you mean?" I asked, startled.

"Why, you are pouring *tea*! Don't you realize that in Washington, tea is outranked by coffee?"

"Well," I laughingly replied, "wherever I am, I would yield precedence to Alice Saltonstall."

I thought she was joking, but within a few days there was a long discussion in the social pages of one of the Washington papers as to the problem this posed to a hostess, one of whom had solved it by having coffee at both ends of the table! Recently, in Boston, we have decided to have *tea* at both ends of the table, as no one wants coffee!

There was another aspect of Washington protocol I found equally ridiculous. Protocol was established under George Washington, and was vested in the State Department, where it still remained in 1953. When I was there, they hadn't caught up with the fact that women had the vote, were people in their own right, and occupied important positions in the government. It was much more comfortable and easy just going along on the old assumption that women were the wives of men.

In 1953 a woman could hold one of the top official appointments in the nation on her own merits, for example; yet in official Washington she was always outranked at feminine gatherings by the *wives* of Cabinet officers.

Wishing to entertain the top-ranking women in official life soon after the Inauguration, a conscientious club president sought guidance from the Chief of Protocol at the State Department as to correct seating arrangements. There she was informed that the ladies must be introduced to the audience in the same order of precedence that applies to the offices their husbands hold, and that they must be seated in the same way.

Thus, the wife of the Secretary of State would come first, said the official arbiter, then the wife of the Secretary of the Treasury, then the wife of the Secretary of Defense, and so on. This made Mrs. Oveta Culp Hobby, a Cabinet officer in her own right, but head of the youngest department, the *last* in order of seating and protocol importance! The fact that

Oveta Culp Hobby, *herself* the Cabinet officer, was seated as of the least important of that group infuriated me.

Many of my friends in Washington were women of the press corps—in particular, Josephine Ripley, staff writer for the *Christian Science Monitor,* Betty Beale, Society Editor of *The Washington Star,* Ruth Cowan, Associated Press, and Bess Furman of the *New York Times* Washington Staff. Not only did they have interviews with me, but sometimes we had lunch together just for the fun of it. Not long before I came home to Boston I was having an off-the-record luncheon with Bess Furman and sounding off about a system in which such a seating arrangement was required. Never mind about private parties, but woman's merit in official Washington shouldn't just be on account of whom she had married. "Oh, Katie," said Bess Furman, with a gleam in her eye and a hopeful note in her voice, "are you going to take on *Washington protocol?*"

ATOMIC TEST

Just after I joined Civil Defense in March, the Administrator, Val Peterson, had gone to Nevada for the atomic test called "Operation Doorstep." A couple of two-story wooden houses were built and furnished. Mannequins representing people were in the houses. One house was 3500 feet from "ground zero" where the atomic blast would occur. It caught on fire and was destroyed. The other one was 7500 feet. The windows were blown in, but there was no fire. It proved that if the occupants of the house were in the shelter in the basement, they would be safe. If they had remained upstairs, they could have been killed by the flying glass.

The test was an "open" one, attended by the press, but the wind shifted and blew across the houses, which became so radioactive that no one could enter them at that time.

Now the Administrator proposed that I go to the next test, a "closed" one. No press, no publicity, but an important atomic test in which many government agencies were participating. This was another first for a woman.

I flew to Las Vegas, arriving in the evening two days before the test, being met, and taken to the Sands Hotel. Gambling was in full swing, but the sleeping quarters were away from the Casino. I had a cabana with living room, bedroom, and bath, and a small terrace where one could look at the huge stars overhead and the desert stretching away.

It was 3:00 A.M. on a very black night when I arose to prepare for the historic event of the test itself. At 3:30 I met my other FCDA colleagues in the casino of the hotel. It seemed incongruous to be eating breakfast in a gambling casino while the evening's entertainment was still at its height, before viewing such an awesome spectacle. The merrymarkers were apparently oblivious of the event that was about to take place, and its implications. The rest of us were not, of course.

At four, in the chilly darkness, we started our drive from Las Vegas out through the town and across the empty desert. I was comfortably clothed in a tweed sport coat, scarf, Davidow wool suit, yellow slip-on sweater, wide red belt, and under all this a dark green cotton dress. I was wearing a small red hat. On my feet were my trusty red loafers as protection against sand and cactus.

As we drove across the desert studded with Joshua trees and hemmed in on both sides by high mountains, the stars faded slowly. The sun came up just as we drove through the gates of Camp Mercury at six o'clock.

With the fifteen Congressmen attending, plus Deputy Secretary of Defense Roger Kyes, I was given a final briefing on the test that was about to take place. We were all given dark glasses to protect our eyes from the glare, and quickly took our places in the viewing area—a rock-strewn hillside some miles away from Ground Zero. Then came the last tense moments as the final seconds were counted off—minus 5, 4, 3, 2, 1...and then the glare—the blast—the heat on our faces, and the hasty exclamations. Ben Taylor of our staff came running up to me. "Take your glasses off now, Mrs. Howard, so you can *see!*"

I looked and marvelled at the white mushroom cloud billowing up and folding under, shot through with orange in the center like a ribbon running through a cloud—amazingly beautiful, and terrifyingly deadly. Then the dust cloud went rushing up to meet the atomic burst, and the resounding explosion of sound echoed from the sky and reverberated through the mountains. I was terribly shaken by the noise and the implied destruction, and so, I noticed, were the most experienced male observers.

From our elevated stand, we could see fires starting on Frenchman's Flats in some of the installations being tested, and troops marching in immediately for maneuvers on the scorched earth. By noon, when we lunched in the cafeteria, it was hot; and immediately afterwards, when I toured the test area with the members of Congress, I shed the coat, suit, and sweater and, I was comfortable in only the dark green cotton dress, the small red hat, and those same red loafers!

In this test, the Bureau of Roads participated, testing the effect of blast on various types of bridges; the Food and Drug Administration, testing effects of radiation on food and drugs. Live animals were in shelters to test the effects on them. This was the first test, too, of the Atomic Cannon. It proved the feasibility of a whole family of atomic weapons. This was 1953—only eight years after the first use of the atomic bomb. Much was still to be learned.

The next day, I was taken to see the test house of "Operation Doorstep." The radiation had decreased sufficiently so that in "Rad-Safe" clothing, I could enter.

The radiation-safe clothing consisted of a white duck coverall, white gloves, which were attached to the sleeves, so that no bare skin was exposed, a white cap on my head, and rubber shoes which came up over the trousers, and were fastened so that no dust could come in. I remarked that the only thing that seemed natural was the white gloves. Thus clad, our Civil Defense staff, Hal Goodwin, Ben Taylor, and Jack Greene, took me to the houses. But first an atomic energy indicator was fastened to my uniform to show how much radiation I received, which became a matter of record.

I clambered all through the house which was not destroyed: upstairs in the bedrooms, downstairs in the living room, dining room and kitchen, seeing with my own eyes what might happen in a typical American home, with the kind of atomic attack we envisioned at that time. Then down into the basement to see the mannequin family, in the shelter, safe and sound.

The trouble with Civil Defense was that just when you thought you had the answer to survival under certain conditions, a new and larger and greater threat would be developed with advancing technology in atomic and hydrogen bombs and the means of delivering them. It was like the Red Queen in *Alice in Wonderland,* running just as fast as she could just to stay in the same place.

After visiting the houses, I was escorted back to the decontamination depot. I was amazed. In the houses I had not seen, smelled, or felt anything unusual, yet when the wand to measure the amount of radiation I had received was carried close to me—from one ankle, up over my head and down to the other ankle—I could see the indicator move like the speedometer on a car, going up and up. Yes, there *was* radiation in the house, although there was nothing to show it was there. Fortunately I was told I was well within safety limits. They would not have taken me there otherwise. It was a warning of the most dangerous weapon in any atomic attack—an *invisible* enemy. I shed the test clothes, went back to my hotel and had a good bath, and the next day in San Francisco, a good shampoo.

XVII

DINNER AT THE WHITE HOUSE— SECURITY COUNCIL

A most memorable evening was our first invitation to dinner at the White House. It was thrilling to me. Charlie came down from Boston, and suddenly the apartment came alive. The dinner, in honor of Vice-President and Mrs. Nixon, was at eight. We rolled up under the porte cochere in plenty of time. As we stepped into the White House I thought how distinguished Charlie looked in his Dunn-tailored tails, silk hat, new silk stock, and gray mocha gloves. I wore a peacock blue satin dress, the pearls Charlie had bought for me in Paris, diamond bracelet, pin and ring, and long white kid gloves. As we came to the East Room, we were announced, "Mr. and Mrs. Charles P. Howard." Then we were escorted across the room to a place in front of the Gilbert Stuart portrait of George Washington. As we looked around, and as more people arrived, there were so many we knew—the Saltonstalls, Sherm and Rachel Adams, Jerry Persons and his wife, Senator Knowland and his wife, Helen. Each time an old friend was discovered, it was a new joy. Promptly at eight o'clock the Marine Band struck up "Hail to the Chief." The President and Mrs. Eisenhower, the Vice-President and Mrs. Nixon, entered and took their places just inside the door. On the arms of our husbands we moved across the room to shake hands with the Eisenhowers and Nixons. Charlie told Mamie what a pretty dress she had. It was a French blue brocaded gown with lace gloves to match. Mrs. Nixon looked lovely in a violet dress, which made her eyes more violet than ever. They all seemed glad to see us. Then the men, who had been given their place cards, found their dinner partners, and we followed the President and Mrs. Eisenhower down the long corridor from the East Room to the State Dining Room. As I went down the hall on the arm of Mr. Slater, the crystal chandeliers were full of rainbows, and the colorful dresses were reflected in the mirrors which lined the walls. All the while the scarlet-coated Marine Band was playing gay music.

As I entered the dining room, I looked up and admired the portrait of President Lincoln over the mantelpiece, looking down on a room filled with distinguished men and women. The dinner table was arranged in an E shape, with the Eisenhowers and Nixons sitting at the center of the straight solid line. Thus they would see everyone and everyone could see them. I was seated at the center table, as near as could be to the President and Mamie. Charlie was across from me and Mrs. Doud ("Miss Min") just down from me. Off and on during the dinner the President and Mamie would raise their glasses to us in silent toasts. Mrs. Doud said to me, "I wasn't coming down till I heard you were going to be here."

Sitting where I was, I was served first of those in our section, and had to break into all the beautiful food which was passed. No cocktails were served, but there was sherry with the soup, sauterne with the fish, claret with the filet of beef, and champagne with dessert. All through dinner the Marine Band played old favorites, and it made a background to our conversation.

The famous gold Monroe set was used with candles gleaming in the handsome candelabra, tall epergnes holding tropical fruits, and candy in low compotes. Mounds of red carnations, blue iris, and white snapdragon made a handsome table, with a white damask tablecloth, gold and white china, and gold knives, forks, and spoons.

I looked on the back of the dinner fork at my place. It said, "The President's House, 1895"; the salad fork was engraved, "The President's House, 1950." The large linen table napkins were monogrammed with "U.S." in the form of a shield. At dinner we talked about the launching of the *Nautilus*; Philip Wylie's book about Civil Defense, *Tomorrow*;

and Charlie's survey which he had made for Governor Herter on the problems of the ageing; golf and Augusta. It was interesting.

At the end of the dinner, the President and Mamie rose, and then we did too. The ladies went to the Red Room where Mamie saw that her Mother and Mrs. Woodrow Wilson were seated on one of the sofas. The rest of us stood around in small groups and chatted. The gentlemen were in the Green Room with the President. There Charlie talked with Stanley High, whose wife had been Charlie's dinner partner, and Senator Bricker and Leverett Saltonstall.

As we walked in to join the gentlemen, Hazel Markel, who had a very popular television show in Washington, said she was sure she had had, in Bobby Cutler, the wittiest and most entertaining dinner partner present. Mrs. High said she would dispute that—she was sure that Mr. Howard would take the honors.

After our dinner partners claimed us again, we returned to the East Room where gold chairs had been set up for a musical program by "The Men of Song." It was light music, with spirituals, and all through the "Noah" piece, a contemporary spiritual, the President's foot was tapping and keeping time.

When we said good-bye to the Eisenhowers and Nixons, I told the President what a marvelous time I had had and how much I had enjoyed the music. "By golly," he said, "I wish there had been a lot more verses to that Noah song!" Mamie said, "Come over and see me soon, Katherine."

As we stepped from the East Room into the hall, groups of people were standing about; Sherm Adams was talking to Congressman McConnell. Sherm turned to me and said, "This is a most capable, but stubborn and hard-to-convince man, Katherine." I said, "Well, you both have a lot in common." "Touché," exclaimed McConnell.

And so home and to bed.

About a week later we were invited to a reception at the White House. As we came down the receiving line—Charlie in white tie again—the President said, "Charlie, your wife is working you pretty hard, isn't she!"

Now it was June in Washington. Congress was struggling feverishly to pass the appropriation bills; the White

House was pressing for the passage of the President's legislative program; there was a flurry of entertaining before the exodus of wives and children for the summer.

The great magnolia trees with glossy dark green leaves were lighted by the big waxy fragrant blossoms. Everywhere roses were in bloom, and the trees and foliage seemed more lush than ever because of the heavy rains in May.

By the end of June the social pace in Washington changed. There were no more official parties. Entertaining was more informal and without protocol. I moved from our apartment at the Westchester to my brother's house on P Street in Georgetown, after my sister-in-law and the children left for New Hampshire.

Our life in Marblehead went on too. Charlie and Herbert and The Cat were there with Jennie and Steve to look after them.

Charlie went to Boston and Cambridge every day. I would arrive Friday night. The air was so delicious after the heat and air-conditioning of Washington. On Sunday night during buffet supper at the Eastern Yacht Club, a taxi would come to pick me up. I would kiss Charlie good-bye and quietly slip away.

Sometimes when I considered my schedule, I would say to myself, "The only way to get through this schedule is *not* to think about it!"

One of the sobering events of June was "Operation Alert." This was a simulated attack on the United States by atom bombs. It was the first continental alert to test the defense warning system of the U.S. and Canada.

The FCDA staff went from our Washington offices to our secret Emergency Headquarters which then had the code name of "High Point" and which we shared with the Office of Defense Mobilization under the Director, Arthur Fleming. Although it was the fourteenth of June, it was cold and rainy. The hills around looked dark and gloomy, as if a disaster had already taken place. The next morning I observed guards outside the iron fence which surrounded our Headquarters, busily engaged in looking for something. When I inquired, they said, "Snakes."

In most cities the exercises began at 10:00 A.M., when the

warning network and Civil Defense organization began functioning. They were brought into play by the Air Defense Command "Alert." "Strong movement of unidentified aircraft over United States and Canada, heading south." When this radio warning was received, the ominous wail of sirens was heard. In New York, Boston, Washington, vehicular traffic came to a halt; pedestrians were hustled to cover in subways, office buildings or air-raid shelters.

The instant after the warning was received Val Peterson and I spoke with the President in the bomb shelter at the White House. Mamie was with him. The President was in contact with us all day by closed-circuit television.

Soon the grim figures began to appear on the immense map in the Situation Room. A "report" went up when a city was first reported hit. Later a confirmation was listed, then came the statistics of the number killed and injured, the availability of food, medical supplies, doctors, and nurses. These estimates were based on the size of the bomb. From tests, it had been learned what the ratio would be between the size of the bomb and the size of the area of total devastation from ground zero (where the bomb hit), to the limit of damage by fire and blast. In a city with dense population it would of course, be much larger than if it fell in the country. We knew that in a nuclear war cities would be prime targets.

Boston appeared on the map. It had been hit and there were estimates of four hundred and fifty thousand casualties. Reports came in of the remedial action Boston was taking: emergency hospitals set up, mass feeding centers, improvised shelters, canteens in operation. The position board showed ground zero, where the bomb fell, the radius of total damage, of fire damage, number of casualties, action taken. I was glad to see that our house in Marblehead, in which we had built and equipped a bomb shelter, was beyond the range of blast and fire. Forty cities in all participated, including New York, Washington, San Francisco, Philadelphia, and Chicago.

In New York, it was reported, fog cast an eerie mask over deserted streets. Taxis, buses and other vehicles were parked along the curb as their occupants hastily ducked into subways and office buildings during the ten-minute alert. Twelve thousand communications workers were on duty, charting casualties, equipment losses and emergency conditions. General Huebner, State Director, stated that New Yorkers' attitude showed that civilians had an appreciation and an understanding of the peril under which we live.

In Washington the streets were deserted too, except for policemen and white-helmeted Civil Defense wardens standing at their guardposts. The entire White House staff of nearly three hundred sought shelter, as did the Federal and District Government staffs. The "bomb," five times more powerful than the one at Hiroshima, was "dropped" over Eleventh and F Streets, N.W.

One could not be at the nerve center of a nationwide operation, with such full-scale participation, without being deeply moved. I felt I should try even harder to warn Americans of measures to be taken for survival if we should be attacked. I always stated the threat, and quoted President Eisenhower's words that an army cannot go on fighting if the civilian population does not have the will to survive.

I was conscious of the people who said, "I don't want to bother. If the bomb comes, I would rather be dead" and of the attitude so well expressed by a member of the Sulgrave Club in Washington. I had been asked to speak there at a dinner given in my honor. Charlie came down to share it with me and my speech went well. Then in the question period a member rose and asked, "*Why* do we have to have Civil Defense? I don't want to even *think* about the atom bomb!" There was a slight gasp from the audience, but when I answered her question, there was spontaneous applause. I said, "I know the whole subject is distasteful. But we have learned from England's example in the blitz that people can stand terrific bombing and emerge alive, because they were educated in first aid, fire-fighting, and rescue work. We remember the story of the woman who was saved from the rubble of a house which had collapsed on her. She was asked, 'Where is your husband?' Her reply, 'Fighting in France, the bloody coward!'"

To increase public awareness of the threat of our atomic age, I decided to invite leading women as my personal guests to witness the "Rescue Street" demonstration at the FCDA Staff College in Olney Maryland. This was the culmination of the two weeks' course in rescue techniques given there every month, with adults from all over the country sent by industrial plants, hospitals, cities, and towns.

For their training and exercises a realistic block of bombed and fire damaged buildings lined "Rescue Street," "Disaster Street" and "Survival Avenue."

Peterson approved my idea of inviting women leaders. We were both firm believers in the old cliché that the three best methods of communications were telephone, telegraph, and tell-a-woman.

We asked a distinguished group. Many came out of friendship for me, others out of curiosity, but they came, with Mrs. Nixon, the wife of the Vice-President, as the guest of honor.

After dinner, served in the cafeteria of the main college building, we went out of doors to Rescue Street. By now it was dark, which made the simulated bomb attack all the more realistic and terrifying—sirens screamed, fires raged, hoses poured water on the burning buildings, hysterical cries came from the rubble of the crumpled houses, where volunteers, made up with wounds and blood stains, moaned and screamed for help. The trained graduates of the staff college rushed to the rescue, fighting the flames, freeing people buried in the rubble, carrying away the badly wounded on stretchers, setting up emergency kitchens, and feeding the walking wounded.

Watching with keen attention was Oveta Culp Hobby, Secretary of the new Department of Health, Education and Welfare and I saw Senator Margaret Chase Smith nod with approval. Also observing were Congresswomen Marguerite Church; Cecile Hardin; Ruth Thompson; Lenore Sullivan; Vera Buchanan; and Edith Nourse Rogers. Ivy Priest came, and Dorothy Houghton; The President's Secretary, Ann Whitman, who rarely went anywhere; Mary Jane McCaffree, Mrs. Eisenwhower's social secretary; and Dr. Martha Eliot, Director of the Children's Bureau.

I was especially pleased that my college classmate and friend, Kay Ascher Engle, President of the National Council of Jewish Women, came down from New York to be there. Others were Miss Nooman Maise, President of the National Council of Negro Women; Mrs. William Dalton, President of

283

the National Council of Catholic Women; Mrs. Oscar Ahlgren, President of the General Federation of Women's Clubs. They represented literally millions of women at home. Peterson was impressed. He said, "Katherine, where did you get all these women?" As we also had many members of the press and radio and television, we were sure of the publicity which we needed, for the public was still a long way from accepting Civil Defense as a way of life.

The success of the women's visit to Olney in June was an incentive for the formation of the National Civil Defense Women's Advisory Council. We included Margaret Hickey, of the *Ladies Home Journal*, the heads of all the national women's organizations who had previously attended. Governor Peterson approved our plans for a two-day conference in October.

Eisenhower showed his approval by allowing us the use of the Indian Treaty Room for our first conference and by promising to open the meeting. It was a proud moment for me when I escorted him in and introduced him to that distinguished group of women leaders. In welcoming them he emphasized in firm military terms that Civil Defense was an essential part of national defense. In the two days that followed there were top-level briefings on the threat, enemy potentials and civil defense measures being taken. At our Conference for National Women Leaders, forty-six heads of organizations attended, representing 25 million women! We stressed the importance of a shelter in each home—who but the woman would see that it was stocked, and that supplies of canned goods, water, etc., were maintained? I was confident that the women who came to our conference would have a sobering appreciation of what a bomb attack would mean to their own community, and what they could do about it. At the conclusion Mamie received the ladies at tea at the White House.

However, more and more, I was beginning to realize that I was part of a man's world. I was accepted; I loved the intellectual challenge; but I was beginning to realize that I rarely saw women or participated in their activities.

The contrast was revealed to me one day at lunch with Jane Weeks, wife of the Secretary of Commerce, and another friend. They had a project for the afternoon; they were going to drive to Arlington, Virginia, in search of a particular shade of sheer nylon stockings. I was going back to my office for a staff meeting, a review of a speech I was to make, followed by a radio-TV recording with a Congressman. I wouldn't have changed places for the world. In the evening we all met at a dinner party given in honor of the Herman Phlegers, who had just returned from the Geneva Conference where Mr. Phleger, Legal Counsel, Department of State, had accompanied Secretary of State Dulles.

Because my working hours were almost exclusively with men, I took every opportunity to lunch with women friends. One day I had to leave a luncheon a little early to go to a meeting of the Interagency Manpower Policy Committee, as FCDA's Representative.

This Committee was made up of members on the Deputy or Assistant Secretary level of the "claimant agencies" on manpower in a wartime emergency. It was my job on the Committee to see that Civil Defense was included in any manpower program for full mobilization. I had to study many documents in order to hold my own in the forthright discussions of this group of top minds with long-time government experience. I was the only woman member.

General Hershey of Selective Services, was a member—a delightful man with forceful and picturesque language—he participated fully in the discussions but he said: "You can make all the plans you want to, but if we have a war, I shall get the men I need, regardless of your plans." I was fighting for Civil Defense for we knew that any future full-scale war would be against civilians.

It was reported to me that one of the men on the committee said, "Mrs. Howard is like a fresh breeze to a bunch of tired bureaucrats sitting around the table."

In September, my sister-in-law Elizabeth Graham and the children returned from New London, New Hampshire, and I moved back to our apartment at the Westchester. After the summer at my brother's, I realized more than ever how little I cared for that apartment, even though for me it was the best possible solution. My apartment had a kitchen so I could cook breakfast. There was a grocery store in the basement of the Westchester so one could easily buy what was needed in a few minutes. I could have dinner in the Westchester dining room, where there were usually friends, or I could have dinner sent up to my apartment. There was everything to make me comfortable. But my chief feeling about the apartment was that it was *sterile*. As I stepped off the elevator on my floor and walked down the long corridor to my door, there was no feeling of coming home. I dreaded putting my key in the door and walking into an empty apartment. Always before I had been the center of a home. There were always people around—husband, children. There was always someone concerned with my comings and goings. Jennie and The Cat would great me at the front door when I came home; The Cat would rub against my ankles and purr; Jennie would bustle around, full of the events of the day, crises and catastrophes barely averted due to her quick action and good sense! I would be home to welcome Charlie when he returned. . . .

There were always plants and flowers, cats and kittens, white mice, alligators, chameleons—whatever the children were interested in at the moment—even Easter chicks in a Beacon Street bathroom. . . .

Now I walked into dark, empty, lifeless rooms. Fortunately I was out a great deal, at cocktail parties or dinners. As the dinner parties began at eight o'clock, there was time to come home, take a bath, a brief rest, before going out again, but still, there was that sinking of the heart as I walked down a long corridor to a lonely apartment.

Then, too it was curious, but as I drove to work each morning in a taxi, the houses I passed seemed to be accusing me of turning my back on family life. To be sure, my children were grown. Peggy was married and away in New York. Herbert was a senior at Harvard College and living in Kirkland House. But behind the doors and windows of those houses I could picture mothers cooking breakfasts and getting their husbands off to work and the children off to school. It seemed the normal way of life.

As we came to the end of August, Val Peterson left for an extended tour to inspect Civil Defense installations in Great Britain, the Scandinavian countries, and Germany. Thus I became Acting Administrator for the next month.

Toward the end of September, Ike returned from a six week vacation in Colorado. He was to attend "Governors' Day"

286

at the Springfield, Massachusetts, Fair, and then go on to a mammoth dinner in Boston. A telephone call came from the White House inviting me to fly with Eisenhower in the Presidential Plane, after which a card arrived saying:

I am informed that
The President of The United States
has invited
Mrs. Katherine Howard
to accompany him on his flight to
Boston, Massachusetts
on
Monday, September 21, 1953
in the Presidential aircraft, The "Columbine"
departing from
MATS, Washington National Airport
Washington, D.C.

The President, by custom, is the last member of the official party to board his airplane before take-off, and the first to leave after landing. Consequently, it will be greatly appreciated if you will be in your seat at 8:30 A.M.

Others who were invited to go were Sinclair and Jane Weeks, Cabot Lodge, Senator Aiken of Vermont, and Sherman Adams.

Wearing a brown suit, a soft hat of a lighter shade, and a yellow and white checkered tie, the President stepped aboard and we were airborne promptly at nine o'clock. Mamie did not come. It seemed like the early campaign days to be flying with Ike again.

Governors' Day at Springfield brought all the New England Governors together. It was an annual event, but made more significant by the President's appearance. At 10:59, the *Columbine* touched down at Westover Air Force Base. The President went nimbly down the steps to be greeted by Governor Herter and Senator Saltonstall, as well as J. Loring Brooks, chairman of the reception at the Fair. "Hello, Chris, good to see you," was Ike's greeting to the Governor—he shook hands with the others, then made a quick review of the troops drawn up at the side of the ramp. Then by motorcade through Chicopee Falls, and downtown Springfield, with crowds lining the streets—to the Exposition Grounds, for a luncheon with the Governors and G.O.P. leaders. My chief recollection is stepping along briskly just behind the President to the tune of "Hail to the Chief."

After an informal talk at the Coliseum following lunch, it was on to Boston on the *Columbine*. This was Ike's first visit to Boston since his election, and he would speak from the same platform in the Boston Garden where he had made his final speech of the campaign in 1952. It was an All-New England Rally with the leading Republican speakers from neighboring states, and with a sell-out crowd of five thousand people. Governor Herter, the genial toastmaster, wittily introduced the speakers who preceded the President and one could feel the tremendous enthusiasm.

The message the President brought was a serious one, for this was his first public reference to the Hydrogen Bomb, and the fact that the Russians possessed one too. He said: "We know the enemies of freedom to be equipped with the most terrible weapons of destruction. We free people will join our efforts with any men truly ready to lift the threat of catastrophe from the world." The President's grim words caused immediate speculation that the administration might be considering a new tax levy to meet the threat posed by the Russian possession of the Hydrogen Bomb.

The seriousness of this note did not quell the ardor or enthusiasm of the gathering. Ike was given an ovation at the end of his nationally televised speech.

We left the Boston Garden amid shouts and cheers, and returned to the *Columbine* for the flight back to Washington, where we arrived a little after midnight.

Two days later I was in the Cabinet Room at the White House participating in a momentous discussion of plans for the safety of the United States. The newspapers for September 24, 1953, carried this notice:

The President's Appointment List
10:00 A.M.: The National Security Council plus the Army, Navy and Air Force Secretaries; Mrs.

Katherine Howard, Deputy Civil Defense Director; Defense Mobilizer Arthur Fleming; and six special Administration Consultants on continental defense.

No woman official had ever attended a National Security Council Meeting, but as Val Peterson was away and I was Acting Administrator, I represented our Agency. The night before the meeting I took home with me all the papers which were not "classified" and studied into the night. This was a momentous meeting. Our Executive Assistant Administrator accompanied me as staff—I don't think he liked it too much when I took my place at the Cabinet table and he sat along the wall behind me. Everyone was in place, when at exactly 10:00 o'clock the door from the President's Office opened. General Robert Cutler, Secretary for National Security Affairs, said—"The President!" We all stood as he entered, then took our seats. I noted that the President sat in the middle of the oval table, with the Vice-President sitting opposite him; the Secretary of State, Mr. Dulles, was on the President's right; and the Secretary of Defense, Mr. Wilson, on his left; and next to him the Chairman of the Joint Chiefs of Staff, Admiral Radford. Sitting near me were Admiral Strauss, Chairman of the Atomic Energy Commission; Harold Stassen, Director of the Foreign Operations Administration; Mr. Dodge, Budget Director; and at the end of the table, Allen Dulles, head of the CIA.

The first business was to hear Allen Dulles' intelligence briefing. He made use of charts—his presentation was clear and concise. The pace of the meeting was rapid, but discussion was frank, and the presentation of opposing points of view was encouraged. The President listened intently, sometimes doodling as he listened, but with no lack of attention. Eisenhower believed in policy planning—it was a technique he had become accustomed to as Commander In Chief in Europe. He believed in the responsible heads of government meeting regularly to give and exchange advice, to become accustomed to working together, to help formulate policy for the President's ultimate decisions. Under General Cutler's direction the National Security Council became as important, if not more important, than the Cabinet. I was fascinated with the ready give-and-take of the President and the Cabinet members, and Agency heads. I even made a very brief statement from the Civil Defense point of view. It was reassuring to have so many people I knew around the Cabinet table, to see my good friends Sherman Adams and Mack Rabb smiling encouragingly at me from their places just inside the door to the President's Office. When the meeting was concluded, Mack said—"You really had the whole show today, Katherine!"

A newspaper account in the *Holyoke Transcript*, September 24, 1953, had this to say:

Ike In Huddle With Top Defense Staff

President Eisenhower summoned his top defense advisors to the White House today to discuss the momentous problem of what the nation can do to meet a possible H-bomb attack.

Members of the National Security Council, secretaries of the Armed Forces, the deputy Civil Defense Director, Defense Mobilizer, and special consultants on Continental defense were ordered to the top secret meeting.

On the agenda were various proposals advanced during the past few months for establishing a strong air defense network to blunt any massive Russian air attack against United States cities and at the same time to unleash a decisive counter blow.

The conferees had the heavy task of weighing the almost prohibitive cost of an air tight system against the administration drive to slash government spending, to balance the budget and cut taxes. Lending particular urgency to the conference is the awesome knowledge that Russia has now exploded a hydrogen bomb device that presumably will give it the power to launch a devastating attack against the U.S.

Mrs. Katherine Howard, Civil Defense Director, said in a TV interview Wednesday night that Soviet development of the H-bomb "startled us" and brought "a turning point in our history." She urged a bigger civil defense appropriation in the next Congress.

On December 8, 1953, the President made an historic address to the United Nations Assembly, laying before the peoples of the world the true facts of the age of peril in which we found ourselves. Ike said:

> Atomic bombs today are more than twenty-five times as powerful as the weapons with which the atomic age dawned, while hydrogen weapons are in the ranges of millions of tons of TNT equivalent.
>
> Today the United States stockpile of atomic weapons, which, of course, increases daily, exceeds by many times the total equivalent of the total of all bombs and all shells that came from every plane and every gun in every theatre in World War II.
>
> A single air group, whether afloat or land based, can now deliver to any reachable target a destructive cargo exceeding in power all the bombs that fell on Britian in World War II.
>
> The free world, at least dimly aware of these facts, has naturally embarked on a large program of warning and defense systems. That program will be accelerated and expanded. . . .

The seriousness of his message had added significance to me as I heard it on the radio in our secret Emergency Command Post where I was making an inspection visit.

During this period world leaders were attempting to work out agreements, based on President Eisenhower's proposals, to harness the atom for peaceful purposes; and the President continued his measures to alert and prepare the American people.

He called a White House Conference of Mayors. The briefings they received were unique in American history. Civil Defense played an important part in the Conference. To them he said:

> Along with our military defense and retaliatory forces, Civil Defense and Defense Mobilization are vital parts of the Nation's total defense. Together they stand as a strong deterrent to war.
>
> It would be unwise to neglect our Civil Defnese Mission because our total defense is incomplete and

meaningless without reliable and responsible home defense. Survival cannot be guaranteed merely with a capacity for reprisal. Equally important is our ability to recover. This means staying power and endurance beyond that ever before required of this nation or any nation.

In Europe General Eisenhower had seen defeat and disaster where civilian morale crumbled—he had seen steadfastness and strength in England which withstood incredible assaults in World War II to hold the fort until America entered the war, and the tide was turned toward victory. It was in this atmosphere that I carried on my Civil Defense tasks with support from the very highest level, the President.

XVIII

NATO—LADY READING

When Peterson returned from his European Civil Defense tour, he said to me, "I would like to send you to the NATO Civil Defense meeting in Paris in November. Would you like to go?"

"Yes, of course," I replied.

"I'll make you Chief Delegate," he said, "and I'll send Colonel Chambers as Alternate Delegate. He knows the ropes."

Thus I entered upon my third area of responsibility as Deputy Administrator—(1) Congressional Liaison; (2) Women's Activities; (3) NATO affairs.

My first introduction to NATO had been in the summer of 1951, when Charlie, Peggy, and I were returning from a pleasure trip to Europe. As we boarded the *America* at Le Havre, I looked inside my passport. There was a small blue slip with a picture of General Eisenhower, and an inscription underneath saying, "Peace Through Strength." Inside there was a short account of NATO. This blue slip was placed in the passports of all Americans returning from Europe in 1951.

General Eisenhower was then the Supreme Commander of Allied Powers Europe. There was already talk of Eisenhower as the Republican nominee for President. But certainly, as I looked at that little blue slip, it never occurred to me that I would be part of an Eisenhower Administration, or that I would represent our country on a NATO Committee.

The next time I saw that blue slip was when I went to exchange my old passport for a new Special passport to go to a NATO meeting as the first woman from any country to serve on a NATO Committee.

The North Atlantic Treaty Organization—NATO to English-speaking nations, OTAN to French-speaking ones—came into being as a mutual security pact after World War II. While Western Europe was still prostrate following that war, Russia, by military might and Communist tactics, took over control of Poland, Hungary, Rumania, Bulgaria, Czechoslovakia, and East Germany. Remembering how the European nations had succumbed to Hitler, one by one, the Western European nations banded together in a defensive pact for mutual protection against the Communist threat.

Lord Izmay, Winston Churchill's great friend, who had served as Chief Staff Officer to the Prime Minister, and Minister of Defense in World War II, was the first Secretary-General of NATO. He had an international staff. In appointing him Chruchill had said, "Well, now, Pug, I hope you won't find that you have to put Great Britain absolutely at the bottom of the heap all the time!"

When Lord Izmay reported to NATO, he called on General Eisenhower at SHAPE, who said, "I wish you'd get something going on Civil Defense." As a result, a Civil Defense Committee composed of the Civil Defense Directors of the fourteen NATO member nations was formed.

The first NATO Civil Defense meeting was held in Paris in February, 1953, just before I joined FCDA. It was the second one, in November, 1953, which I was now to attend as Chief U. S. Delegate, with Colonel Chambers as alternate. I traveled under the auspices of the Department of State, although the staff work was done by our organization. When I returned, I reported to Val Peterson and to Livingston Merchant, then Assistant Secretary of State for European Affairs.

Peterson suggested that before the NATO meeting in Paris, I confer with the Civil Defense officials in The Netherlands and in Great Britain to learn about their methods, and to exchange Civil Defense information. I took the American Export Line to Cannes, ten days at sea instead of five hours by air—spent a cold, rainy late-October morning in the shuttered resort city, took the noon train to Paris, arriving at midnight, then to the Meurice Hotel.

The next day I checked in with the American Embassy, and they advised that I take the train to Amsterdam. There was an American couple in my compartment. They recognized me by my face and voice from television at the Republican National Convention of 1952. They were interested in politics, had been to the Inauguration, and they gave me a good guide book about The Netherlands which was very helpful. Some diplomatic-looking Dutch gentlemen were with us part of the way and they said that the proper tip for all my luggage—four pieces—was one guilder, the equivalent of twenty-five cents. This proved to be true. In Amsterdam I had a free day, and I took great pleasure in seeing the newly cleaned and restored Rembrandts, almost startling in their freshness.

Then on to The Hague where my official duties began. Mr. Schneider, a secretary of the Embassy met me, took me to the Hotel des Indes, and outlined the program for the next day. In the morning we went first to the American Embassy to call on the Acting Ambassador, then to the Holland Civil Defense Headquarters to meet Mr. Franken, the Director. He offered us coffee. We were accompanied, Schneider and I, by Colonel Hoffman, assistant Military Attaché at the Embassy and a charming man who was extremely interested in the whole day's proceedings. Mr. Franken gave me a well-worked-out and well-presented picture of civil defense in Holland. He knew exactly what they were doing, why they were doing it, and the reasons for some of the things they were not doing.

We proceeded from there to call on Mr. Kloosterman, the Ministerial Representative of Civil Defense. A maid brought coffee and we were offered cigarettes. Then Mr. Kloosterman sat rather pompously behind his desk and talked from notes about President Eisenhower and Civil Defense, and the moral and organizational valued of C.D. At the conclusion, he asked us all to lunch. There was an omelette for the first course, sole meuniere for the second, with salad, and with white wine; and cheese for dessert. Then we had coffee in the lounge. I asked Mr. Kloosterman for a copy of his remarks.

Next we drove seventy-five miles to see the Civil Defense Staff College, where the course of study was explained, and where we saw two official Dutch Civil Defense films. One showed the work done by C.D. in the spring floods. The other film was an official Dutch Civil Defense film, "The Lesson of

London," depicting the great devastation Rotterdam suffered, when in one day the city was leveled by Nazi bombs. The people of Holland said to their government, "Give up, give up, we can take no more." The Government capitulated, and the Nazi occupation of Holland began.

The film showed that London was subjected to even greater bombing, but survived because of the Royal Air Force and because the people were trained in Civil Defense. It was amazing to me that this film should be part of the training course at the Netherlands Civil Defense Staff College.

We were offered Bols gin or sherry, which I took, and then Mr. Franken drove me back to the hotel, talking to me of the hardships during the German occupation of his country, when food was so scarce that he had to eat his precious tulip bulbs to keep from starvation.

Mr. Schneider was giving the party of the season that evening with all the diplomatic corps as guests. I went briefly. Then an Embassy car came and drove me through the cold and fog and rain to the Hook of Holland where I took a boat for the crossing to England. I had expected to fly, but the Embassy wisely advised against it and booked a stateroom for me on the boat. I laid me down and slept till I was awakened at 6:30 A.M. by a steward with tea and biscuits. We were approaching England, also shrouded in fog. Breakfast was served on the train to London.

I had been invited by Pauline Fenno, of Boston and London, to visit her and Lady Reading at their manor house in Sussex. Pauline had been active in Civil Defense all through the blitz, and Lady Reading was the leading figure in the world in regard to the participation of women in Civil Defense. I accepted with alacrity. From Victoria Station in London I took the train to Lewes, in Sussex, where I was met by Miss Fenno in her Jaguar, and we drove through typical English countryside with rolling "downs" (small rounded hills). Finally I looked ahead and said, "What a delightful place that is!" and Miss Fenno said it was theirs. She and Lady Reading (the Dowager Marchioness of Reading) lived together in Lewes and in London and worked together in Civil Defense. We drove into a courtyard with rounded cobblestones, and thence to the manor house.

The butler greeted us at the door and took my bags upstairs to a marvelous big guestroom. It had a vaulted ceiling, walls two feet thick with windows in the recesses, twin beds with tufted headboards, a beautiful tapestry behind each bed, great tiger skins on the floor from the days when Lord Reading was Viceroy of India, a modern dressing table, antique desk, two bedside tables piled high with books, a great chest, wing chair by the fireplace, and settle. There was a small radiator and two electric heaters going full tilt. The color scheme was peacock blue and apricot, and the bedsheets and pillowcases were apricot color.

Miss Fenno said, "Would you like to be unpacked?" I hesitated a minute. She said, "We always do—only some people don't like to be unpacked." I said I'd be delighted. I hate to unpack and pack, and so at Lewes and at London I didn't have to, and when I reached the Meurice and had to go straight to the Conference, I asked to have my bags unpacked and the concierge looked so pleased and happy as if here was a lady who knew how to live, the proper clientele for the Meurice.

Miss Fenno said, "Put on your oldest clothes." So I put on a blue cashmere slip-on sweater and the navy blue cardigan sweater from Bermuda with my gray flannel skirt and red "loafers" and the Graham plaid scarf from Edinburgh and a tweed coat. By now it was raining. Pauline Fenno and I started out of doors, when in came Lady Reading from planting bulbs. She had a bandana handkerchief tied over her head, heavy jacket, and skirt and shoes, heavy dark apron over her skirt. "Come on," said she, "and I'll show you my garden." Then—"Have you got proper shoes?" "For an American," I said, "pretty good," showing her my shoes. She smiled and nodded, still a bit uncertain of me, and she apologized for her appearance. She had just planted a thousand bulbs. "Are you interested in gardens?" said she. "Yes," I said. "What are those sticks down there?" "Ah," said she, and we were off. "Those sticks down there" were rosemary, a new rosemary hedge she had had set out, with forsythia, then rosemary again, then fuchsias along the roadside. "This will make a nice screen for you along the road," I said. "Yes, but better still," she replied, "it will make something lovely for the people who pass along the road to look at."

Swanborough Manor was in existence, or a small part of it

was, in 600 and King Alfred wrote his will there.

The main part was built in 1400 and my bedroom was the upper part of the great hall; a floor had been put across, making the living room below me and the bedroom above.

So then she and I toured the gardens. Amazingly, gardenias will grow out of doors there. Many, many flowers were in bloom. Like all proper English gardens it had a kitchen garden, too, with beautiful head lettuce and strawberries growing on the plants and asparagus in "feather" in November, a lovely color; deep green parsley and great yellow chrysanthemums too.

She said, "How nice you like gardens. Most Americans are just interested in hothouses." "So now," she said, "we'll go in and have a drink." I had arrived at noon and by now it was about one o'clock.

We went into the big living room with a bright fire burning, sofa in front of it, long bench before it covered with needlepoint, deep chairs on either side, the walls mostly booklined, flowers all about, chintz curtains at the windows. A maid brought in a tray with fixings for drinks and two other guests were there. Lady Reading quickly changed to a dark blue pleated skirt, white shirtwaist, navy blue cardigan sweater. By this time we were all easy, and good friends.

Lady Reading was one of the truly great women, or people, in the world, not in the slightest because of her title, but because of her mind and heart and spirit. I wish I could remember the things she told me, every word, for she talked to me from her heart, and from her vast experience.

Her husband died in 1936. He had been a great jurist, Viceroy of India, Lord Warden of Cinq Ports with a large castle shaped like the Tudor Rose. They had lived, too, in Deames Castle. These two castles are now depicted on the placemats they use at meals.

In 1938, the British cabinet, fearing war, asked Lady Reading to organize the women of Great Britain. She organized the Welfare Service of Civil Defense, and an organization called the Women's Voluntary Services. She was still the head, and could call out one million women. The members were amazing, but her character, the standards she had set, her humility and simplicity, her deep religious feeling, the way she had welded noblewoman and charwoman into a team working together happily, was a major achievement.

After lunch, Pauline Fenno suggested a nap for me then at 3:30 she and I drove off to see the countryside. It was raining hard and was very cold. I had my sealskin coat and was thankful for it. But it seemed right for it to be raining. We drove through villages straight out of storybooks, passed Ann of Cleves' house, finally came to the ruins of Pevensey Castle, a huge fortified castle from the fourteenth century, now just a shell. Then we went into an ancient house, now an antique shop, where once Edward the Sixth had stayed, and with a concealed entrance into the attic where the smugglers once hid their wares.

As we drove away, a herd of cattle came into the village square and went ahead of us toward home in the gathering dusk. In the medieval setting it seemed hard to think of modern wars having touched England.

Back to Swanborough through the rain, talking Civil Defense in Massachusetts and in the United States, for Pauline Fenno was the woman head of C.D. in Massachusetts until she resigned in 1953. Lady Reading had changed into a shirtmaker sports dress, and we had, Pauline and I, a warming whiskey by the fire. Then upstairs for a hot bath. Lady Reading suggested that I wear a tea gown for dinner. I had brought along a velvet one, just right for what they wore. We had grouse with bread sauce and red wine and a delicious treacle tart which didn't taste a bit like molasses. After dinner we talked and talked. Lady Reading and I talked to each other with complete understanding.

At bedtime they suggested that I ring for my breakfast whenever I wanted it. There was a fresh hot water bottle in my bed and ·I snuggled down cozily for a long sleep, until about ten next morning. A morning paper came up with my breakfast tray. At eleven-thirty I came downstairs. Lady Reading had been hard at work all morning on letters. She has a dictaphone machine which she takes about with her.

There was a guest for lunch and about three-thirty we all left for London. They had asked me to stay with them there, too, although I had a reservation at the Savoy, which they cancelled for me. We drove along the coast in what we would call a line storm with great surf and driving rain, through Brighton with its beautiful regency houses.

About six-thirty we arrived at Smith Square in London, a square of small, perfect houses around a bombed-out church called Anne's Footstool.

Next morning it developed that Colonel Chambers, who was going to make plans for me in England, was leaving in ten minutes for France, and that I had been misinformed as to the date of the NATO meeting. I was scheduled to leave England on Tuesday, and the meeting began Tuesday morning at 10:30. However, we got busy. The Embassy put me on the night train and ferry which would arrive in Paris at 9:00 o'clock with an hour to spare the next morning.

Lady Reading had arranged Monday for me, which included visiting the Women's Voluntary Services Headquarters, being told about their welfare work and shown filmstrips used for training; lunching with Lady Lucas-Tooth, whose husband was Parlimentary Secretary for Civil Defense; to the Home Office to see Sir Arthur Hutchinson, Permanent Civil Service Under-Secretary for Civil Defense, and finally back to W.V.S. Headquarters where General Irwin, the British representative to the NATO Civil Defense Committee, came to see me and showed me the agenda for the next day's meeting. He was going on the same Paris train ferry I was going to take.

So back to 9 Smith Square for dinner at 7:30 instead of 8:00. My bags had been packed and were downstairs. The Embassy car came for me, and Pauline Fenno and Lady Reading went to the station and saw me off. The train left at nine. Breakfast was served on the train.

On arrival in Paris, I went to my hotel. There was no word from Colonel Chambers, so I took a taxi to the Palais de Chaillot, which is on a hill, just beyond the Eiffel Tower, and in front are fountains and a long flight of steps. The taxi had left me at the wrong entrance.

I clambered up many steps, finally arrived at the proper door, was passed by the guard, and walked into the lobby alone. There was Colonel Chambers having a good time with all his old friends. He greeted me, and introduced me as his "boss." Soon the bell rang, and we took our places at the round table, Colonel Chambers and I side by side. The countries were arranged alphabetically around the table, according to the French nomenclature. Thus as "Etats Unis" we were high up in the alphabetical order, sitting just ahead of

"Grande Bretagne," whose chief delegate, General Irwin, I had met through Lady Reading. The President of the Committee was Mr. Labourie of France, the Secretary, Peter Anninos of Greece, Oxford-educated with a pronounced Oxford accent. They sat together at the head of the table, with the flags of all the NATO countries behind them.

The proceedings were conducted in either French or English. Earphones were at each place. You could turn on the French or English translation. All of the delegates spoke English except the delegates of France and Belgium. At one time, while the Turkish delegate was struggling in English, General Irwin whispered to me, "I wish he'd speak in French, and then I could get a good translation. As it is, I can't make out *what* he is saying."

The countries represented were Belgium, Canada, France, Greece, Denmark, Italy, United States, United Kingdom, Norway, Holland, Turkey. Portugal is a member, but was not represented.

In anticipation of this meeting questionnaires on various subjects had been sent out. For some reason, all this is classified information. Then the questionnaires are studied and summarized and presented to the Conference by one country. As to the Conference itself, it was in its beginning stages as an organization. At that time it worked as a clearing house for information. It moved very slowly, with long deliberations between Mr. Labourie presiding and Mr. Anninos, the Oxford-educated Greek permanent secretary, before announcements were made by Mr. Presidente. Usually the ball was carried by Irwin, Worthington, or Chambers, with Greece and Denmark speaking too. After discussion the necessary vote was taken. In NATO deliberations there must be agreement by every country or no action is taken. The last word must be: "It is agreed."

Colonel Chambers spoke for us both during the deliberations. My part was to show the film of "Operation Doorstep" and to tell of my personal experiences in attending an atomic test. The delegates listened with keen interest as I described the Atomic Bomb test at Yucca Flats. No one there, not even Chambers, had ever seen in person the blinding flash of the bomb as it burst, nor heard the delayed reverberations of the sound, nor witnessed the effects on buildings and trees, bridges, and other installations—nor been impressed, as I was, with soldiers moving in for maneuvers immediately after the blast.

Following this came the film, "Operation Doorstep." It showed the two typical American two-story wooden houses, one 3,500 feet from the atomic detonation, the other 7,500 feet away. The nearer one was destroyed by blast and fire, the second one had its windows blown in, but the building stood and the mannequin occupants were safe in the bomb shelter in the basement. I described visiting this house in Radiation-Safe clothing, clambering all through it unaware of the radiation, and my dismay in finding that when tested before I shed my Rad-Safe coveralls, that I had acquired a measurable amount of radiation, but within safe limits. With the film and my first-hand accounts, I brought a touch of reality to the theoretical discussions.

That evening Colonel and Mrs. Chambers, General Irwin, General Worthington of Canada and I went to dinner together. "Worthy" and I became great friends, and he said he wanted to have someone like me in the Canadian Civil Defense set-up. In the course of dinner General Irwin was discussing negotiations. He said, "In war, you've got to win. You'll promise anything, Israel to the Arabs—or anything at all."

Next morning I went out to the Conference. I had been allocated some money for entertaining, so I arranged a cocktail party in the name of the United States Delegation. I specified that it must not be ostentatious.

It was given in the Wagram Hotel, Rue de Rivoli, at the conclusion of the second day's session (the United States Embassy owns the Wagram) and was a great success. The conference didn't end until six. The guests mostly arrived at seven and stayed on until 9:45! I found myself talking French, and making them laugh at my description of the French interpreter's illustration of Colonel Chambers' remarks—*with* Gallic gestures—whereas Colonel Chambers always kept his hands quietly in front of him. Before they left, the French invited me to go with the Chambers to Versailles Friday afternoon. I thanked them but declined, telling of all the things I wanted to buy—"Must do my shopping," I said, "a dress, perfume, presents for my family, books, pictures." Mr. Labourie said,

"But Madame does not need to buy hats; she *has* charming hats!"

Saturday morning I had a nice visit with Ambassador Hughes, our representative to NATO. He was just back from Germany where he had seen the U. S. High Commissioner James Conant. I told him Harvard had never been able to understand why Conant gave up being President. He said, "Well, at this moment Conant can't either!"

My trip to NATO as the first woman official from any country was newsworthy. When I returned I was asked to appear on the Arthur Godfrey Show, then the prime radio and TV show. With some trepidation I went to New York. I remember stepping on to the platform, Arthur Godfrey over to the right, a big audience out in front. Arthur Godfrey introduced me, and asked me a question about NATO. Facing the audience, I started to talk. I expected him to interrupt me and ask more questions, but he didn't. I talked and talked without notes, thinking in the back of my mind, "Why doesn't he say something, or cut me off?" However, I kept going, and when he finally thanked me, it had been almost fifteen minutes of extemporaneous talk. I may say I enjoyed it once I got going.

Radio and TV appearances continued. One of the important ones was the nationwide National Broadcasting Company's TV show, originating in New York, called "Mrs. U.S.A." As I sat beside the host of the show, Mr. Peter Roberts, waiting for the light to indicate that we were on the air, he must have felt my tenseness, for he turned to me with a smile and said, "Shall we dance?" I responded with a smile, all of a sudden feeling at home and even somewhat glamorous, and we were off for another successful, unrehearsed nationwide TV show.

Delightful invitations started the New Year off on a happy note. We were bidden to the White House to the first State Reception of 1954, on January twelfth. This was a double-barreled evening as we were also asked to the British Embassy for a party in honor of the Sadlers Wells Ballet after their performance.

Charlie came down for the reception, which was a white-tie affair. Washington was deep in snow, but it only seemed to add to the gala mood. At nine o'clock President and Mrs. Eisenhower descended the White House staircase to the stirring blare of drums and bugles. Then they went in to the Blue Room to receive the guests. Mamie looked particularly pretty in a black lace over coral evening gown.

They greeted each guest with more than a how-do-you-do and were warmly welcoming to Charlie and me. After being received, we passed through the Red Room into the State Dining room. Here, there were so many friends to see, including Secretary of the Treasury Humphrey and Mrs. Humphrey, lovely in a rose lace gown. Pam Humphrey was the most loved of the cabinet ladies. She was kind, gracious, thoughtful of others; she had simplicity and dignity. She was the moving spirit in many happy occasions, in some of which I was included. She had tea at home on Foxhall Road every afternoon. From time to time she would say to me, "You haven't been to tea lately. Do come." I would leave my office a little early and join the group around the tea table.

We had come to the Reception with the Sinclair Weeks, in their official Cabinet limousine, and we went on with them to the British Embassy party. This was a happy mingling of the Sadlers Wells company, with Margot Fonteyne always surrounded by admirers; and of diplomats, government officials and Washington society. It was notable that the Soviet Ambassador and Mrs. Zaroubin were there, and he was asked how his talks with Secretary of State Dulles were coming along. He replied, "We are still talking." Mrs. Zaroubin was asked "Would she go to the Berlin Conference with Ambassador Zaroubin?" She smilingly said, "If my husband goes, I don't want to be left behind." She spoke English with perfect ease. It was such a successful party that it lasted until 1:30, a very late hour for a Washington weekday party. Sir Roger Makins, the Ambassador, and his American-born wife, were very popular. I told him about going to England and visiting Lady Reading to learn about Civil Defense. I said, "I literally sat at her feet." "That is the only posture you can take with Lady Reading," he replied.

The next morning I was at the White House for the presentation of the National Achievement Award to Senator Margaret Chase Smith. Bobby Cutler said to me, "What's the matter with Joe Chambers? He went to Paris with you, and he's been in the hospital ever since." Sherm Adams spoke up, "She doesn't have that effect on me."

In early January the President delivered the State of the Union address. Speaker Joe Martin had given me a ticket, a front row seat in the gallery, beside Alice Longworth. Joe Martin always reserved one of the seven tickets allotted him as the Speaker for Mrs. Longworth. He said, "A daughter of a President, and widow of a Speaker of the House is properly entitled to a seat in the gallery whenever she wishes it." She boasted that she had never missed a single such occasion since her father, Theodore Roosevelt, was President, and she was the debutante daughter of the White House. She commented afterwards, "I'm deeply grateful to Joe for making it possible for me to come."

To me, it was a thrilling experience, and I couldn't have had a better view of the President. In a gray suit, with pale blue shirt and navy blue tie, he looked lean, tanned, and vigorous as he strode down the aisle. Glancing down, I saw Leverett Saltonstall, slender and ruddy; Sinclair Weeks; handsome Henry Cabot Lodge; and Sherman Adams, all from New England. *The Boston Herald*'s Bill Cunningham wrote, "It was harder to get into the Capitol to hear the President's speech today than it was to pass the same lines when the gentleman was inaugurated. . . . In the gallery were wives of members and diplomats. Some were party V.I.P.'s in their own right. Mrs. Charles P. Howard from our town, for instance, sat at rapt attention in the gallery's front row. She looked very pretty, too, in a dark suit, a red hat, and a big red bow across the general vicinity of where a gentleman tucks his napkin."

On February 2, 1954, President Eisenhower told Congress that the U.S. made "the first full-scale thermonuclear (hydrogen) explosion in history" at Eniwetok in 1952.

This was the first official confirmation that the vast explosion, which wiped out an island, was a full-scale test of devices leading to the dread hydrogen bomb. The President called the experiment "a necessary first step in the hydrogen weapon program of the U.S." and implied the country is now far ahead of that stage. The statement accompanied the showing to the legislators of the film "Operation Ivy," the Eniwetok test.

We, at FCDA, had just seen the film for the first time. It sent me out of my office and to the nearest church to kneel and pray that this dreadful device of destruction might never be used.

It was this film which, as Chief U.S. Delegate to the NATO Civil Defnse Committee, I was asked to show to that committee at its next meeting in Paris in the spring. It was a sobering responsibility to be the one to reveal the terrors of the hydrogen bomb to an international group.

In early February the Joint U.S.-Canadian Committee on Civil Defense met in Washington. Val Peterson appointed me to the Committee, and asked me to plan a dinner meeting at the Sulgrave Club. The Candian Delegation was headed by the Hon. Paul Martin, Canadian Minister of National Health and Welfare, and included my good friend from NATO, General Worthington.

Our delegation, headed by Val Peterson, was equally distinguished. We met for three days, exchanging information and making arrangements for mutual aid in continental civil defense warning, welfare services, evacuation, reception of refugees, medical aid, emergency hospitals.

A pleasant diversion soon after this was a meeting of "The Friendly Sons and Daughters of President Franklin D. Pierce," at Fred Seaton's house. This informal group of the top echelon on the Campaign Train met on the train when there happened to be an evening with no rally, no speech, no crisis. Tom Stephens, and Fred Seaton were the prime movers, President Eisenhower was Honorary President, but he did not attend. Sherman Adams came occasionally, but Rachel Adams, with her sense of fun and merriment sparked the meetings, and with inimitable charm led in the singing of our theme song—

> How Ike's Train keeps rolling
> With so many men controlling. . . .

sung to the tune of "I'm Looking Over a Four Leaf Clover."

The cardinal rules for membership were—"You mustn't take yourself seriously," and "You must have made a mistake—not a teeny one but a great big blooper." With songs and banter and good cheer, tensions were released, problems laughed off for the moment, and friendships forged.

The unlikely name of "The Friendly Sons and Daughters of President Franklin D. Pierce" just came from nowhere. He was the little known fourteenth President of the U. S. There was no "D" in·his name but he was a Democrat and we borrowed the initial from FDR!

Peter Edson, a Washington correspondent, got word of the forthcoming meeting and wrote, "One of the most exclusive and elusive inner-circle organizations in Washington, and in the world, for that matter, is The Friendly Sons and Daughters of President Franklin D. Pierce. . . .

The State Directors of Civil Defense met in Washington once a year in March. Their two-day meeting was an important event for FCDA. They were appointed by the Governors of their states and had to be handled with gloves. Most of them were retired Colonels, Generals and Admirals who were used to command, but now had diminished authority.

I was asked by Val Peterson to preside at the morning meeting of the Directors. Perhaps I was being handed a hot potato, but I took the assignment as a compliment and as a sign of confidence in my ability. The agenda for the morning was a heavy one. There was the acceptance and adoption of the "Home Protection Exercises" on which we at FCDA had been working for so many months; there was to be a discussion of Labor's support of Civil Defense; and Lady Reading, who had come to America on my invitation, was to make the concluding address.

To my surprise, there was some opposition by the Directors to the adoption of the now completed Home Protection Exercises. Each Director considered that he was the last word on what was good for Civil Defense; he wanted to take the floor, state his views of what was wrong with Civil Defense, and have them recorded. As the morning wore on, the debate became acrimonious. Each General or Admiral was used to being heard and this was particularly true of General Huebner, State Director of New York, and General Robertson of California, two outstanding commanders of the Second World War. The debate raged on, hot and heavy: Huebner and Robertson were firing away in a duel of wits and we had to leave time for Lady Reading's address. I glanced at my watch. Giving General Huebner the opportunity to finish his statement, I rapped the gavel sharply and announced that "the Chair rules that only one more question will be entertained." There was a pause; General Robertson eyed me to see if I would get away with it; I did. We finished the morning's business. The Home Protection Exercises were accepted. The Labor problem was resolved. And I proceeded to introduce Lady Reading.

She was a brilliant speaker and a commanding personality. It was a great opportunity to have a woman of such proven ability speak to the all male group of State Directors about utilizing the volunteer services of American women. In introducing her I spoke of the fact that she had built the Women's Voluntary Services from nothing to a trained organization of a million and a half women. I recalled that I had once said, "You had the prestige of a great name to help you." "Yes," she replied, "but I could not bring disgrace to that name. When I started out," she said, with an expressive gesture, "I had nothing but the gloves on my hands!"

To the largely military group of State Directors she began her talk with a reference to the American GI in England, who, seeing her in uniform, called her "sister," and she loved it. "In England," she said, "only women forty or under are called 'sister,' after that you are 'Auntie'." She spoke with gratitude of the American aid to England, during the time of the blitz and the V Bombs. Then she told of the methods used in recruiting and training the members of the Women's Voluntary Services of the Welfare Branch of Civil Defense. When the worst Nazi attacks came, the women were trained and ready and they were referred to as "The Army Hitler forgot."

Her advice to us was that it was all very simple. It was a question of getting women ready in preparation for disaster. In England they developed films and slides for teaching, courses for training teachers, and for the teachers to use in training recruits. She said, "The training programs must be so simple that the maximum will understand and the minimum will misunderstand." She said that in her no-rank army of volunteers no leaders were picked who did not have a sense of humor.

While it was a practical talk, one felt the force of the great personality whose "army" cared for the veterans returning from Dunkirk, in the evacuation of the children from London, in all the darkest days of England's dogged fight for survival. When Churchill proclaimed, "We will fight them on the beaches, we will fight them from behind the stone walls...." Lady Reading later said: "One reason he could say those words was that we were prepared to do just that."

In the late afternoon Charlie and I gave a reception for Lady Reading at the Sulgrave Club. In spite of having had a full and busy day, she was dynamic and engaged in animated conversation with the many guests. Her gray hair was set off by a black dress of simple lines, brightened by diamond clips from her tiara. She and Pauline Fenno received with Charlie and me. I wore a taffeta afternoon dress, which was described as "Howard Blue."

It was fun to look out over the gathering, which filled the second floor of the Sulgrave Club, and see Representative and Mrs. Gerald Ford of Michigan talking with Joe Alsop. Miriam Summerfield said happily, "At last I've gotten my husband out to a party." He seemed to be enjoying himself. General Huebner and General Robertson had made their peace with me and with each other. Bertha Adkins, pouring tea, looked stunning in a jacketed ivory-colored lace dress with red shoes and a red hat. Opposite her, my sister-in-law, Elizabeth Graham, was pouring coffee. Mrs. Wilson was there, the wife of the Secretary of Defense, Sinclair and Jane Weeks, the Saltonstalls, and a large group from Massachusetts. It was a good party.

My Congressional Liaison duties occasionally brought me in touch with the American Federation of Labor. George Richardson, an official of the American Federation of Labor, served as one of the twelve-member National Civil Defense Advisory Council. Bowie Johnson and Bill Price were our regular liaison men. Each year, we sought the help and backing of the Legislative Council of the A.F.L. in our work on Capitol Hill to secure an adequate budget for FCDA. Because of this I was asked to speak at the Annual Meeting of the National Legislative Council of the A.F.L. in their hall. I considered it quite a challenge.

That March morning is indelibly engraved in my mind. I

was to appear at ten o'clock, and my legislative assistant, Bowie Johnson, would go with me. He was known and liked by the A.F.L. He would introduce me when I arrived, and break the ice. He was my strong right arm. But when I walked into my office at eight-thirty, no Bowie Johnson. In a few minutes the telephone rang. I pressed the proper button and answered. It was Bowie calling from his home in Silver Spring, Maryland.

"Mrs. Howard, I am really distressed. My wife is having a miscarriage, and I cannot leave her. I am dreadfully sorry not to be able to go with you to the Legislative Council." Oh dear, I was to be fed to the lions all alone. I went over my speech for the last time, rang for my car, drove off to speak to a hall full of labor leaders. Afterwards, word of it got to Max Rabb at the White House; (he knew what was going on everywhere) and he said to me, "There was no question that you made a deep impression on the American Federation of Labor group that heard you." This was a far different audience than the ones I was accustomed to. I continued to work with their leaders and they gave their support to our budget appeals on the Hill.

The U.S. Mission to NATO must have made a good report on me, for when spring came, I was asked to go again as Chief U.S. Delegate to NATO, this time not with Chambers but with a lesser member of our staff.

But in the month before my departure, each day was brimful of activities, and often the evenings too. One of the most pleasant was a small dinner at the apartment of General and Mrs. Snyder. The other guests were Sherman and Rachel Adams and Bobby Cutler. Everyone kissed me in greeting, even Bobby. The conversation was mostly about Eisenhower's TV talk on fear and hysteria the night before. Rachel said, "Too much Robert Montgomery." Dr. Snyder agreed. Bobby thought it was perfect. After dinner Sherm sat at the piano and played. We all sang hymns. Then we recited poetry.

Bobby said, "Thank God we aren't going to have war," (referring to our sought-for intervention in Indochina). He said, "I went in to see the President about noon, and he was calm and sure. Everything was all settled then and the Security Council met in the afternoon." This was in the middle of

310

the crisis over Dien Bien Phu, April 6, 1954.

The next two days were given over to the National Republican Women's Conference, organized by Bertha Adkins. Fourteen hundred women were there from all over the country, and the cherry blossoms cooperated by being in bloom.

Bertha asked me to preside at the luncheon. The President spoke first and left. Mamie sat at my right, and gave me a "Pink Lady" lipstick to go with the pink hat I was wearing. She told me a lot about the Gettysburg house now at the point of decisions on paint, paper, and draperies.

Her mother, Mrs. Doud, and Bertha's father were sitting together on the floor of the huge dining room. I introduced them, and also Mrs. Robert Taft, there in a wheelchair, looking rather lost and troubled, but receiving a tremendous ovation. At the Head table were Mrs. Nixon, wife of the Vice-President, all the Cabinet ladies, Bertha Adkins, of course, and the speaker, Alice Leopold. I introduced them all, beginning with Mamie.

Before my departure for NATO, I was scheduled to speak in Washington at the Continental Congress of the Daughters of the American Revolution in Constitution Hall. I had worked long and hard over what I was going to say, and the title of my talk was "The Ramparts We Watch." My main point was that no American city was now beyond the range of enemy bombers, and that there is no way of stopping all the planes which might attempt a raid.

"From one-half to two-thirds of them," I said, "would get through to their targets. . . .

"As a result, we civilians might suffer many times more casualties in a single day than our armed forces have suffered thus far, in all the years of all the wars of our history."

The audience was so still that I could feel that they were shocked. Then I urged the D.A.R. delegates to check into the local civil defense needs when they returned home and concluded by saying that it is possible to alert a large part of the millions of American families against the worst effects of such attacks.

From the D.A.R. speech I took the train to Tampa with my bags all packed for sailing to NATO. Tampa was a workout! When I arrived at 8:30 A.M., the officials meeting me said hopefully, "Have you had breakfast?" Fortunately I had, for immediately we did a fifteen-minute radio show, met the Mayor, had a press interview, visited Civil Defense Headquarters, went to St. Petersburg, met the County Commissioners, did a radio show, had a press interview, half an hour for lunch, did a TV show, back to Tampa, another radio show and a newscast tape recording. I ended the day with a speech to five hundred people! My stateroom on the boat would be a relief.

I had a superb cabin on the S.S. *America*. The State Department paid minimum first-class passage. If the U.S. Lines had luxury accommodations vacant, they sometimes made them available to government officials, or others, and I was fortunate to be given one.

Charlie had sent me American Beauty roses, which reflected in the mirrored walls as they opened wide. My quarters included a living room, a bedroom, a bathroom with tub, and an entry for bags. I wrtoe my family, "If you were all along, I'd be perfectly happy."

There was a telegram from Val Peterson saying, "KNOW YOU WILL DO A GRAND JOB FOR THE U.S. KINDLY EXPRESS MY REGARDS TO THE ASSEMBLY. HAVE A GOOD TIME. VAL PETERSON."

From my two secretaries: "RECOMMEND IMMEDIATE SURVEY FOR AVAILABLE OFFICE SPACE FOR THE AGENCY'S D.P.s. PREFER LEFT BANK. WILL TRAVEL. JEANNETTE AND HANK."

And from Hugh Gallagher, Assistant Administrator and Donald Sheehan of the Public Affairs Department: "AVAILABLE SUMMER ENGAGEMENTS FOLIES BERGERE. NEW SONGS AND JOKES. HAVE A GOOD TRIP. GALLAGHER AND SHEEHAN."

It was heartwarming. Off to a good start.

Among the interesting group of passengers was Mrs. Woodruff of Atlanta, whose husband was President of Coca-Cola. She was going as a U.S. delegate to the World Health Organization. Her friend, Mrs. Schneider, travelling with her, had been asked to look me up, and I had been asked to look her up. Mrs. Woodruff was a friend of the Eisenhowers and a delightful person. The only drawback was that I had a toothache.

The Coca-Cola Paris representative, Burke Nicholson, met

her at Le Havre. I was with them in the same compartment on the boat train to Paris. There I was met by William Walker of the NATO mission, who drove me to the Meurice Hotel. After unpacking and having lunch, I went to the "Talleyrand" Palace, headquarters of the NATO mission, for a conference with Bill Walker. As we talked, my toothache got worse. I realized it was Friday afternoon, and with Saturday and Sunday and no relief in sight, I asked Walker if he could possibly get me an appointment with a dentist.

Bill Walker got through to Dr. Halley Smith, who said he could see me if we came immediately. So Bill accompanied me to the address at 23 Place Vendome. There was no sign anywhere which suggested a doctor. Bill inquired of the concierge who said, "quatrieme étage." We went up in the lift and stepped out—no sign—just one of those expensive-looking doors painted black with a big brass knob in the middle. Bill pressed a bell and the door was opened by a manservant in tails! Quite naturally I thought we were in the wrong place, but we stepped into a drawing room with oriental rugs, oil paintings, beautiful French furniture with white linen slipcovers for summer, crystal chandeliers, and Bill said this was it. The man in tails went off to summon an attendant. I gasped to Bill, "This certainly looks expensive." "Yes," he said, "you'll find that you contribute heavily."

I bade him good-bye as a nurse came in and conducted me down a long corridor to a small room at the end. Then a gray-haired woman in a white operating coat and hair done up in a dustcloth emerged from somewhere. I still had on my hat and mink jacket and no one seemed interested in my removing them. However, I succeeded in giving them to the nurse who had escorted me so far. I asked the doctor's assistant if she spoke English; she did not, but I made her understand where the pain was, and then I saw she was about to take an x-ray which seemed to me a sound idea.

So then I was escorted to the petit salon where my coat was over the back of a chair in front of a beautiful directoire secretary. I sat on one of the petit point chairs with its linen dust cover neatly tied on until I was summoned into the doctor's operating room which looked quite normal except for a desk, chair and sofa in one corner.

Dr. Smith came in, took a look at the x-ray and said the

tooth must come out. However, when I told him I was only here for a week, and had conferences to attend, he agreed to treat it. He put some penicillin ointment where it could get at the infection, and the pain lessened. At the end of the treatment he called for his assistant and told her that I would come in tomorrow for a treatment if my tooth continued to pain me. "Main non, monsieur, demain est le premiere Mai." So he turned to me and said, "Well, Madame, you are from the city of Mary Baker Eddy; tomorrow you must practice Christian Science."

The next morning, Saturday, Mrs. Woodruff called to invite me to go to lunch at the Eiffel Tower with her, Mrs. Schneider, and Burke Nicholson. I accepted and then tried to make a hair appointment but was told, "Non, madame, aujourd'hui est le première Mai," as if that explained everything. I went downstairs and when I stepped up to buy a paper, "Mais non, there are no papers today. It is the First of May!" (Through that day and those that followed I felt a dull insistent pain, but Christian Science sustained me, and the tooth was pulled out when I got home.)

When Mrs. Woodruff arrived to pick me up in a large car with chauffeur, Burke Nicholson said he would go on ahead in a taxi. But before we pulled out of the driveway, he came running back and rapped on the window and climbed back in with us. "Today is the First of May and quite naturally there are no taxis." He bought for each of us a small bouquet of lillies-of-the-valley, for it is traditional to give your wife, mother, sweetheart or friend such a bouquet on the First of May.

We had a marvelous lunch at the Eiffel Tower looking off to Sacre Coeur in one direction, and to the left the Seine, and further to the left the Palais Chaillot, and down below the soft yellow-green of the trees coming out, and a garden with lilacs in bloom. Lunch was something to dream about—fresh asparagus an inch thick and yellow-white, served with melted butter and grated hardboiled egg; chateaubriand steak, and wild fresh strawberries with wonderful thick cream; and the appropriate wines, of course.

By now my papers had arrived by diplomatic pouch at the U.S. NATO Mission, 2 Rue Florentine, the Hotel Talleyrand. The Talleyrand Palace is a handsome building, and one of

France's historic sites, so that no exterior or interior changes could be made. Removable partitions of plywood were put up on the second and third floors to make the offices. Outside, the building was guarded by U.S. soldiers with guns. One had to show a pass to enter. Inside, you sign a book with your name, the date and hour. If you are to see the Ambassador or Minister or any of the deputies, you are given a card. Then you go up the broad impressive marble stairway to the office, present the card as you present yourself. The officer signs it and you turn it in when you leave.

You can never travel with NATO papers or leave them in your hotel room. The material given me to study on the *America* was all nonclassified background material. I had to study the NATO papers at the U. S. Mission.

The first meeting of this session of the Committee on Civil Defense was on Tuesday, May 4, 1954, at the Palais Chaillot in Paris. Bill Walker came for me in a car. I presented the U. S. paper—"Industrial Dispersion." Questions and comments followed afterwards by Belgium, Italy, and France which I summarized and answered. It is a strange feeling to have one's American words turned into another language almost as quickly as they can be spoken. I would look up at the glass cage where the translators were, and see that my words were being translated with much emphasis and with gestures. But the most impressive experience of all is to hear oneself saying, in response to some grave question from a foreign dignitary, "I am instructed by my government to state that the position of the United States is as follows. . . ."

The next day, May fifth, was one of the most important ones in my life. Val Peterson and the State Department had entrusted to me the responsibility of showing to our NATO Civil Defense allies the fearsome film of the U. S. detonation of the first hydrogen bomb. This was "Operation Ivy" which had so overwhelmed me when I saw it that I had sought out the first church I could find to kneel and pray. I have never ceased to wonder that they sent me to Paris on such a mission.

Before the film was shown, I made a statement along the lines suggested by the State Department. I said, "The U. S. Government realizes that the development and successful detonation by the U.S. of the world's first Hydrogen Bomb has caused alarm among all nations including our allies. It is only natural that there should be questions in our allies' minds. So far as possible I will answer them after the showing of the film called 'Operation Ivy,' taken at the test on Eniwetok Island in the Pacific." I continued, "It is the feeling of the U. S. Government that the American Hydrogen Bomb is the free world's shield against aggression. The United States will never be the first to use it. It is our hope that our possession of it will be a deterrent to attack against our NATO Allies."

Then the film in color was shown. As the enormous flaming fireball flashed on the screen, it seemed as if hell itself had erupted into the world. At its conclusion there was a stunned silence.

The questions came. One delegate asked, "How big is the Hydrogen Bomb?" I explained, "The atom bomb dropped on Hiroshima had a yield of the equivalent of about twenty thousand kilotons of TNT. The Hydrogen Bomb has a yield of a million kilotons." There were looks of concern and distress. Another question, "What is its area of total destruction?" With some agitation they awaited my answer.

I said, "The area of total destruction is 3½ miles, large enough to take out the heart of a city." The delegate from the Netherlands pursued the subject, "And what about the devastation from blast and fire?" I replied, "About twenty miles—far enough to reach the outskirts or suburbs of many cities."

There were frowns on many faces, but a look of relief came over the face of the Belgian delegate.

"Oh," he said, "Mrs. Howard has relieved my mind. Until now I believed that this fearful weapon might wipe out my whole *country*. Now I know better." Heads nodded in agreement; faces relaxed; the worst was over.

I continued, "New methods to deal with the new peril must be considered and acted upon. We must give serious thought to the new concept of evacuation and dispersal. Rural areas must be prepared to receive evacuees, provide food and shelter, and reunite families. There is hope, for many more would survive than perish."

The delegates accepted my statements with grave concern but some relief, as voiced by the Belgian delegate, and the meeting ended. When it was all over, Bill Walker looked at me earnestly and said, "Mrs. Howard, you served with distinction."

At the end of the conference, the car of General Gruenther, who had succeeded Eisenhower as Supreme Commander, Allied Powers Europe, was waiting to drive me to their house in Marne le Cocotte. There I had a drink with him and Mrs. Gruenther and saw the comfortable dwelling which the Eisenhowers chose and Mamie decorated. Appropriately it was a white house.

It was a beautiful drive through the Bois de Boulogne with the white horse chestnuts out, and the pink ones just beginning to come. The house was full of lilacs and the garden had tulips and hyacinths and lilacs in bloom. Al Gruenther mixed a long bourbon and water for me and we sat and talked about NATO. He said, "Imagine a woman official at NATO!" and we talked about the budget for FCDA, and Indochina, and Mrs. Woodruff, and Homer Gruenther and General Snyder and the Eisenhowers. Before I left, they showed me the drawing room and dining room and garden. I signed the guest book.

Then I went to a party the French minister of the interior gave for the Civil Defense delegates to NATO. Bill Walker took me, and we both came back to the Meurice where Ambassador Hughes was giving a party for the delegates to the Organization for European Economic Cooperation. We ended the evening with coffee and eggs at the Palais Athenee Coffee Shop. I fell exhausted into bed and to sleep even though my tooth was still bothering me.

It had been a challenging assignment but never to be forgotten.

Next day I sailed home on *The United States.*

When I returned from NATO, I was called on to make many speeches and have radio and TV interviews. I took all I could manage, but I also had to get ready for two Commencement addresses, one at my first Alma Mater, Salem College in Winston-Salem; and one at the Kingswood School, Bloomfield Hills, Michigan.

The Salem College one came on May 30. Having been the first Alumnae Trustee, I became the first graduate of Salem College to give the Commencement Address.

At the Kingswood School, again in cap and gown, I spoke from the pulpit of the Chapel, taking as my title, "To Thine Own Self Be True." Assistant Secretary of Defense Hannah spoke at Cranbrook, the Boys School. When I saw him a few days later, I was amazed that he had chosen, quite by coincidence, the same title for his talk! Commenting on my speech, the Head of the School said, "Even the young ones listened," and a senior came up to say, "You really talked to us!"

At this time, too, I was asked to write an article for *The Armed Forces Chemical Journal* entitled "Civil Defense Progress." It was a rather commonsense article in the course of which I said that in future wars, chemical warfare would be conducted against civilians as well as the armed forces and concluded, "As I see it, my job is to prepare people to live through an atomic attack, not to die in one. . . . to survive and win over any attacks, not to give up in abject helplessness."

Admiral Radford, then Chairman of the Joint Chiefs of Staff, was in the same issue of the *Journal*, with an article entitled, "Problems and Progress in Defense Planning." I felt I was in very good company.

XIX

HOME, SWEET HOME

It was May and Washington was as beautiful as ever. Each thing I did took on a special meaning, for I felt in my heart it would soon be over. All through the spring the conviction had been growing on me that in due course I was going to resign and return to Boston. There were many factors involved, but the overriding reason was the increasing feeling that interesting and worthwhile as I felt my work to be, this was not the kind of life I should continue. In the end, Charlie won. He refused to go to Washington—he freely let me go; he came down to go to official functions with me, but "home" was still Boston. More and more, as I was given increasing responsibilities, I saw less and less of my women friends. I rejoiced in the daily stimulus of new and challenging situations, but there were frustrations also. There were days when I was tired and discouraged and homesick.

In March I had written Charlie, "Mamie called me up today just to say 'hello' and chat. It was nice. My love, and I'm coming home soon."

On May 13 I wrote in my diary, "This day I definitely decided to go home. Looked at my calendar and said, 'This is it'." A few weeks later, June 2, I went to see Sherman Adams about resigning. "We certainly will miss you if you feel you have to go," he said. "Let's consider another possibility. If the President can be persuaded to run again, he would want you to help line up the women delegates." He went on talking about the President, who was fed up with the McCarthy business and in no mood to start thinking about another term. Sherm said, "If there should be a congressional defeat, a recession, or 'another Korea', the President would feel someone else should cope with it. Now he is longing for his farm." He continued, "I don't know how Mamie feels about it, but I think she is enjoying the White House."

I asked him if it was his opinion I would be wanted in this capacity. He replied, "If I have anything to do with it, and I assume I will, you would be my choice."

The next step was to talk with Val Peterson about my decision.

Val had said to me once, at the conclusion of one of our Monday morning policy meetings: "Katherine, I think you fear no man."

"Except you, the President, and Charlie," I replied.

"I'm interested in your sequence!" he laughingly said.

Now Charlie *was* taking precedence.

When I told Val, he was upset by my decision, much more so than I had anticipated. He knew that in the main I had found happiness and satisfaction in my work; my health had been remarkable with the strenuous program I pursued. I had never had a day's sickness. I had many friends. I had everything but family and home life, and he did understand my natural desire for them. Regretfully he said, "After you have seen the President, we will talk again."

So now I was to see the President. Tom Stephens, his appointment secretary, scheduled me for 9:00 A.M. on June 29. When Tom opened the door and ushered me into the President's office, Ike was sitting at his desk. He rose and greeted me cordially and motioned me to a chair facing him close to his desk.

I told him how much I appreciated being part of his administration, how much I liked working with Val Peterson, and how rewarding my job was, but that, as he realized, it was at a considerable sacrifice on Charlie's part and my part, and that I had reluctantly come to the conclusion that I must offer him my resignation.

He was surprised; he got up from his chair and started walking about. "I can understand your situation," he said. "You have carried a hard job under difficult circumstances. I can understand that it is a sacrifice to you and your family. . . ." Then pausing, looking at me earnestly, he contined, "But we don't want to lose you. Why don't you become a Consultant?"

I thanked him, told him that was a possibility I had not thought of. I said I would not leave Washington until my Congressional liaison work was completed, with the passage by Congress of the appropriations for FCDA, and I thought this would be by the end of July. I sent my love to Mamie, and he walked with me to the door.

In my letter of resignation, dated that day, I expressed the same sentiments:

June 29, 1954

Dear Mr. President:

It has been a privilege and a pleasure to serve in your administration as Deputy Federal Defense Administrator. I appreciate the opportunity for service to our country which this appointment has given me.

The Civil Defense work in which I have been engaged for sixteen months has been challenging and rewarding. I firmly believe that the success of the program is vital to the security of the nation, and that women will make an increasing contribution to its success.

However, my service has necessitated a sacrifice on the part of my family. In their best interests I feel that I should now relinquish this post. I am, therefore, requesting that you accept my resignation, effective July 31, 1954.

Please be assured of my devotion to you and Mrs. Eisenhower, and of the real pride I feel in having been part of your official team. You know, of course, I shall be happy to be of any future service to you.

With my warm personal regards,

Katherine G. Howard

The next day was the Eisenhowers' thirty-eighth wedding anniversary, *The New York Times* in a long article noted the President's activities on that day:

Signed 21 bills, including a year's extension of the Reciprocal Trade Act; conferred with the National Security Council; authorized flood relief for Texas; sent a message to Dr. Adolph Ruiz Corbines expressing his sympathy in the flood disaster which struck the country along the Rio Grande; received a message from Chancellor Konrad Adenauer of Germany expressing satisfaction with the Eisenhower-Churchill statement of June 29 dealing with Western Europe; wrote a letter to Mrs. Katherine G. Howard accepting "with reluctance" her resignation as Deputy Administrator of the Federal Civil Defense Administration; conferred with Charles E. Wilson, Secretary of Defense.

Amusingly enough, illustrating the news article was an excellent Associated Press picture of me, with the caption: "Leaves Post. Mrs. Katherine G. Howard, who resigned as Deputy Federal Civil Defense Administrator to return to family."

The President's letter, released to the press with my letter on July first said:

Dear Katherine:

Since I have been aware for some time of the tremendous personal sacrifices you have made in connection with your duties as Deputy Federal Civil Defense Administrator, your decision to resign does not come as a shock, but nevertheless as a matter of deepest regret. I must, of course, accept your resignation, but I do so with reluctance despite my complete understanding of your situation.

To your post you have brought the ability, tact and charm I grew to admire during our days together in the '52 campaign. You have had a difficult, and often, I fear, unpopular job in trying to alert the people of our country to a terrible threat that many would naturally prefer to disregard. I congratulate you on your successful efforts and the concrete results you and Governor Peterson have achieved.

It is good to know that we in the Administration can count on your friendship and continuing support, even if we are no longer to have the benefit of your day-to-day participation in the national picture.

Mrs. Eisenhower joins with me in warm good wishes to you and your family for a happy future.

Sincerely,
Dwight D. Eisenhower

Press clippings from all over the country noted the president's letter, quoting his acceptance of my resignation "with reluctance," "with deepest regret." One noted another *first* for me—"The first woman official to resign her post."

The day the news broke a long-time friend in the Commerce Department called me up.

"What happened?" he asked. "Why did you resign?"

When I told him, he was relieved. He said, "Now that I've heard your voice, I know it is all right."

When I resigned, I expected to make a clean break. I had been Deputy Administrator. Now I would be a private person. But Val Peterson was upset. Whether he spoke to the President or the President with him, I do not know. Val said to me, "I can understand that you want to return to a normal family life, but we want to keep you with us in some way, on a consultant basis. I'll send Paul Wagner in to work out details with you." Paul was his young, capable troubleshooter and personal assistant. He and I were always great friends.

Paul came in, really shaken up that I had gone and done it. I don't know why they wanted so much to keep me on, but it was evident they did. He came in and sat by my desk. I was thinking in small and limited terms of continued activity. He was thinking in larger terms. We talked about what I would do, and we decided I would keep full responsibility for NATO affairs, using the title conferred on me by the State Department "Permanent Alternate U. S. Delegate to the NATO Civil Defense Committee." (I was actually chief U. S. Delegate except when Val Peterson attended; then I served as Alternate.) This would take me to Paris twice a year to attend the meetings. I was to continue to be in charge of Civil Defense foreign relations, which would involve me in considerable correspondence. Hank Parker in the Washington office and I at home could manage it, keeping the mails busy.

"Val wants you to be Special Advisor to the Federal Civil Defense Administrator," Paul said. That seemed quite a good mouthful and would cover just about anything. He went on to explain—I would have an office near the Administrator's in Washington, and Hank Parker, my attractive, efficient secretary would hold the fort there. When I was Deputy Administrator, I was based in Washington and I went home each weekend at my own expense. Now I would be based in Boston, and when I went to Washington, maybe one day a week, my fare would be paid by FCDA and I would receive a consultant's fee for the days I worked in Washington. For all the work I did at home I made no charge.

July first, my diary records: "Today at a meeting of the Assistant Administrators of FCDA, Val Peterson first reported on the Security Council meeting he had attended. Then he announced my resignation as Deputy Administrator. There was a stunned, incredulous look on several faces. After the meeting Hugh Gallagher came to me and said, 'I think you are the finest woman I have ever known'."

Tonight going out to dinner on Massachusetts Avenue there was a full rainbow in the sky. An omen?

The day of my resignation was a heartwarming one. In the afternoon I went to a meeting of the Interagency Manpower Committee; General Hershey was there. He said, "I noticed in the paper that you had an appointment with the President this morning." "Yes," I replied, "I went to see him to resign as Deputy Administrator." "Oh no!" he exclaimed, "that's a tragedy!"

Mamie was disappointed too. She said, "Ike tells me you are going home. I'm sorry. I guess we can't appoint any more married women." That distressed me. But all married women officials didn't have husbands like Charlie. Oveta Hobby's husband was older and retired and happily came to the Capitol; Ivy Priest's husband sold his business and came along; so did Dorothy Lee's husband. Pearl Pace was a widow; Bertha Adkins was not married. So it went!

The day ended on a happy note, with a dinner party which Charlie and I gave at the Westchester, our "home" in Washington. It was a coincidence that this party, planned some weeks before, should come on the very day I made my retirement official. I was glad it happened that way, for Charlie was there.

Around the table in the private dining room of the Westchester were so many friends of whom we were fond—some were new friends made in Washington. Others went back to years before that. Charlie, who loved Austria, had Mrs. Gruber, the wife of the Austrian Ambassador, at his right; and Jane Weeks (Mrs. Sinclair Weeks) a very special friend, on his left. Ambassador Heeney of Canada was on my right (Mrs. Heeney was in Canada); and Ambassador Gruber on my left. Sinclair Weeks, the Secretary of Commerce, was there; Charlie and Julia Thomas, Charlie was Secretary of the Navy; and the Chapman Roses (he was Assistant Secretary of the Treasury); Homer Gruenther (of the White House Staff), Homer and Bess, close friends from the Campaign Train; General and Mrs. Snyder (he the President's personal physician on the Campaign Train and at the White House), both of them close friends; the Frank du Ponts; Laurence Curtis, our Congressman from Boston; and Senator Eve Bowring; my sister-in-law, Elizabeth Graham; and Rachel Adams (Sherm was away). There were thirty-four good and true friends around the table. There was wit and gaiety—it was just the right ending for that day. Charlie and I went to bed in our apartment knowing that in another month I would be at home.

Life went on at FCDA. On July 8, I went with the Administrator to a briefing in the most deep, dark, hidden secret part of the Pentagon. To be admitted to this region was an experience I won't forget. As we were escorted down corridors and past guards, my eyes were busy taking in every detail until we were ushered into the brightly lighted conference room. Since I was to continue as Special Advisor, the briefing was not wasted on me.

My resignation took many people by surprise. Letters in regard to it started coming in. Bobby Cutler wrote in characteristic fashion:

> Dear Katherine:
> I did not realize that you were leaving the nest

until I saw the exchange of letters between you and the President.

The old home won't seem the same without you!

Sincerely yours,

S/Bobby

Robert Cutler, Special Assistant to the President

July 2, 1954

One of the nicest was a handwritten one from Colonel Brewer of our staff. He said, "I have appreciated your leadership, sincerity and helpfulness from the day I met you. That you have been personally kind and courteous simply adds lustre to your laurels. . . ."

One which surprised and pleased me came on American Federation of Labor Stationery from Mr. W. C. Hushing, Chairman of the National Legislative Committee of the AFL. It took my thoughts back to that March morning when Bowie Johnson's wife was ill, and I had had to go alone to the prestigious meeting of the National Legislative Council of the A.F.L. to address that group.

Mr. Hushing's letter said:

Dear Mrs. Howard:

I have learned recently that you are resigning effective at the end of the current month. I regret very much to learn of this because my observation has been that you have done a wonderful job in your present position.

I know that your job has covered many different phases of the Civil Defense Program, and while I am not fully informed in detail of all your activities, I do know of some of the wonderful things you have done in the field of legislation.

May I say further that our Legislative Council was greatly impressed by the address you made in March regarding your legislative problems, and the National Legislative Committee of the American Federation of Labor *for the first time* found able, competent and highly cooperative support from

326

your staff. I credit you with being responsible for this. It is my sincere hope that this cooperation will continue after your departure.

With best wishes for your future undertakings, I am

Sincerely yours,
S/ W. C. Hushing

Before I left Washington, I wanted to give a party for Mamie and the Women Officials. She was constantly with the Cabinet wives, but except for me, she rarely saw the women appointed by the President to high government positions. She readily accepted my invitation, and set the date for July 22.

I had planned to have the luncheon at my brother's house in Georgetown, where I was spending the summer, but as the guest list grew to sixteen and his dining room was small, he suggested that we ask his close friends across the street, the Frank Wizners, if we could have the party there as they were away for the summer. Polly was pleased to help and sent her butler over to see me and her caterer to make plans with me. Her handsome house was a fine setting for the party.

And what a day! Sunny—warm—cool breeze. The house and grounds were perfect inside and out—lovely flower arrangements on the two tables in the dining room.

All the guests had arrived at the P Street house when Mamie's car drew up. As she stepped out to be greeted by me on the sidewalk, the strains of the campaign theme song, "The Sunshine of Your Smile," pealed from the house where I had had a phonograph and the record placed. We embraced, sharing memories of the Look-Ahead-Neighbor Train.

Mamie was radiant and animated, looking lovely in a flowered print. I wore a pale blue tucked crepe de chine dress, and Mary Lord was down from New York in a sheer navy dress with white hat. Mamie's ease and friendliness and charm made the luncheon an instant success. We laughed and chatted, had pictures taken in the garden, and finally sat down to a perfect summer menu.

Cold Watercress Soup
Chicken in aspic on slice of tongue
Hot Rolls

327

After the main course the table guests, except for Mamie and me, changed places so that everyone would have been at her table during the luncheon.

For dessert we had cool, ripe, juicy cantaloupes filled with lime sherbert and fresh fruit.

Small cups of coffee were served in the drawing room. Then Mrs. Eisenhower said, "Katherine, I 'd like to see where you are living. Why don't we go across the street?" So we strolled over to the Graham's house and settled down in their attractive living room.

Among the guests were Alice Leopold, of the Department of Labor, as well as Ivy Baker Priest, U. S. Treasurer; and Dorothy Houghton of the Foreign Operations Administration, her nickname "Bubbles." From Congress came Edith Nourse Rogers, Marguerite Stitt Church, Ruth Thompson, Cecil Hardin, and from the National Committee, my good friends Bertha Adkins and Anne Wheaton, both in high government positions subsequently.

Mamie was comfortable, settled on the sofa, and conversation was going at a great rate, when at four o'clock, Mary Lord said, "In spite of protocol, I must go, because I have to take a plane back to New York for a dinner appointment." All at once everyone realized how late it was and the party reluctantly broke up.

As a gesture of appreciation I had bought a guest book for the Wizners. The first name written in it was "Mamie Doud Eisenhower."

One of the fascinating things about Washington was its many facets. The next day I was lunching with Mr. Kiplinger, of the famous *Kiplinger Letter*, and his staff, at Kiplinger Headquarters, 1729 H Street in Washington. Mrs. Eva Bray of the staff had invited me to come to luncheon, talk informally and answer questions about the Civil Defense program. It was the custom to ask people to the weekly staff meetings to probe their minds and size them up. When I arrived I was received by Mr. Kiplinger in his office which was a delightful surprise. There was a fireplace, bookshelves and many books, and early American furniture. It was as if I had stepped into a seventeenth century living room in New England. He had an incisive mind and asked penetrating questions. At first he was sceptical, but I think I opened his mind somewhat. When Mrs.

Bray said to him toward the end of the luncheon conference, "I am considering writing an article on Civil Defense for the Kiplinger magazine," he replied. "I think Mrs. Howard has some good points, and it might be a good thing to do." After lunch, I conferred with Mrs. Bray in her office, and she asked me to send her some material for an article in *Changing Times.*

I sent her material on dispersal, urban analysis, and the medical and hospital program with my letter of thanks in which I said: "I can't imagine anything more suitable for a magazine with the title *Changing Times* than an article on how to adapt and survive in the air-atomic age in which we live."

I also asked her to tell Mr. Kiplinger that the mock cat which he gave me caused great interest and merriment over the weekend.

One day in the middle of July the telephone rang in my office. It was Homer Gruenther calling from the White House. He had been a favorite with me since our days together on the Campaign Train. He had been one who had rattled and banged on the empty train with Mamie and me, when we made the long trip back from San Antonio to New York. And in the final days on the train, he was closeted in one of the compartments in our staff car busily going over records and files, the door tight shut, a sign outside saying: "Do Not Disturb. Men Working." He had a warm, friendly nature and was universally liked. Now he was saying, "Katie, some of us here at the White House want you to come over and have lunch with us in the Staff Dining Room before you go home. Would such and such a date be convenient? I said, "Yes, and I'd love to come." A few days later he called again, this time to change the date to two days later "because some of the people who want to come can't make it on the previous date."

So on the appointed day, July 29, Champ, my driver, drove me through the White House gates, and up to the door through which I had entered the White House to be sworn in by the President, a year and a half ago.

A car was just ahead of me, and a woman stepped out and entered. When I came in the door she was walking in the direction of the President's office. The press, whose quarters were then just to the right of this door, came over to speak to me. I inquired who the lady was. "Oh, that's the nurse from

Dien Bien Phu," they explained. It was Lieutenant Genevieve de Galard-Terraube, whose ministrations to the wounded in the besieged Indochina fortress won her the title, "Angel of Dien Bien Phu." Her bravery in the siege there, before the French were defeated and capitulated, had won her worldwide acclaim, and now she was here to be decorated by the President with the Medal of Freedom. I thought to myself, "She's probably going to have lunch with Ike and Mamie." It must have been a short ceremony. After a brief wait on my part (I was always early), Sherm and Rachel and Homer Gruenther appeared from the opposite corner, where Sherm's office was. After warm greetings, they escorted me to the steps leading to the Staff Dining Room. As we started to go down, the familiar strains of "The Sunshine of Your Smile" were heard. I began to get an inkling of what was in store.

Down we went, and there was a party for me, and Ike and Mamie were there! They were the two who "wanted to come" and for whom the date was changed. It was a real surprise.

A long table was gaily set. The President and the First Lady were in the middle, Mamie on the President's right, I on his left. Those of us who had been together on the Campaign Train "and had loved it," as Stanley High wrote, were there. Among those ranged up and down the table were Sherm and Rachel, Fred Seaton, Homer Gruenther, Bobby Cutler, Bernard Shanley, Leonard Hall and several others. The place cards were snapshots taken in the campaign. The President's which he gave me, showed him at an outdoor rally. Mine was a snapshot taken inside one of the cars in a motorcade. Congressman Hall and I were smiling and talking and Fred Seaton, his head through the back window, was listening.

It was all so nice! I was so happy! Sherm and Bobby made speeches. The President had some gracious words and presented me with an autographed photograph, with the inscription:

"For Katherine G. Howard—

With lasting appreciation of distinguished
government service—and with best wishes to her
and her charming family—

Dwight D. Eisenhower"

I don't remember what we had to eat, or what I wore, I

Above: Katherine G. Howard, Secretary of Commerce Sinclair Weeks, and Charlie Howard. *Below:* Friendly Sons and Daughters of President Franklin D. Pierce.

Press conference in office of Deputy Administrator of FCDA,
Katherine G. Howard.

just remember the warmth and friendliness and gaiety of everyone there. I said my thanks, and with a warm handshake of the President, and a kiss from Mamie, I said good-bye.

With the days running out, my staff had been busy toting up statistics as to what I had been doing in the months of my Civil Defense activities. It added up to quite an impressive record. It seems I had travelled 99,763 miles on official business (to say nothing of those trips home each weekend).

I had made sixty-two speeches in thirty-two cities in twenty-two states, and in Canada and France. Each one was tailor-made for the occasion and the locale. But in all of them I stated the threat, Civil Defense measures for protection and survival, and what the group which I was addressing could do. These were all "major" speeches to statewide or national organizations. I was not permitted to take "local" engagements.

I had appeared on twenty-eight radio and fourteen television shows. It seemed like a lot more.

I had held twelve press conferences outside of Washington, and several in Washington, including a press interview with Helen Thomas, which was widely quoted. I enjoyed fielding the questions.

I had visited officially the tornado areas in Vicksburg, Mississippi, and the fireworks plant explosion in Chesterton, Maryland, grim warnings of what might come.

And I had attended the atomic tests at Yucca Flats, Nevada; and shown the Hydrogen Bomb film to our NATO Civil Defense allies in Paris—once seen, never forgotten.

When I sent a summary to Val Peterson, he wrote: "Katherine, a great record and a colorful one!"

There was still one more party before I packed my bags. This was given me by FCDA in a hotel near our offices on Columbia Road. Much thought and care went into it. It was a heartwarming affair. The invitation said:

Farewell Party
for Mrs. Howard at
The Highlands

Friday   5 P.M.

Val Peterson was there, of course; the Assistant Administrators; my secretaries, Hank Parker and Jeannette Thuman;

333

Paul Wagner, and the majority of those who with me, believed in Civil Defense and made up the FCDA force. There were probably two hundred people present. Of course, Jack deChant and Chick Ellsworth had had a lot to do in planning it.

Val made a flattering speech and presented me with an engraved sterling silver tray. The inscription said:

Presented to
Katherine Graham Howard
For inspiring leadership and notable service as
Deputy Federal Civil Defense Administrator
1953-1954
by her F.C.D.A. Associates

Then, for traveling home, and in the future, back and forth to Washington, and to Paris and NATO countries, I was given two handsome sky-way suitcases in my favorite blue and initialed K.G.H.

After all this, my heart was full. It was a happy, happy gathering. I stepped to the microphone to say my thanks and to respond with lines I had thrown together:

> I came from Back Bay to FCDA
> To work for Governor Val
> In this high estate
> It was my happy fate to administrate
> Although I am only a gal.
>
> The things I have learned
> As the midnight oil burned
> Have been many and varied and queer.
> But through it all we worked with good cheer.
>
> I went way out yonder
> When the Atom went off
> And now I ponder
> How can anyone scoff?
>
> So now the job is over
> I'm turned loose in clover
> But I'll never be the same again
> After all of you attractive men!

I'm sure you all know
That I've loved the show
The days were too short
The hours too few
To do all the things I needed to do
But husbands won't wait
While wives administrate.

You're all tied to my heart
As now we must part
Good luck to you all as I go on my way
Good luck to you all
Friends of FCDA.

Just doggerel, but heartfelt.

It was Friday evening. With deep content I was going home. Home to a loving husband—to Marblehead—to Herbert—and Peggy when she came from New York; and Jennie and Steve—and The Cat. I was going home to family and friends and Boston activities. People may have wondered why I was so adventurous as to go to Washington anyway. I knew why. It had been good. But now I was home again.

AFTERWORD

It was August when I came home to Marblehead. In the late Fall, Charlie proposed that we take a Mediterranean trip in the New Year. He was to be appointed to a new post in the Spring—that of Commissioner of Banks for the Commonwealth of Massachusetts. The word was not out, but we could take this golden opportunity to travel together. Charlie planned everything to perfection. We would sail from New York to Naples, stay there a few days, then visit Egypt, Lebanon, Turkey, Greece, return to Italy, and home on the new *Andrea Doria*—a trip of about six weeks duration. With Charlie's acquiescence, I wrote the State Department that we were taking a pleasure trip at our own expense, but since we were visiting several NATO countries, we would be glad to give one day in each country to confer with Civil Defense officials if it was desired. Egypt was not a NATO country, but we had entertained their officials seeking Civil Defense information in Washington. Each nation was pleased at the opportunity and responded generously. In many countries Civil Defense was part of the military establishment, so we were always accompanied by the U. S. Military Attaché, and Charlie was always addressed as Colonel.

In Egypt we were entertained at the Egyptian Army Club, where Britishers are never invited, and Americans very rarely. The Minister of the Interior, Zakaria Mohi el Deen invited Charlie and me to his office and had a picture taken there, which appeared in the press, along with an interview in which I was quoted about the hydrogen bomb, the importance of Civil Defense and President Eisenhower's proposals for Atoms for Peace—a friendly article.

337

In Turkey, where we stayed a week, they placed at our disposal a staff car with an English-speaking Air Force Captain as our escort. They asked for two days instead of one—and the meetings were held in the handsome Army Headquarters with marble floors, crystal chandeliers, murals, and elaborate furniture. They were a keen, intelligent and interested group.

The high spot of our stay in Greece was being received by Queen Fredericka at the Summer Palace. In addition we conferred with the Greek Civil Defense officials and were entertained by them.

In Athens, of course, we went to the Parthenon, and to the Forum, thinking of St. Paul's words uttered there. Charlie engaged a car, with Niko, a well-known guide, who drove us to Eleusis and Corinth through countryside beautiful with fruit trees in bloom, figs and grapevines sprouting and even a whole field of blue grape hyacinths in bloom, with a white goat stock still in the middle of it. Niko was very knowledgeable, and as we stopped to admire the amphitheatres, temples, and even the marble plumbing arrangements, he made the ancient civilization come to life. We spent the night at an inn at Nauplia, returning next day by way of Epidaurus. It was hard to believe that we had actually stood at the scene of so much history and mythology.

Back to Italy—a reception at the American embassy, and then staying on to a private dinner with Ambassador Clare Boothe Luce, and two friends of hers from *Life* Magazine. Home on the *Andrea Doria*. She did not sink on this trip.

When I returned, I wrote a report for the State Department and FCDA—but in my heart was recorded one of the happiest times Charlie and I ever had.

His swearing-in by Governor Herter as Commissioner of Banks took place soon after. He was glad to be back under the golden dome of the State House and just across the street from his luncheon group at the Union Club. He became a popular and respected Commissioner, and served with distinction until his retirement when he reached seventy years of age in 1957.

As for me it was good to be at home. It was good to have Charlie's love and companionship—to pick up some of my Boston activities, and rejoin my friends in pleasant gatherings.

It was also good to still belong to FCDA, but on a more manageable basis. The change in title from "Deputy Administrator" to "Special Advisor" seemed to make very little difference, officially. In addition, I was now, by Presidential appointment, a member of the National Civil Defense Advisory Council. I was still asked to participate in Operation Alert Exercises, and given "Deputy" responsibilities. After almost a year Val Peterson said to me, "Any time you want to come back and be Deputy, I'd like to have you." I was pleased, but smiled and shook my head. Not too long after that, a successor was named. But I did attend other Atomic tests, this time as a member of the National Advisory Council. I went to Washington perhaps one day a week, staying at the Sulgrave Club—going to my office—seeing Washington friends also. I did an enormous amount of work at home. My secretary and I had envelopes going back and forth almost every day—and speech requests still came in.

In addition, I was asked to make official inspection trips to Germany, and to Denmark, Norway, and Sweden, in connection with my trips to Paris as U. S. Delegate to the NATO Civil Defense Committee.

From 1922 up to the present, always, always, my concern has been that women should participate in political life as voters, members of the party organizations, and officeholders. When I began, the Women's Suffrage Amendment had just been passed, but once they had the vote they did not use it. "Woman's place is in the home," was the cry and both men and women had to be convinced that women could be in the home and still reach out into the business and political world.

It was my husband's decision to run for the State Senate in 1922 which started my political life. At that time, most wives of candidates did not participate, but Charlie wanted me with him, and when it came to the actual things to be done for his election, he asked me to organize friends to address envelopes, to help line up the cars to take people to the polls, and to supervise those working on the check lists at the polls. At the victorious end of his campaign, I was asked to go on the Republican Town Committee, and to be a delegate to the Republican State Convention.

In 1938, when he ran for the Republican nomination for

Lieutenant Governor, again he wanted me to be with him and I came to know the Party leaders in the state, so that at the end, I was asked to become a member of the Board of Directors of the Women's Republican Club, then a powerful organization, with headquarters at 46 Beacon Street. Charlie went off to war, and I kept busy serving as Vice-President and President of the Club.

In his long absence, I was promoted to Republican National Committeewoman; and by Sinclair Weeks, made a member of the Massachusetts Republican Finance Committee, and of the Massachusetts Policy Committee, and his working partner, in the innermost circles of Massachusetts politics. It was he who suggested that I might become Secretary of the Republican National Committee.

When Charlie returned, I, who had always been accepted in political circles as Charlie Howard's wife, now had won laurels on my own. It troubled me. Charlie went back to being Treasurer of Middlesex County, but his three and one-half years' service in the War had cost him advancement in the political world.

After Eisenhower's victory in 1952, I hoped he might be called to the capitol, but in the end he declared, "I'll be darned if I'll go to Washington. I live in Boston."

He always helped and backed me up, and we shared my last assignment at the Brussels World's Exposition. It came at just the time when he retired. So after a banquet in his honor, we could sail together for me to take up my position as United States Deputy Commissioner-General to the Brussels International Exposition. President Eisenhower had offered me the position, carrying the State Department rank of "Minister" (the Commissioner General had the rank of "Ambassador"). Our stay in Brussels was from January, 1958 to October, 1958. We had a beautiful house, an adequate salary, an allowance for entertaining, a car and chauffeur, perfect household staff, a beautiful office, with a regular secretary and a social secretary. There was a little concern about the form of our invitation cards. It was finally decided that the most acceptable form for Belgium would be:

Mr. Charles Pagelsen Howard
and the
Deputy Commissioner-General, Mrs. Howard
cordially invite you. . . .

Charlie had to open the bank account for me and he stocked the wine cellar, as a connoisseur should. He returned to America from time to time, but the Brussels experience made a fine transition from Commissioner of Banks, to opening a law office, which he did when we returned.

In Belgium, our son, Herbert, met and a year later married Margaretha Vandaele, now our dearly loved daughter-in-law.

After I took up my duties in Belgium, I became more and more convinced that part of our program should be to demonstrate the important part women play in every phase of life in the U.S. That I was the only woman official from any of the participating nations, made it all the more important. But I realized the difficulties. All exhibit space in our pavilion had been assigned, and all money in the budget allocated.

After a good deal of thought I presented to a staff meeting a plan for presenting distinguished American women. I proposed asking the Women's Bureau in the Department of Labor to send me a bipartisan list of American women who, by their accomplishments, would make an impressive appearance on our program. To this list the Commissioner-General and I would send a letter saying: "If you are coming to Europe this summer on an official mission, or a pleasure trip, we would like to present you, as a speaker, to an international audience in the U.S. Pavilion." I pointed out to the staff that I was asking for no budget or space allocation, and would direct the program. Since no money was involved, and I would do the work, the Commissioner-General and top staff agreed.

From the Women's Bureau I received a list of forty names and I wrote to them individually, inviting them to speak in the U.S. Pavilion before an audience composed of the diplomatic corps, the Commissioners-General, Deputies from the forty-four participating nations and their wives and officers and members of the women's organizations in Belgium.

The Program began on May twelfth with Mrs. Oswald

Lord, U. S. Delegate to the United Nations General Assembly, and U. S. Representative on the Human Rights Commission of the United Nations.

Each program began with the playing of the "Brabaconne," the Belgian National Anthem; followed by the "Star Spangled Banner," then I introduced the speaker.

Mary Lord was an instantaneous success; she spoke in French in describing the work of the United Nations. Following her came Miss Hazel Palmer, President of the National Federation of Business and Professional Women, who was joined by her Belgian counterpart, and groups of business and professional women who came from Brussels, Antwerp, and Malines.

The most ambitious program was a double-barrelled one featuring Alice Leopold, Assistant to the Secretary of Labor, and Head of the Women's Bureau; and Betsy Blackwell, Editor of *Mademoiselle* and promoter of American fashions. In addition to the two stars we had a fashion show by a group of ten representative American women who were employed at the U. S. Pavilion, showing their own ready-to-wear clothes. Alice and Betsy were both dynamic and attractive. Alice spoke first, in French, on "The Mutual Goals of Women." As for Betsy Blackwell the French press reported, "Sous un étonnant beret de velours violet Miss Blackwell abrite une tête aussi rempli d'ideal que de realisme et de psychologie." It was the violet velvet hat which stole the show.

A mature contrast was the American Mother of the Year. We were able to find the Belgian Mother of the Year, widow of a political prisoner who died during World War II in a concentration camp. They were fine women about the same age and congenial.

When Jacqueline Cochrane came we decided to have an evening meeting, knowing that she would attract the men. A famous aviator, she was, at that time, President of the Federation Aeronautique Internationale, whose members were mostly men. She was attractive and glamorous and said to me: "I don't like women, but I like you." She made an arresting talk and showed a film on the future of aviation in interplanetary travel. (This was 1958!) She was a hit.

Mrs. Eleanor Roosevelt was the star attraction and her appearance lent added dignity and prestige to the program.

Governor Christian A. Herter swears in Charles P. Howard as Commissioner of Banks of the Commonwealth of Massachusetts, 1955, in the Governor's Office, State House, Boston. Left to right: Governor Herter, Katherine G. Howard, Hon. Frank S. Viola, Charles P. Howard.

Undersecretary of State Christian Herter, and Deputy U. S. Commissioner-General, Katherine G. Howard—in U. S. Pavilion, Brussels Exposition.

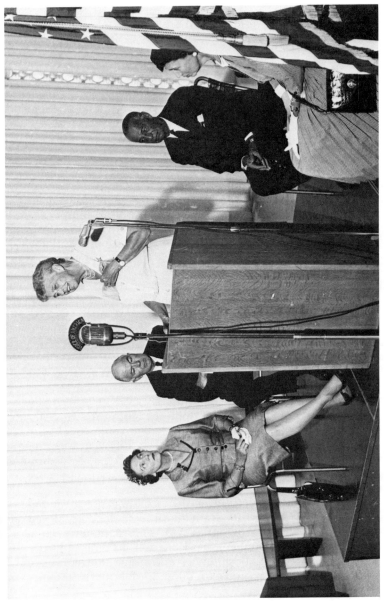

Mrs. Eleanor Roosevelt speaks in "Distinguished Women's Program," Brussels Exposition.

Wearing a light-colored dress in the unexpected September heat, she spoke in an intimate and friendly fashion about her impressions of the Exposition and of its contribution to international understanding. Naturally members of the Diplomatic Corps attended; Commissioners-General and Deputies and their wives, leading men and women, but the person who seemed to mean the most to her as we mingled after her talk, was Harry Belafonte. She greeted him and his wife warmly, with a kiss for each.

Congresswoman Edith Green, Democrat from Oregon, was present, and spoke.

Judge Mary Donlon, appointed by President Eisenhower to the U. S. Customs Court was next. A long-time friend of mine, she was our house guest. She aimed her remarks at the women lawyers of Belgium, many of whom were present.

Perle Mesta was a drawing card. She had recently been Ambassador to Luxembourg, Belgium's next door neighbor, and she recalled her lively memories of her appointment there. I was pleased that on this occasion she acted so naturally and did not demand Ambassadorial treatment.

Our program concluded on October 2, with Mrs. Robert Whitelaw Wilson, National Chairman of Volunteers of the American Red Cross. We had Belgian Red Cross Officers, both men and women, at the head table. She had with her a letter from President Hoover, asking her to say for him, "There was never a greater outpouring of voluntary service than that of the Belgian women during both world wars.

"Occupied by German armies and blockaded by the Allies, the meager food and clothing supplies in both wars were distributed through the devotion of over 50,000 volunteers."

Janet Wilson said: "I perhaps fall into a different category than those who have preceded me, for my career is a voluntary one, though I would like to think we are becoming more professional volunteers."

Her appearance ended the series. It had been a meaningful one. It demonstrated in dramatic fashion the role played by women in law, government service, international affairs, aviation, journalism, volunteer service. I felt it carried out the basic purpose of the Exposition, to encourage and stimulate the people of many nations to know and understand one another better.

In addition to the women's program, I also had a heavy program of administrative and representational duties; of greeting Kings and Queens and Heads of State and entertaining visiting dignitaries.

In my lifetime there have been enormous changes in the attitude toward women. Women have risen to be admired executives in government and industry. We think of the two women holding Cabinet positions under President Carter: Mrs. Patricia Roberts Harris, Secretary of Housing and Urban Development; and Juanita Kreps as Secretary of Commerce. Anne Armstrong had previously served as a ranking member of the White House Staff and was then appointed by President Ford as Ambassador to The Court of St. James. We think of Governor Ella Grasso of Connecticut, Lieutenant Governor Krupsak of New York; and Susie Sharp Marshall, Chief Justice of the Supreme Court of North Carolina. No list of influential women would be complete without Barbara Ward. Two pioneers in medicine were Dr. Martha Eliot and Dr. Alice Hamilton, and in the present day, Dr. Anne Phillips is an international expert on the treatment of burns. It is no longer surprising to find Mrs. Carl Gilbert serving as Chairman of the Board of Overseers of Harvard, or Mrs. Harold Hodgkinson, Chairman of the Board of Trustees of Smith College and of the Science Museum of Boston. In industry and banking, Catherine Cleary is President of the First National Trust Company of Milwaukee, and a Director of General Motors. These are but a few of the many distinguished women in high ranking positions.

Early in my marriage I followed my husband into politics, and the war gave me a chance to play an increasing part, in state and then in national affairs. Women have come a long way and will go further. Others will enjoy, as I have, the pride of accomplishment, and they will find, as I did, that it is imperative never to neglect the joy of being a woman.